J. C. (Johan Carel) Voigt

Fifty Years of the History of the Republic in South Africa

Vol. II: 1795-1845

J. C. (Johan Carel) Voigt

Fifty Years of the History of the Republic in South Africa
Vol. II: 1795-1845

ISBN/EAN: 9783743386259

Manufactured in Europe, USA, Canada, Australia, Japa

Cover: Foto ©ninafisch / pixelio.de

Manufactured and distributed by brebook publishing software (www.brebook.com)

J. C. (Johan Carel) Voigt

Fifty Years of the History of the Republic in South Africa

FIFTY YEARS OF THE HISTORY OF THE REPUBLIC IN SOUTH AFRICA
1795-1845

Fifty Years of the History of the Republic in South Africa

(1795–1845)

By J. C. VOIGT M.D.

Of the Cape Colony Volunteer Ambulance Service in the Transvaal in 1881

IN TWO VOLUMES

VOL. II

NEW YORK
E. P. DUTTON & CO.
LONDON T. FISHER UNWIN

"Nicht allein der Triumphator,
Nicht allein der sieggekrönte
Günstling jener blinden Göttin,
Auch der blut'ge Sohn des Unglücks,

"Auch der heldenmüth'ge Kämpfer,
Der dem ungeheuren Schicksal
Unterlag, wird ewig leben
In der Menschen Angedenken." HEINE.

CONTENTS OF VOL. II

PART II (*Continued*)

	PAGES
RECORDS AND CHRONICLES OF THE VOORTREKKERS (*Continued*)	1-81

Maps and Illustrations:

Sketch Map to illustrate the Narrative of the Massacres of 11th February, 1838. Laagers of Emigrant Farmers on Mooi, Bushman's, and Blauwkrans Rivers, with the position of Umkungunhlovu and of Italeni . . 50

CHAPTER XVII

Trek under Jacobs and Jacobus Uys—Retief's Mission to Natal 1-18

CHAPTER XVIII

Campaign of the Mariqua—Massacre of Umkungunhlovu . 19-48

CHAPTER XIX

Zulu onslaught on Emigrant Laagers—Massacres of 11th February, 1838—Battle of Italeni—Death of Pieter and Dirk Cornelis Uys—Battle of the Tugela—British Government Proclamation—Foundation of Potchefstroom—The Winter of 1838 in Natal—Arrival of Andries Pretorius . 49-81

CONTENTS

PART III

	PAGES
THE REPUBLIC OF NATAL	85-283

Maps and Illustrations:

Sketch Plan of the Bloed River Battlefield . . .	97
Diagram to Illustrate how Bart Pretorius cut the Zulu Army in two at the Battle of the Bloed River . . .	101
Sketch Plan of the Battle of the White Umveloosi Plain .	105
Diagram showing Zulus converging and attempting to surround Column of Emigrants	110
Diagram showing Column of Horsemen advancing over Plain and keeping back Zulu Front Ranks . .	110
Map showing Republics of Natal and Winburg, and Vassal Zulu State	159
Sketch Map of the Congella Battlefield . . .	223
Sketch Map : Battle of Durban Bay . .	246

CHAPTER XX

The Campaign of the Win-Commando .	85-119

CHAPTER XXI

Major Charters' Occupation of Port Natal .	120-136

CHAPTER XXII

The Conquest of Zululand .	137-158

CHAPTER XXIII

The Federated Republics of Natal and Winburg .	159-173

CHAPTER XXIV

Second Seizure of Port Natal by a British Expedition .	174-208

CONTENTS

Chapter XXV

Second Seizure of Port Natal by a British Expedition (*continued*)—Captain Smith's March—Commencement of Hostilities—Battle of Congella . . . 209-228

Chapter XXVI

Siege of Captain Smith's Camp . . . 229-244

Chapter XXVII

Battle of Durban Bay—Defeat of Pretorius . 245-252

Chapter XXVIII

Submission of the Republicans in Natal . 253-269

Chapter XXIX

Republicans Recross the Drakensberg . . 270-283

APPENDIX

England's Native Policy in South Africa . . . 287-307

Index to Vol. II 311-316

ERRATUM

VOL. II.

P. 263, second side-note: *for* "No Hollander, Clergyman," etc., *read* "No Hollander Clergyman," etc.

PART II *(Continued)*

RECORDS AND CHRONICLES OF THE VOORTREKKERS *(Continued)*

CHAPTER XVII

THE PROMISED LAND

Pieter Jacobs and Jacobus Uys—Preparations for Expedition against Umsiligaas—Quarrel between Potgieter and Uys—Retief's Mission to Natal—The British Emigrants at the Bay—Request for Annexation—Refusal—Cape of Good Hope Punishment Bill—British Government, although Refusing to annex Natal, claims Magisterial Jurisdiction—Emigrants move Eastward—Retief at the Drakensberg—In the Passes—Among the Summits of the Range—Peaks and Crags—First View of Natal—A Sea of Hills—The Solitudes—Towards the Upper Tugela—Natalian Flora and Fauna—View of the Sea from Mount Inchanga—The Africander Balboa—National Aspirations—Pieter Retief Welcomed at Durban—Co-operation of English Settlers to Establish the Republic.

ALREADY before Retief's arrival several small parties of Emigrants, besides the main bodies or treks under Potgieter and Maritz, had come from the Colony (chiefly, one may say almost entirely, from the Eastern districts), and settled in and around Winburg. Now larger numbers were on the way. Pieter Jacobs and the men of Beaufort district with him had arrived; and the patriarch Jacobus Uys with his sons and daughters; their respective wives and husbands; their children and grandchildren—all the members of the several families together numbering over a hundred. This clan came from the Uitenhage district. The old man was then

_{Pieter Jacobs.}
_{Jacobus Uys.}

about seventy years of age. His son, **Pieter Lafras Uys**, had distinguished himself in the Kaffir war; and when the old father, with all his relatives, passed through Grahamstown, the British settlers there presented him with a large family Bible as a mark of their esteem and respect.

This old veteran and his party, all members of one large family, were in themselves a powerful host. On nearly every battlefield in the history of the Republic one or more of the name of Uys have signalised themselves by brilliant deeds of gallantry and valour, and not a few of them have given their lives for their country's cause. It is a name of which South Africa may well be proud.

A missionary teacher called **Erasmus Smit** was, in 1837, appointed chaplain. For, so far, not a single minister of the Dutch Reformed Church had come forward to throw in his lot with the Emigrants, and to perform religious services for them.

Preparations for Expedition against Umsiligaas.

Retief, in the name of the Emigrant Farmers, now sent word to Umsiligaas, the Matabele King, that, on condition of his restoring everything which had been taken by his Impis, peace would be granted to him; but that, if he did not comply with this demand, hostilities would be resumed against him. No reply was received to this communication. The Commandant-General had in the meantime visited the friendly Chiefs, Moroko, Tawane, Sikonyella, and Moshesh, and concluded alliances with them. When the second expedition against Umsiligaas was being organised, Tawane, Moroko, and Sikonyella offered their services and active co-operation in the campaign. But large numbers of Emigrants from the Colony were then reinforcing those already north of the Orange river; and Retief thought it would be their best policy to fight out unassisted by Native allies the quarrel with the Matabele. He therefore declined the proffered help of the Chiefs. As there was some talk of a probable attack on the Emigrants by the Griquas of Waterboer and Adam Kok, the expedition against Umsiligaas was postponed for a time. Unfortunately, the quarrel between Potgieter and Maritz was revived, about September, 1836. Retief was unable to succeed, as he had done before, as peacemaker. On the contrary, things went from bad to worse. Not only did Potgieter and his followers declare their intention of separating from the main body of the Emigrants and setting up a Government of their own in the territory which they had purchased from Makwana; but Uys and his relatives, taking offence at some rather injudicious restrictions of the movements of smaller sections of Emigrants away from the main trek, also announced their resolve to separate and settle somewhere east of the Drakensberg range, in the territory of what is now the Colony of Natal. Retief himself was in favour of the entire body of Emigrants settling in Natal; but before definitely deciding on this, he resolved to make a journey of exploration in person, and to obtain a cession of territory from the Zulu King, Dingaan. *Quarrel between Potgieter and Maritz.* *Retief's Mission to Natal.*

All the country between the Tugela and Umzimvubu had been previously overrun and conquered by those tribes which fled from Chaka's armies, and the

Zulus were now looked upon as holding dominion over the soil by right of conquest. The former inhabitants who had not been killed or reduced to vassalage by the invaders had been driven over the Drakensberg into the countries now known as the Transvaal, Orange Free State, and Basutoland; and also towards the south into Pondoland and Kaffirland. According to Theal, all Natal did not then contain more than 5000 Natives. These owned the supremacy of Dingaan, and were the remnants of the tribes which formerly possessed the land. Retief, knowing that, according to Native law and custom, the country belonged to the conquerors, even although they might have had no moral right to it; being anxious to avoid hostilities and anything that might even look like illegal occupation of territory; and considering his own life and safety as nothing where what he deemed great issues to his country and his people were at stake: formed the daring resolve of visiting the Zulu monarch in his own stronghold.

The number of European inhabitants at that time in the country between the Drakensbergen and the sea, and between the Tugela and Umzimvubu mouths, was about thirty. They were English and Cape Town adventurers, and were located, for at least three months every year, a little further inland than the present town of Durban. They were nearly all elephant hunters and traders, and many of them were Chiefs ruling over small kraals of Kaffirs, and acknowledging the supremacy of Dingaan, to whom they paid tribute (in the form of substantial presents of money). Captain Gardiner, formerly of the British Navy, had settled at the Bay in 1835. Previous to that year the houses were mere wigwams, hidden in the bush. Only one house was built on the European model; but the walls were of mud, and the roof was of reeds. In June, 1835, a public meeting had been convened, and it had been resolved to lay out a town where Durban is now built, and to call it after Sir Benjamin D'Urban, who was then Governor at Cape Town. As has been mentioned on a preceding page, a petition was then signed and sent to the Governor for transmission to the Home Government. It asked for the establishment of a British Colony, with a Governor and Council—appointed by the Crown—to rule over the inhabitants through the medium of a Legislative Assembly selected by themselves. This petition was forwarded by Sir Benjamin D'Urban on the 4th of December, 1835 (THEAL). Earl Glenelg, then Colonial Secretary, replied on the 29th of March, 1836, that "his Majesty's Government was deeply persuaded of the inexpediency of engaging in any scheme of colonisation, or of acquiring any further enlargement of territory in Southern Africa." *[margin: The British Emigrants at the Bay.]*

[margin: Request for Annexation.]

In January, 1834, a meeting had been held in the Commercial Exchange Buildings at Cape Town, where resolutions were passed to request the British Government to annex Natal. The petition conveying this request was also rejected by the Home Government, on the ground of the expense that would be involved in any scheme of further extension of the British dominions in South Africa.

The British Government had, therefore, definitely refused to have anything to do with the new settlement, when, in June, 1837, Captain Gardiner, who had been on a visit to England, again returned to the country, bringing with him some other missionaries, and establishing himself at Berea, a mission station which he had previously founded. He had gained Dingaan's favour by taking back to the Chief's residence four miserable Zulu fugitives, who had sought refuge with the English settlers on the Bay. These poor wretches were, by order of the King, when the missionary Captain took them back to him, starved to death.

<small>Refusal on the Part of the Home Government.</small>

In 1836, Earl Glenelg's administration had passed through the British Houses of Parliament an Act known as the Cape of Good Hope Punishment Bill. This measure enacted that all British subjects committing any crime in any part of the Dark Continent south of latitude 25° rendered themselves liable to be brought up for punishment in the Courts of the Colony of the Cape of Good Hope. The Government of the Cape could grant commissions to suitable persons to arrest and bring to trial any of his Majesty's faithful subjects who had rendered themselves liable to punishment by committing crimes south of the 25th parallel of latitude. At the same time, the Act distinctly stipulated that the King's Government refused all responsibility of administrative rule over any territory beyond the actual Colonial border, and that the provisions of the Bill were not to be construed as meaning any extension of the Empire beyond what were then the frontiers.

<small>Cape of Good Hope Punishment Bill.</small>

<small>British Government, Although it Refuses to assume Governmental Responsibility, claims Magisterial Jurisdiction.</small>

The missionary ex-Royal-Navy Captain, who had

propitiated Dingaan by delivering up to Zulu justice the four fugitives alluded to, seems to have been considered by the British authorities a suitable magistrate under the provisions of the Cape of Good Hope Punishment Bill, and received a commission to act as such at Durban. The English settlers of those days, however, refused to acknowledge his authority, arguing that, as their petition for incorporation with the British Empire had been refused, they must look upon themselves as beyond the jurisdiction of that Empire. As they did not share its benefits, said those hardy pioneers, they would have none of its Royal-Navy missionary justice.

It was in the beginning of October, 1837, when Retief, accompanied by Marthinus Oosthuizen, Abraham C. Greyling, B. Liebenberg, and two others, started from Thaba 'N Chu, and rode across the plain to the east. Their mission was to cross the Drakensbergen, visit the Bay of Natal, and from there proceed to the head kraal of the Zulu Chief to negotiate with him for a cession of territory. Large numbers of the Emigrants were already on their way towards the mountain passes. They had been trekking slowly with their waggons and cattle; but their progress was stopped, as they had reached a region where very extensive grass fires had destroyed all vegetation—so that they now found all the "*vlakte*" in front of them scorched and black, without a blade of grass left for their oxen and sheep. They had, therefore, to await the advent of the early summer rains before they could again pass on towards the east.

Emigrants move Eastward.

Retief and the horsemen with him rapidly traversed the burnt-up plains where the fire had been raging, and, as most of that country lies between five and six thousand feet above the level of the sea, they soon found themselves riding into the first of those mountain passes by which they were ascending and crossing the range of gigantic mountains which lay between them and the land of Natal. On either side of their course, huge rocky heights towered to the skies; and, as their path wound up the slopes and led them further into the centre of the range, the wild grandeur of the scenery around them presented a striking contrast to the dull monotony of the level plains across which they had recently travelled. Rugged and scarred by the thunderstorms and torrents of ages, here with little rills of water—tiny streamlets only, for it was the dry season—trickling down their steep faces; there with dry and arid slopes of rock, bleak and bare of all vegetation; yonder, again, with heaths and grass lining their mighty crags: those silent sentinels that had watched the dusky legions of Chaka and of Ma 'Ntatisi marching past, frowned down on the half dozen bold pioneers—the first White men who had invaded their majestic solitudes, and who were now, guided by Destiny, advancing into that unknown land to the East. As the travellers ascended to still higher regions, they saw huge cloud banks floating around some of the loftiest summits of the range, while others reared their topmost peaks, even beyond the clouds, into the blue African sky. And then extensive ravines and "*kloofs*" could be seen,

Retief at the Drakensberg.

Among the Summits of the Range.

stretching downward towards the east. In the deepest of these glens, forests of trees fringed the mountain stream, and bright-coloured heather and other flowers covered the slopes of some of the rocks. Here and there, high up the precipitous cliffs, the brown coneys were sunning themselves in the October sunshine. The deep stillness in the mountains was broken only by the occasional shrill, piping cry of the little rock rabbits when the shadow of an eagle's wing, from high overhead, flitted across the face of the rocks; by the clatter of stones falling into the depths below, after having been set rolling by the horses' hoofs; or by the subdued sound—wafted upwards by the breeze—of water running down the face of the steep rocks in the ravines. *The Lonely Peaks and Crags.*

When emerging from the last pass, the travellers saw, towards the south, an endless succession of mountains and mountain tops—the continuation of the Drakensberg in that direction. Straight before them, to the east, were rounded and irregular-shaped hills, covered and obscured from view by a hazy mist, but all diminishing in height with distance. It was the land which Pieter and Jacobus Uys had explored further east, and where now White men dwelt on the seashore; it was Natal—the Land of Promise to the Emigrants. Standing in that wild mountain pass, with their faces to the east, Retief and his companions looked upon the vast expanse of country gradually sloping downward towards the distant Indian Ocean—a succession of hills, the nearer ones of which lay radiant in African sunshine, while those more distant were obscured and only *First View of Natal.* *A Sloping Sea of Hills.*

dimly visible in the cloud of vapour which hung over them. Under the veil of mist lay the banks of the Tugela and Buffalo rivers, of the Blauwkrans and the Mooi, and of the Bushman's, where the town of Weenen was to arise to commemorate the sufferings and misfortunes of the Voortrekkers. To the north-east, the white curtain hid from view a great part of the landscape. To the north, the continuation of the Drakensbergen stretched onward without interruption. In that direction, also, clouds obscured the more distant view.

Standing in the mountain pass and looking around them, the pioneers were once more struck with the stillness and the solitude, as the breeze wafted towards them the soft melodious sound of water falling over the edge of a deep glen, where huge tree ferns grew.

Let us try to recall from the Past—to bring into the Present—one or two salient features of the scene.

The Mountain Solitudes.

Hidden from view by some of the mountain ranges to the north, far away in the distance, towards the thickly-wooded slope of Amajuba, where the Spitskop rises at one end of the huge mass of rock, flocks of wood-pigeons are winging their way through the air. The *klipspringer* stands on the highest pinnacle of one of those groups of huge rocks away to the north, where the tops of the Drakensbergen are concealed in the clouds. The wild Bushman crouches in the shelter of a dark crag, perhaps watching the White strangers in the passes far below his feet. He grasps his bow and tiny arrow. High overhead in the hot sky, a black vulture sails lazily along. He, also, is watching. Then the shrill piping cry of the little brown rock rabbit is heard once again, as, again, the shadow of the mountain eagle's wing flits across the face of the overhanging cliffs; and Pieter Retief and his companions ride down the eastern slope from the last mountain pass, into the unknown land, and under the veil of mist.

Travelling down the slope, which in several places they found so steep that they had to dismount and lead their horses, they gradually made their way past frowning precipices and immense ravines, often between huge stones and boulders overgrown with long reeds and grass, to lower ground, where they found the country well watered and with better pasturage for cattle. They were now on the affluents of the Upper Tugela, and this new land which they were exploring for their fellow-emigrants presented a remarkable contrast to the flat plateau plains which they had left behind them to the west of the giant mountain range. The hills, rising terrace upon terrace, one above the other, from the great Indian Ocean to the Drakensbergen; the well-wooded slopes and sheltered *kloofs;* the abundant water supply derived from the mountain streams combining to form magnificent rivers; the good pasturage and the great variety of climate and soil: all these were points of such importance as at once to attract the attention of the Emigrant leader and his companions. So far, they had not seen any Natives. The entire country seemed to have been depopulated by Chaka's savage battalions.

Downward towards the Upper Tugela.

There were numerous wild animals in Natal in those days, and as the explorers came into the more eastern region, away from the mountains, they observed elephant paths leading to the banks of the streams where those animals came to drink. Some of the plants—the bright-coloured scarlet flowers on the trees, the llianas and creepers, the fan-palms and tropical shrubs, as well as other features in the vegetation; the bright-coloured plumage of some of the birds which they saw; the strange insects and reptilia of this eastern zone: all these spoke to the Emigrants of the characteristics of a more genial, more salubrious climate than that which they had just left, and warned them of their near approach to the shores of that ocean, whose warm current, flowing southwards from the equatorial regions, tempers the cold of the upland slopes, even in the depths of winter (when the highest peaks of the Drakensberg are covered with snow), and throws that hazy curtain of vapoury mists, which had been observed from the passes, over the rounded hills of Natal.

Natalian Flora and Fauna.

As they had been advancing down the mountain slopes towards the sea, this veil of smoke-like clouds had limited the view of the explorers. Now that they were on lower ground, the sky was clear all round them; and they could see objects plainly (and un-obscured by mist) at a much greater distance than before.

The traveller, coming from the west by the Pietermaritzburg road, first obtains a view of the Indian Ocean from the summit of the Inchanga mountain, or from one of the other elevated positions in the tract of beautiful country forming the watershed between the Umlaas and Umgeni. It was from one of these heights that Retief's party saw the blue waters of the great sea before them in the distance. As far as is known, they had been the first people of European blood to traverse the country intervening between the inland plateau, where they had left the other Emigrants, and the point which they had now reached near the coast of Natal. With no other provisions than such as they could easily carry with them in the saddle-bag—dried camp biscuits, sun-dried antelopes' meat (*springbok biltong*), and perhaps a little coffee—varied now and then by the meat of such game as they could succeed in shooting along the way, they had arrived, after more than a fortnight's journey, within sight of the Indian Ocean. Far to the west, and thousands of feet above them, now lay those vast grassy plains and plateau lands where their countrymen were awaiting their return. Still higher up among the clouds, frowned the topmost peaks of those stupendous mountains in whose lonely defiles and dark passes their horses' hoofs had recently re-echoed; and further down the slope from the Drakensbergen, where mist and hazy vapour obscured the view, were the magnificent streams in which they had discovered the fords, and by the banks of which they had lit their camp fires at night. With the canopy of the Southern sky and its stars overhead, they had more than once, as the glow of the firelight lit up the adjacent thickets and brought out in strong relief the dark outlines of the distant mountains and of the wooded river banks, been impressed by the solitude of the wilderness around them. Occasionally they had heard the heavy tramp of elephants approaching to drink, and even the roar of the lion had sometimes sounded in their ears.

During the daytime, they had often noticed abundance of game in many parts of the country through which they had ridden. The *spoor* of elephants and rhinoceri was especially well marked as the horsemen came to the low-lying districts of country towards the east. Koodoo, and many of the other South African antelope species also, were met with in large numbers.

But, though the land seemed to possess a variegated and plentiful fauna, and to be characterised by great variety of vegetation, human beings appeared to be scarce; for Retief and his companions saw, it is said, no Natives anywhere between the Drakensberg and the sea. The desolating scourge of Chaka's armies, or rather—to be more exact—of the hordes of refugees driven south of the Tugela by the Zulu Impis, had swept the country of its inhabitants. Year after year, the conquering hosts had overrun the fertile land. In the track of the Zulu conquest, flame-scorched ruins and the sun-bleached bones of human skeletons testified to the sufferings of the vanquished. The victors had taken a keen delight in slaughter. The legions of Dingaan, Chaka's successor, were as cruel and as merciless; but their predecessors had done the work of conquest and destruction so thoroughly, that no victims were left for massacre. The few thousands of Natives remaining alive in all Natal had concealed themselves in the woods and in the mountain caves to escape from their tyrants.

The White strangers had ridden through what was, indeed, a desolate land; and now, when they were at the Inchanga mountain, Retief and his fellow-travellers obtained their first view of the Indian Ocean.

As he saw spread out before him that vast expanse of deep blue waters, which in the far distance appeared to be merged into the sky, the Africander leader, no doubt, once more reviewed in his own mind the great projects which he entertained. On the shores of that Ocean would be the harbour for the free Nation which he would bring to this land. Here would be, for his countrymen—driven from the homes of their forefathers by unjust government and bad laws—liberty; for the remnants of Native races—cruelly oppressed by their conquerors—protection and life in place of extermination and destruction. <small>View of the Sea from Mount Inchanga.</small>

In the history of the Western world the picture of Balboa first viewing the Pacific Ocean from the mountains of Panama has been handed down to our age enshrined in all the glamour of romance. The portrait of Pieter Retief in sight of the Indian Ocean has not yet been painted. What subject is more worthy the artist's brush? <small>The Africander Balboa.</small>

We Africanders are called "an inarticulate people," a Nation without a Language: as yet, we have no Artists.

Another pale reflex, then, of the Past:—

As Balboa stood on the mountains of Panama, gazed on the magnificent expanse of the great Pacific Ocean, and, fired with all the enthusiastic Crusader-like ardour which characterised the explorers of those days, prayed to God that he might be able to navigate the waters of the unknown seas, so also stand Pieter Retief and his five companions on that ridge of Mount Inchanga, viewing the Indian Ocean. For a moment they rest their weary steeds, there where now goes the road to the sea from the town still named in memory of the great Africander leader, and look out upon the broad waters stretching towards the horizon. They, also, are stirred by enthusiasm. Ardent patriotism and love of liberty have led them—disgusted with a stupid Government, which desired to treat them as subjects, but which forgot justice and ignored their rights—to leave the land of their birth and the associations and surroundings which were dear to them, and to found a new home for themselves and their descendants by transforming the wilderness into a new Fatherland, where they will be free to make their own laws and establish their own Government.

We are justified in supposing that, as Retief's eyes rested on the blue waters to the east, he, also, prayed heaven to help him in realising his aspirations—freedom and independent nationality for his people; and for the new land through which he and his companions had travelled—not the cross and the sword, but peace and prosperity. As he came to that Ocean's shores from those mountains in the distance, he had seen around him a fertile country without inhabitants—the desolation wrought by the cruel conquering regiments of the Zulu Kings. For the surviving remnants of the oppressed and persecuted Natives, now hiding in the mountains and in the forests, the White strangers brought protection. The laws of the new State would give them security of life and property. The Republic would save them from further destruction. Retief's noble nature abhorred cruelty and tyranny. In founding a Republic for White people, he did not forget the rights and interests of the Natives. This is proved by the special clauses in the Constitution which he framed.

To look once more on the reflex :—

Beyond the mountains to the west, on the great plains thousands of feet above him, his countrymen are awaiting his return. And thousands of feet above them again, high up among the clouds, are the giant silent rock sentinels of the Drakensberg summits, which in former days have heard the thundering tread of Chaka's Impis, and which, for aught we know, in the dim, distant past, may have witnessed the march of Arabian or Phœnician legions. They have seen the White men pass eastward to the sea. They have witnessed the advent of the herald of the Republic in Africa. Veiled in mist and crowned with clouds, lie the thickly-wooded glens, the steep ravines, the frowning *kransen* of the Amajuba, predestined to be an eternal monument through the ages which are to come.

Pieter Retief at Inchanga, gazing on the rolling waves of the Indian Ocean in the distance, is the representative and the embodiment of Africander aspirations. *Africander Aspirations.* The sea itself is emblematic of those aspirations—of his people's unconquerable determination to advance towards the achievement of their independence and to fulfil their destiny.

Trichard and his party had previously found a way to the ocean much further north. This fact only became known to the southern pioneers after Retief's death, when Carel Trichard, one of the few survivors of the first trek, reached Natal.

Having now ascertained for themselves the suitability

of Natal for settlement by the Emigrants whom they represented, Retief and his fellow-travellers rode down to the Bay to visit the small Colony of English hunters and traders. They arrived at Durban on 19th October, 1837. The inhabitants seem to have given them a very hearty welcome. An address was publicly presented to the leader of the Emigrant Farmers. In this document the residents at the Bay of Natal expressed themselves as ready and willing to co-operate with the Farmers in the formation of their new Commonwealth; and, on Retief stating his intention of proceeding to visit the Zulu King, Dingaan, and getting that potentate's consent to the occupation of the country, the Englishmen at once sent a messenger to Umkungunhlovu to announce this to the Chief.

Pieter Retief welcomed at Durban.

Co-operation of English Settlers to Establish the Republic.

The loyal co-operation of the English settlers with Retief, and afterwards with Maritz, will astonish no one who has carefully read the history of South Africa. For, whoever has, could not fail to notice how, repeatedly, when civilisation has had to engage in mortal combat with barbarism, all the different sections of the White inhabitants — whether of Dutch, French-Huguenot, British, or German origin—have remembered that they had interests in common, that they were Africanders; and have stood by each other in the hour of peril, in the death struggle against the forces of savagery. The Kaffir wars in the Old Colony formed the first connecting bond between the two main European elements in the White population. The establishment of the Republic in Natal, and the war against Dingaan, made the second bond of union.

CHAPTER XVIII

THE MARTYR SENTINELS

THE ACELDAMA OF THE CHLOOMA AMABOOTA

Journey to Umkungunhlovu—Dingaan's Welcome—The Captured Cattle—Proposed Cession of Territory—Account of the Second Expedition against Umsiligaas—The Campaign of the Mariqua and the Capture of Kapayin—Abandonment of Territory by the Matabele—Potgieter's Proclamation—The Foundation of the Transvaal—The Crossing of the Drakensberg—Retief at Matawaan's Kop—Sikonyella—Second Journey to Umkungunhlovu—Dingaan's Treachery—The Cession of Territory—The Dance of Death—The Last Cup—Doomed—On the Chlooma Amaboota—The Faithful Sentinels—Pillars of the Republic.

On the 27th October, 1837, Pieter Retief and his five fellow-travellers, accompanied by John Cane and Thomas Halstead as interpreters and guides, left the Bay of Natal for Umkungunhlovu. The Emigrant leader, having ascertained for himself that the White settlers at Durban were not only willing, but eager to co-operate with him in establishing an independent State in Natal, was now anxious to obtain the permission of the Zulu King to form a settlement. *Journey to Umkungunhlovu.*

Travelling in a north-easterly direction, through a country in which game (elephant, buffalo, eland, koodoo, water-buck, etc.) was then plentiful, the Voortrekker delegates saw before them a park-like land, forests alternating with grassy plains and hills. They crossed the Umgeni, Umvoti, Tugela, Lalazi, Umslatoosi, and one or two smaller streams, as also the ridges and watersheds intervening between those rivers, and then arrived at the Chief's kraal on the right bank of the White Umveloosi, where they met with a very cordial reception. Quarters were assigned to them, to rest after the fatigues of their journey; and they were supplied with abundance of meat, maize, and other food. They were honoured, as distinguished guests are among the Kaffirs, by the performance of an elaborate war dance in their presence by large numbers of young warriors.

Dingaan's Welcome.

Then some thousands of old veteran Zulu soldiers followed the younger men to dance before the King's guests. Troops of cattle—trained to execute various military movements: ranged in rows and mixed with the men of the Zulu regiments; or, after representing the loot of the conquering army in this mimic warfare, filing off, at word of command, into a kraal set aside for them—took part in the entertainment. The King sent friendly messages expressive of his pleasure in welcoming them, to the Emigrant leader and his followers; and, when receiving Retief in audience, agreed with him as to the desirability of establishing a settlement for White people in the unoccupied country south of the Tugela, at the same time stating that he would consider the matter of a cession of territory, and give his decision in a few days. Near the Zulu kraal were some sheep, which had been brought from the plains to the west of the Drakensberg by Dingaan's armies. About July or August, 1837, a large Zulu expedition had been sent to invade

Umsiligaas' territory. A great battle was fought in the Marico district between the Matabele and these invaders under Tambusa and Salela. The latter were victorious. One of the Matabele regiments, which made a very brave stand against great odds, was entirely destroyed. But the remnants of Umsiligaas' defeated army, after losing all their cattle, fell back, received reinforcements, and, again advancing against the invaders, were led to victory by the Chief's favourite general, Kalipi. The Zulus were completely beaten and driven out of the country. They managed, however, to retain and carry off with them quite a number of the captured cattle. Some of the oxen and sheep thus carried off by the Zulus had previously been taken by the Matabele in their attacks on the Emigrant encampments on the Vaal river. One of Retief's companions now recognised a few of the sheep as having belonged to the members of Potgieter's trek. When this was pointed out to Dingaan he had all that could be found collected. There were a hundred and ten. These he asked Retief to take back, and stated at the same time that the others which were captured by his armies, and which had formerly belonged to the Farmers, had been slaughtered. It is also said that Dingaan offered to give the skins to the Farmers. Retief, in his capacity as leader and representative of the Emigrants, probably asked more questions about these sheep than the Zulu Chief liked. The bold and fearless Africander had already made a great impression at Umkungunhlovu. The outward show of respect and the

The Captured Cattle.

marks of distinction with which the treacherous Chief received him proved this. The crafty savage stood in awe of these White strangers, whom he supposed to be very powerful and mighty wizards. He was always very ready to take offence, even where none was intended. It is quite possible that he may have felt piqued and angered when this matter was discussed. If so, however, he was skilful enough in diplomacy to conceal his displeasure. When, on the 8th of November, Retief and his party left Umkungunhlovu, the Chief gave him a written statement, which had been drawn up (in English) by Mr. Owen, a missionary resident at the King's kraal. In this document, Dingaan professed himself ready to cede to the Emigrants the land for which they asked, on condition of their restoring to him some cattle which had been carried off from a Zulu outpost by horsemen armed with guns and wearing European clothing. These robbers were Basutos, belonging to the tribe of Sikonyella, on the other side of the Drakensberg (on the upper Caledon river). Dingaan stated that the Zulus believed the cattle to have been taken by the Emigrant Farmers, and he wished to give Retief the opportunity of disproving this.

Accepting the conditions thus laid down by Dingaan as to the cession of territory, the Voortrekker leader now returned by way of Natal and the Drakensberg passes to the plateau regions to the west of the mountains.

Second Expedition against Umsiligaas.

Meanwhile, while Retief was coming back from Dingaan's kraal, hostilities against Umsiligaas had been resumed. After the battle of Mosega, Potgieter and his followers had founded the town of Winburg (named in commemoration of their recent victory on the Rhenoster river). Large numbers of Emigrants were then arriving from the Colony. Many of these settled and built homes for themselves at Winburg. The first township established by the pioneers of the Republic grew rapidly in size. The houses were mostly little cottages with white or clay-coloured walls, and with straw-thatched roofs. It was at Winburg that Retief's Grondwet, the first Constitution of the Republic, was promulgated, and the first Volksraad and Uitvoerende Raad or Executive Council were elected, on the 6th of June, 1837, as has been described on a previous page.

The expedition which was undertaken against Umsiligaas, towards the end of 1837, was under the joint command of Andries Hendrik Potgieter and Pieter Lafras Uys. This Commandant, who, with his father, the patriarch Jacobus Uys, came from the district of Uitenhage, had already distinguished himself in the Kaffir wars of the Old Colony, and had also (in 1834) undertaken a journey of exploration to Natal. The family of Uys was held in high estimation by the English settlers in the Eastern Province. It will be remembered that Retief, before starting for Natal and Zululand, had made preparation for an expedition against the Matabele. The object of the commando which was now organised at Winburg was to ensure the safety of the new settlement. Umsiligaas, although his forces had been defeated and his kraal at Mosega destroyed by the previous expedition under Maritz and Potgieter, was still in command of a powerful army, and had plainly shown his hostile intentions by disdaining to make any reply to the Commandant-General's demand for the restitution of the cattle which his impis had taken from the Emigrants on the Vaal river. To have left the Matabele power unbroken would have been to court a repetition of the disastrous massacres of 1836 whenever small parties of the Emigrants ventured northward on hunting expeditions. The campaign of Mosega had been interrupted by the rainy season, and by the necessity for further preparation. The force which now took the field consisted of three hundred and thirty men.* There were two separate commandoes, one under Potgieter, and the other under Uys. No auxiliary Native fighting force was taken; but some Barolongs, under Mongala and two other brothers of Matchawe, acted as scouts and herdsmen.

In October, 1837, the expedition left the Vet river, and, pursuing the same course as had been followed by the commando at the beginning of the year, crossed the Vaal and proceeded in a north-westerly direction towards Mosega. The country was found as desolate and unoccupied as before. Scouts were sent out in all directions; but no hostile Natives, indeed no inhabitants whatever, were found. The ruins of the towns and kraals, and the skeletons of the Natives who

---

* This is the figure given in his diary by Cilliers, who took part in the expedition. Theal puts the total number of Farmers in the united commandoes at a hundred and thirty-five.

had been massacred by the Matabele hordes, were seen along the way; and, when the camp fires of the expedition were lit in the valley of Mosega, where the great battle had been fought in February, no opposing impis had so far been encountered. The entire neighbourhood, as well as the immediate site, of the former regimental town, was found abandoned by the enemy. When once this fact was definitely ascertained, when it was known that by a forward movement no hostile force would be left in their rear or on their flank, the leaders of the expedition lost no time in moving northward towards the Marico,* where, it was then known, Umsiligaas had his main fighting force. The intervening space of fifty miles or so was rapidly traversed by the advancing commando; but no precaution was neglected to guard against being taken unawares by the enemy on the march northward. The mounted scouts of Uys and Potgieter rode well in front of the column. Where the country was covered with bush and acacia forests, special care was taken to avoid falling into an ambuscade; and, at the night encampments, the laager formation was adhered to, and sentinels were placed all round the main body. The horses were picketed, well within reach, in the centre of the laager. *Commando under Potgieter and Uys.*

It was early in November when the Marico Poort— the region where the Marico river makes its way, through wild forest-covered mountain gorges, to its point of junction with the Limpopo—was sighted. Three mountain ranges are here pierced by the Great Marico river in its northward course. These mountains run *Expedition to the North.*

---

* Great Marico, Mariqua, or Marikwa.

almost at right angles to the river basin. The southern range is known as the *Dwarsbergen;* and where the river finds its way through the range is the wild cañon of the *Eerste Poort.* Between this and the second transverse range of mountains, known as the *Witfonteinbergen,* the river winds by a somewhat tortuous course through a well-wooded valley. The gorge by which the Marico penetrates the second mountain range is known as *Tweede Poort.* To the north of this is another valley, stretching up to the *Derde Poort* or cleft through the third mountain range. This valley, also, has dense vegetation covering the mountain slopes, and the tract of country to the north of the third range of mountains is quite tropical in climate. The southern boundary of the region, the Dwarsbergen, lies almost directly under the 25th parallel of latitude.

This wild mountainous region of the Marico was the scene of the nine days' campaign in which Potgieter and Uys broke the power of the Matabele King. Little, or next to nothing, has been written about this contest, the issue of which was to decide whether the regions north of the Vaal should pass under White dominion, or remain the hunting-grounds of the fierce Matabele and the Aceldama of the hunted Bakwana. There was no scribe with the expedition. Sarel Cilliers, alone of all those who fought under Potgieter and Uys, in his journal, published subsequently, has made reference in a few brief lines to the fighting that took place during those nine days. His statement is to the effect that three thousand Matabele fell in the series of battles on the Marico.

The passes in the first range of mountains were soon seized by the attacking columns. Then followed in- *Campaign of the Mariqua.* cessant fighting; first, in the valley to the immediate north of the Dwarsbergen; then in the Witfontein mountain range; afterwards in the valley to the north of these mountains; and, finally, in the third range of mountains to the north. Where the country was much broken by bush and rocky ridges, the detachments of Uys and Potgieter fought on foot, and—always with their horses close at hand, to guard against the enemy making a flanking movement in strong force, and thus cutting them off—by a constant and well directed fire, drove the Matabele further northwards. Where broad stretches of open country favoured their tactics, the Matabele Chiefs adopted the old Zulu battle formation. *Nine days' Fighting.* From the front corners of a central mass or square, two long lines or columns of attack were thrown forward across the plain, attempting to surround the horsemen before attacking them at close quarters. Then the burghers fell back, galloping over the Veld, keeping parallel with the advancing lines of the impi, and directing a withering fire at the extremities or points of the columns. There would be no time for dismounting to fire on the enemy. Every one would fire from the saddle, and then load again, as well and as quickly as he could, with his horse cantering all the time. When the retreat had been kept up long enough to scatter and divide the Matabele, then the horsemen would wheel round and charge the disorganised masses, chasing them back over the plain, and inflicting heavy losses on them. Valley after valley, and mountain range

28   HISTORY OF THE REPUBLIC

Defeat of the Matabele.

upon mountain range, was stubbornly contested by Umsiligaas' soldiers. But, on the ninth day, they broke and fled with hardly a show of resistance, believing that the White horsemen were invincible, and that it was useless to continue the contest any longer. They were pursued into the desert, and the foundation of

Annexation of Mataboleland and Dependencies.

the Transvaal Republic was laid by the victory which Potgieter and Uys had gained. Between six and seven thousand cattle were captured, and Commandant Potgieter immediately issued a proclamation claiming (as compensation for losses sustained by the Emigrants) authority and government, by right of conquest, over the dominions previously ruled by Umsiligaas. These territories, which the Chief had in previous years himself acquired by conquest, and which were now uninhabited, comprised more than half the modern South African Republic, as well as a large portion of the present Orange Free State Republic and all Southern Bechuana-

District of Potchefstroom.

land. The new district of Potchefstroom was now formed. It embraced all the territory north of the Vaal

Original Boundaries.

river, as far as the Zoutpansberg ranges. Its western boundary was the edge of the Kalahari Desert, so that it included a large part of what is now British Bechuanaland. Eastward, it extended as far as Rhenoster Poort.

When the early summer rains had fallen, and the grass was again sprouting on the plains to the west of the Drakensbergen, the main body of the Emigrants on their way to Natal once more approached the mountain

The Crossing of the Drakensberg.

passes. They travelled with their waggons and cattle across the large plains which now form the eastern part of the Orange Free State; and then undertook the passage of the Drakensberg.

The difficulties which they encountered in crossing the range have been thus graphically described by Cachet:

"A little to the south-west of the present main transport road along the Van Reenen's Pass one sees a grey stripe, which appears to descend almost perpendicularly from the top of the mountain and soon loses itself among the boulders and bush. It is as if some thoughtless young baboons had here constructed a glissade, which, however, to prevent accidents, had been again destroyed by the older ones scattering rocks and digging furrows over its surface. That stripe, that glissade, is the commencement of the old road used by the Farmers in 1838-39 in their trek over the mountains.

"Let us join the waggon of the Farmer whom we already know, and see how the crossing was effected. For days previously the 'path' has been taken in hand to make it somewhat practicable. The larger rocks and boulders, hurled downwards from the crest of the mountain by the lightning, or gradually loosened by the action of continuous rains, have been removed out of the way, the deepest clefts filled up with earth and stones; the steepest places somewhat levelled by the spade; branches of trees and bush removed by the axe, and the numberless water-courses and gullies made passable. But .... there are curves in the road, along projecting rocks and on the edge of precipices a thousand feet deep, which can neither be avoided nor changed; and masses of rock three or four feet high—specially constructed, apparently, for the gymnastic exercises of gems-bok and klipspringers—from which the waggon will have to be made to jump after the manner of those graceful antelopes. Only a practised Africander waggon-driver will dare to cross the mountain by this 'baboon path.'

"The whole waggon, and especially the *trek*-gear, must be once more thoroughly over-hauled before the journey is commenced; the front box-seat must be fixed by means of an extra rope to the side supports of the waggon, and all articles in the vehicle must be fastened as securely as possible, to prevent the load shifting its position and landing on the oxen. A select *span* of trek oxen must be yoked to the waggon: the leaders to step out well, those immediately in front of the rear or hindmost pair thoroughly trained to back at steep places, and the rear pair accustomed, in case of dire necessity, to let the waggon press against their bodies. The *baas* (owner or master) himself drives and his brother takes the '*touw*'—the thong by means of which the leaders are coupled together and by which they are steered. Under other circumstances this is the work of a Kaffir or Hottentot servant (often, also, on the journey, when servants are wanting, the task of the girls) but the road is so dangerous that the '*touw*' can now only be entrusted to some one who, without anything being said to him, knows how to steer the oxen. Thongs have also been fastened to the waggon, which a number of friends accompany in order to balance the vehicle—where such a proceeding becomes necessary—to save it from total destruction, by pulling at these ropes. No one remains on the waggon except the driver, who will, every now and then, have to cling with hands and feet to it, so as not to fall off, and the aged mother-in-law, who cannot walk, and places more confidence in the skilful driving of her son-in-law than in her tottering knees. When everything is ready, and when still on level ground, the oxen are deftly whipped up—'warmed,' as it is termed—and now, with double brakes on the wheels, the waggon goes slowly down the mountain side. Woe to our friend if his brake-chain gives way or the waggon-pole snaps; if his oxen shy at an ugly curve; if he does not know how to steer between that big boulder on the left and yonder hole on the right; if his rear oxen are not reliable at this and his leaders at that other spot, or the whole team does not pull evenly in that muddy hollow at the foot of the first ridge. Now the road is so slanting that five or six men are hardly able to prevent the waggon from being upset; then again so steep that the oxen can barely hold the vehicle back or drag it onwards. The worst trial comes when the heavy waggon has to jump from the rock masses three or four feet high, in imminent danger of being dashed to pieces. One faulty move, and the vehicle lies in the ravine a thousand feet deep. But it is as if a Higher Power has stretched forth a protecting hand, and, after hours of arduous labour, the farmer can enjoy the satisfaction of outspanning at the foot of the mountain on Natal's soil, surrounded by wife and children. In this way the apparently impossible passage of the Drakensberg was completed, and thus, marvellous though it may seem, the thousand waggons descended almost without accidents. Only one waggon, as far as is known, was lost—happily without sacrifice of human lives—by being dashed to atoms over a precipice." *

Retief, in returning from Umkungunhlovu to the mountains, passed through the Klip River district of Natal. He met some of the advance parties of the pioneers who had crossed the Drakensberg. They were then laagered at Matawaan's Kop. Here future plans were discussed between them and their leader, who specially warned them not to scatter their encampments too much over the country, but to keep well together, so that, in case of necessity, they could at once concentrate their forces. This shows that he was not altogether unmindful of treachery on the part of the Zulu Chief. He was not blind to it as far as it affected others—his followers. But for himself, for his own safety, he never had a thought.

A thousand waggons of the Emigrant Farmers were by this time over the Drakensberg. Most of them had crossed by the defile already referred to (Van Reenen's Pass). Others had travelled by a pass lying more to the north (De Beers). All were now at the foot of the mountains, on the Natal side, and yet others were following from the plains to the north of the Orange river. While Retief was preparing for his second journey to Umkungunhlovu, some of the Emigrants begged him not

marginal note: Retief at Matawaan's Kop.

* "Worstelstrijd der Transvalers aan het volk van Nederland Verhaald."

again to risk his life by placing himself once more in the power of the Zulu King. They were beginning to have forebodings of evil, and many of them were of opinion that the Zulu Chief had treacherous designs. Retief's life, they said, was too valuable to the community that it should be endangered; some one else should be sent to negotiate with Dingaan, and to take back the Zulu cattle.

Several brave spirits offered to take the task upon themselves rather than again see their beloved leader endanger his own life. Maritz was one of these noble and unselfish volunteers. Truly, this man's name deserves to be remembered with love and respect by his countrymen—always self-denying, ever ready to do more than his duty.

The historians of South Africa have pointed out—some with scorn, others in sorrow—the too frequent quarrels and dissensions among the Emigrants, about this time and at a later date. But instances of such generous loyalty to each other and to the common cause, as we find in this proposal of Maritz, go far to make us forget the apparent want of cordial co-operation which was sometimes noticeable.

Returning to the western side of the Drakensberg, the Emigrant leader at once took steps to recover the Zulu cattle. Sikonyella's Kaffirs had also stolen some horses belonging to the Farmers. A small commando having been quickly organised, these were retaken, and the Chief himself was surprised and captured without any difficulty. He was now informed that, unless the cattle taken from the Zulus were immediately given up,

Sikonyella.

Second Journey to Umkungunhlovu.

he would be detained as a prisoner. This energetic action had the desired effect, Dingaan's oxen soon made their appearance, and preparations were made to return to Umkungunhlovu with them. Retief argued that he should himself go a second time. Were another, he said, deputed to negotiate with Dingaan, the Zulu Chief and his people would look upon the mission, unaccompanied as it was by the leader, as showing distrust and suspicion on the part of the Emigrants; and failure to secure the desired cession of territory would be the result. Rather than that this should happen he was prepared to risk anything. But, as to the question of danger, why, there was none. He would even consent to take a strong body of volunteers with him. His followers, when they saw that Retief was determined to go, insisted on permission for volunteers to accompany him, and he made no objection. The Zulu Chief, he said, had, by way of compliment, entertained them with great display of warlike pomp. Let them, in return, show him a small body of their fighting forces, armed and mounted. Volunteers at once came forward, and about seventy were allowed to accompany Retief. A much larger force should have been taken; but neither the Commandant-General nor his followers knew the real character of Dingaan and his councillors, Tambusa and Salela. Their treachery and deceit were soon to be revealed.

At this day it seems almost incredible that greater care was not taken to guard against surprise. Implicit trust appears to have been placed by some of the Emigrants in Dingaan's word and good faith. And why?

Did they—most of them men from the Eastern Province of the Cape Colony; nearly all born and bred on the frontier; well acquainted with the character of the Kaffir races; and knowing the history of the early Kaffir wars—did they believe the Chief to be incapable of treachery? This is very unlikely, to say the least of it. Besides, we have direct evidence that many of them had their suspicions. The representations which were made to Retief point to this assumption.

The truth seems to be that they believed in Dingaan because Retief believed in him—at least they thought he did. Did he in reality? It is probable that the Commandant thought no better of Dingaan than of other savage potentates, and believed that he, Dingaan, would keep faith with a White man only as long as that White man showed his strength and was to be feared—that the Zulu Chief would not hesitate, should the opportunity offer, to destroy any one whom he no longer feared. It seemed as if Retief realised to the full that there was danger to himself; and those of his followers who placed themselves as a guard around him, and who afterwards died with him, also realised this. Coming forward in such numbers as they deemed sufficient to overawe the Zulu Chief should he meditate treachery, they accompanied their leader to Zululand. There were Bothmas and De Klerks, names honoured among the inhabitants of the frontier since Slachtersnek —as borne by those who had suffered and died for South Africa. Liebenberg, Pretorius, Botha, Basson, Cilliers, De Beer, Oosthuizen, Marais, Meyer, Greyling, Van Vuuren, Malan, Labuschagne, were some of the other names of those who now rode to their death with Retief.

There were sixty-six Europeans in all. They were followed on horseback by about thirty Native servants, leading spare horses and taking charge of baggage and provisions. In passing through Natal, Retief once more impressed on those of his countrymen whom he found encamped along the line of his route the necessity of keeping well together, and of not spreading themselves out over too large an area of country before everything was settled and the cession of territory finally ratified by Dingaan.

The last injunctions, the last commands of the Emigrant leader were for the safety of his people. But his instructions were not attended to. In fancied security, large numbers of the Farmers spread their encampments over the new country into which their arduous passage of the mountains had brought them. Finding everywhere delightful pasturage and abundant water for their cattle, they looked upon the land as already theirs. Retief, their leader, had carried out his part of the agreement entered into with Dingaan in their name, and was even now taking back the King's cattle to Umkungunhlovu. They had such confidence in their Commandant, that they scattered their encampments along the Klip, Bushman, Mooi, Buffalo, and Tugela rivers. Others—those who had crossed by the more southern passes of the Drakensberg—were now encamped on the upper waters of the Umgeni and Umkomanzi.

Meanwhile, the Zulu Chief and his councillors were

awaiting Retief's arrival at Umkungunhlovu. There can be no doubt whatever that Dingaan had been much impressed by the striking personality of this remarkable man on the occasion of the first visit, and, while pretending to be very well disposed towards the Emigrants, had procrastinated and evaded as much as he could when discussing the question of cession of territory. Fearing the power of the Emigrants, the Chief's policy had been to gain time, and, meanwhile, to find out more about these strangers. In his previous intercourse with White men, Dingaan had found them always ready to propitiate him with gifts. These new arrivals had brought no presents. Boldly their leader had spoken to him. He whose very name was a terror to all surrounding nations, he who had slain Chaka, had listened to the fearless words of the White Chief who had dared, in the very stronghold of the Zulu nation, to lay claim to cattle and sheep which had been taken in war by the Zulu armies.

And now, while Dingaan was waiting for the return of the audacious strangers, there had come to Umkungunhlovu the tidings of the complete defeat of the great Matabele Chief whose army had but recently conquered that of Dingaan. Then had followed the news of the crossing of the Drakensberg by large numbers of the Emigrants. Intelligence is rapidly conveyed to a great Kaffir Chief from even the remotest frontiers of the territory over which he claims authority. The traveller passes through what appears to him a desolate and entirely voiceless wilderness. True, the country is uninhabited; but on the tops of the lonely hills, here and there, Native sentinels are stationed. Soon a tiny column of smoke, perhaps quite unobserved by the uninitiated, rises from the side or from the very summit of one of these mountains. This signal, even if noticed by the White traveller, is to him quite meaningless except as an indication of the probable presence of a stray wild Bushman among the barren rocks. To the Kaffir sentinel on that other hilltop away towards the horizon, however, the little column of smoke is a telegraphic message. When he has deciphered it, which he does in some mysterious way— God knows how—by carefully noting the outline, direction, volume, etc., of the smoke column, he either repeats the signal by lighting on his own signal post a fire, the smoke of which is watched, and its message deciphered, by a sentinel on a more distant mountain summit; or, in case there is no other signal hill near enough to telegraph to, he runs across the intervening plain to the nearest post previously agreed on as a station for the King's intelligence department, and there delivers the message.

Kaffir Telegraph Service.

It may seem almost incredible to European readers, and yet it is a fact, that some of the express runners in the service of the great Abantu Chiefs travel at a rate of speed which is fully equal to that of a good horse. They carry the King's messages across the plains where no hilltops can be utilised for the smoke telegraph signals, which serve where the country is mountainous. The entire system, which has been used by all the principal Kaffir races from time immemorial, works so expeditiously that, over and over again in the history of South Africa, it has been proved to convey intelligence more rapidly than the European horse-express. To take only one instance out of many. In the Transvaal War of Independence, when the Republican Executive was at the town of Heidelberg, news of the disasters to the British forces in the Drakensberg was brought by Native messengers sent by friendly Kaffir Chiefs. These messengers invariably reached their destination some considerable time before the arrival of the Transvaal express riders; and it is well known that the latter get over the ground more quickly than English cavalry scouts.

By the South African savage every superior acquirement of the White race, every art, every accomplishment which the Natives do not themselves possess, is looked upon as witchcraft. Nothing is so much feared, nothing so much respected, as the power of magic. Quite as much as the Aztecs had been astonished and awed by the Spaniards on horseback, were the Zulus also impressed and astounded by the first appearance among them of large bodies of Europeans with firearms—of White men riding on horseback, and bringing their household goods and chattels, as well as their families, into the country by means of the ox-waggon. The smoke signals and the King's runners rapidly carried the tidings to Umkungunhlovu, and thus ran the message:—

"They come in thousands across the great mountains. They bring with them their wives and children; they mean to dwell in the land, and their huge houses are drawn along the ground by trained oxen. They also bring horses with them—the animals on which they rode when they conquered the Matabele nation; and they carry those weapons by means of which they hurl thunder and lightning, and death. The most powerful wild beasts—the lion, the rhinoceros, and the elephant—are struck down by their magic and die, as the antelope dies by the Zulu assegai."

There is reason to suppose that Dingaan was informed as to the attitude which Retief and his followers had taken up in relation to the English Government in South Africa. In the archives of the Colony of the Cape of Good Hope is a letter, dated Port Natal, 20th July, 1838, and addressed to Major Charters (Secretary to Governor Major-General Napier), at Cape Town. It was written by a Mr. John Parker. Mr. Parker accuses John Cane of having caused the massacre of Retief's party by treacherously sending a message to Dingaan: that the Emigrants, who had run away from the Cape Colony against the wishes of the English Government, would try to drive him from his country, and that the English would not assist them. Parker states that Daniel Toohey, a clerk in Maynard's business at the Port, informed him that he, Toohey, had it from Cane's own mouth that such a message had been sent.* There does not seem, however, to be any other evidence against Cane than this hearsay statement; and the subsequent career of the man—his co-operation with others to help to organise an expedition against the Zulus in order to punish them for their treachery, and, most of all, his own death on the battlefield while fighting bravely

* Theal: "History of South Africa."

against Dingaan's army—tends to disprove Mr. Parker's statement altogether. Theal himself discredits the accusation.

Had such a message really been sent to Dingaan, it was more likely to have emanated from Henry Ogle than from John Cane. Both were Chiefs under Dingaan. Both had about an equal interest in land which, had the cession made by the Zulu Chief taken effect, would have passed into the possession of Retief and his followers. Cane, however, had co-operated with Retief, and had acted as guide and interpreter on the occasion of the Emigrant leader's first visit to Umkungunhlovu. Ogle had held aloof, and at a later stage of his career showed bitter hostility to the Emigrants. He and Richard King afterwards rendered themselves notorious by organising marauding bands of Kaffirs, who carried off cattle belonging to the Emigrants, and, after murdering White men, committed atrocities on defenceless women—the wives of Farmers who had taken part in the war against the British in Natal. Besides, Ogle's previous history was not without stain. He had put to death, by order of Dingaan, a Chief named Hlambamanzi; and, as a consequence of this act, had Retief's Government become established in Natal, it is not unlikely that he would have been tried for murder.

But Dingaan needed no message from any White adventurer or outlaw to make him decide on the destruction of Retief. The Chief was possessed of an almost maniacal passion for putting to death whoever he feared. His own brothers, and all the great Indunas

Dingaan's Character.

who had been faithful to Chaka, as well as all their followers, had shared that fate; and the favourite Councillor was he who always advised Dingaan to inflict the penalty of death. Dingaan's brother Panda, as well as all the Indunas whose evidence was taken before the *krygsraad* in Zululand in 1840, testified that the Zulu King never committed a murder without first consulting Tambusa, and that this Chief had taken a leading part in advising the massacre of Retief and of all the Emigrants.

On the 3rd of February, the Africander leader and the cavalcade which accompanied him rode over the hills which brought them in sight of Umkungunhlovu. They were received with every possible demonstration of welcome by the Zulus. The cattle which they had recaptured from the Basuto Chief, Sikonyella, were now restored to the King, who was, apparently, delighted at this proof of Retief's sincerity and good-will. As on the occasion of their first visit, elaborate war dances were performed in honour of the Emigrant delegates, and soon the day arrived on which the cession of territory was to be ratified by Dingaan in Council.

The Rev. Mr. Owen, a missionary who was then resident at the Zulu town, was asked to draw up a document embodying this cession, and the King and his councillors affixed their marks in lieu of signature. Three of the burghers also signed as witnesses.

"UMKUNGUNHLOVU, *4th February*, 1838.

"Be it known to all and everybody: that, as Pieter Retief has retaken my cattle which Sikonyella had stolen, which cattle the above-mentioned Retief has now delivered to me, therefore now I, Dingaan, King of the Zulus, declare and certify that I have deemed it right to cede to him, Retief, and to his countrymen, the region Port Natal with all the land attached to it, that is to say, from the Tugela as far as the Umzimvubu River to the West, and from the sea to the North, as far as the country may be suitable for occupation, and as far as it belongs to me—which I hereby do, and give to them as their property in perpetuity.

<small>The Cession of Territory.</small>

As Witnesses	† Mark of Dingaan.
M. Oosthuizen.	Chief Councillors
A. C. Greyling.	✗ Maoro.
B. J. Liebenberg.	✗ Julavusa.
	✗ Manondo."

Such was the wording of that historic document.

Retief's mission was accomplished. His people would have a free harbour. The commerce of the world would be drawn to their coasts. Their flag would take its place among those of other free nations. The Republic would arise on the shores of that ocean. But its founder and his brave companions would soon be no more. It was part of the wily strategy of Dingaan to lure them to their destruction by his feigned candour and straightforwardness. So completely had the crafty Chief succeeded in concealing his real intentions from the Emigrants, that they would not listen to the warnings of the Rev. Mr. Owen, who seems to have understood Dingaan's character well, and who appears

<small>Dingaan's Treachery.</small>

to have repeatedly urged on Retief and the other leaders the necessity of extreme caution in all their dealings with the Zulus. Thomas Halstead, the interpreter, also seems to have feared treachery, and to have warned Retief to be on his guard. The latter, however, firmly maintained that there was no need whatever for any apprehension, that he was quite positive the King was acting honestly, and was friendly towards them.

After Dingaan's formal ratification of the cession of territory, the Farmers began to make preparations for their return journey. But the Chief sent a messenger to Retief, asking him to tarry another day in order that more war dances might be performed. It was requisite, the messenger stated, that this should be done, so as to properly honour the King's guests. The Emigrant leader readily acquiesced. On the 6th of February, after the performance of another great war dance by some of the most distinguished regiments, and when the Emigrants were on the point of departing, having already sent their servants to fetch the horses, Dingaan requested that they would come into the enclosure of the kraal and drink a parting cup of Kaffir beer (*Yuala*) with him before commencing their journey.

The Dance of Death.

The Last Cup.

Putting an unaccountable trust in the good faith of their hosts, Retief and his companions went forward, and even laid aside their arms at the entrance to the kraal. This was the fatal mistake.

It is said that Halstead and one or two others remonstrated with Retief, and advised that they should go armed, but that the leader thought that, by so doing, they would show that they distrusted the Zulus. Large numbers of Natives were noticed inside the enclosure. Another war dance was performed, apparently in honour of the strangers. Two of the most famous Zulu regiments, the *Umshlanga Umjama* (Black Shields) and the *Umshlanga Umshlopa* (White Shields), were circling round with earth-resounding, thundering tread. The ground trembled with the incessant heavy thump of the feet of two thousand dusky warriors. Accompanying voices intoned the cadences of the battle song. Loud and clear rang out the herald's mimic challenge to the foe. Stalwart captains, whose head circlets were ornamented with plumes of splendid ostrich feathers, muscular Indunas, whose loins and shoulders were partly covered with massive leopard-skin karosses, roared and bellowed their words of command in deep-toned basso; and, from all the line of Zulu soldiers, came the answering echo of deep bass voices, as once more the earth seemed to tremble under the heels of the dancers. Then the vessel containing the maize brew was brought, and, as the Emigrants sat down to drink the parting cup, Dingaan, giving the signal to his warriors, called out: "*Bulala Amatagati!*" ("Kill the wizards!") and stepped backward towards his hut. In an instant the doomed men were seized. Halstead shouted out in Zulu: "Let me speak to the King," and, at the same time, remarked to his companions: "We are done for." Dingaan merely waved his hand, to signify that he had decided; and then the unfortunate victims were set upon by the crowd of Zulus armed with battle-clubs and assegais. One or two of the

<small>Doomed.</small>

Farmers managed to draw their pocket-knives and despatch a few of the murderers before they were themselves slaughtered. Most of the others were dragged away to the hill Chlooma Amaboota, which overlooked the kraal, and is situated at the top of a precipice. Here they were killed, in most cases by blows on the head. From the accounts that have been obtained from Zulus who took part in the massacre, it appears that Retief himself was first made to witness the execution of all his companions, that he was then struck on the head and killed, and that, after his chest had been ripped open by the sharp cutting blade of an assegai, his heart was taken out and brought to Dingaan. According to Captain Cornwallis Harris, who, in his work on South Africa, gives an account of the murder, Halstead, who was one of those who succeeded in drawing a knife before he was secured, and in killing with it two of his assailants, was tortured by being flayed alive. The bodies of Retief and the others were not stripped by the Zulus, but were all impaled on stakes driven into the ground on the hill Chlooma Amaboota. There they remained, for more than ten months, until the 21st of December, 1838, when the victorious commando, under Andries Pretorius, captured Umkungunhlovu. On that occasion, the deed of cession of Natal, signed by Dingaan, was found in a small leather despatch bag on the dead body of Retief.

* * * * * * *

In all history there are few more tragic pictures than that of the martyred leader keeping guard on that hill—his faithful heart torn from his body, his sixty-five murdered companions keeping watch with him, guarding the document for which they had given their lives, and on which their Nation's claim to independence in their own land of Natal rests.

The days, the weeks, the months, roll on, and, still stationed on that precipice, stand those faithful sentinels, the guard of death, waiting for the advent of those to whom they have bequeathed the inheritance of their people's freedom. Through all their lonely vigil their leader holds clasped to his side, even in death, that document which will give life to a new Nation. The Faithful Sentinels.

The savage Zulus look with awe on the silent watchers when the darkness of night falls upon the mountains. Even the vultures and wild beasts respect the dead sentinels.*

The Republic in South Africa is not built on sand. Its foundations are on rocks. Mountain summits— Slachtersnek, Chlooma Amaboota, Amajuba—are the central supporting pillars of the enduring edifice. Pillars of the Republic.

Names of those who were murdered at Umkungunhlovu (from Theal's "History of South Africa"):

"Dirk Aukamp, Willem Basson, Jan de Beer, Matthys de Beer, Barend van den Berg, Pieter van den Berg the elder, Pieter van den Berg the younger, Jan Beukes, Joachim Botha, Gerrit Botma the elder, Gerrit Botma the younger, Christiaan Breidenbach, Jan Brits, Pieter Brits the elder, Pieter Brits the younger,

---

* "Aasvogels en wilde dieren schenen eerbied gehad te hebben voor de lijken dier braven, en ze onaangetast te hebben gelaten."—CACHET.

Pieter Cilliers, Andries van Dyk, Marthinus Esterhuizen, Samuel Esterhuizen, Hermanus Fourie, Abraham Greyling, Rynier Grobbelaar, Jacobus Hatting, Thomas Holstead, Jacobus Hugo, Jacobus Jooste, Pieter Jordaan, Abraham de Klerk, Jacobus de Klerk, Jan de Klerk, Balthazer Klopper, Coenraad Klopper, Lukas Klopper, Pieter Klopper, Hendrik Labuschagne, Barend Liebenberg, Daniel Liebenberg, Hercules Malan, Carel Marais, Jan van der Merwe, Pieter Meyer, Barend Oosthuizen, Jacobus Oosthuizen, Jan Oosthuizen, Marthinus Oosthuizen, Jacobus Opperman the elder, Jacobus Opperman the younger, Frederik Pretorius, Jan Pretorius, Marthinus Pretorius, Matthys Pretorius the elder, Matthys Pretorius the younger, Pieter Retief, Isaac Roberts, Jan Roberts, Christiaan van Schalkwyk, Gerrit Scheepers, Jan Scheepers, Marthinus Scheepers, Stephanus Scheepers, Stephanus Smit, Pieter Taute, Gerrit Visagie, Stephanus van Vuuren, Hendrik de Wet, and Jan de Wet."

CHAPTER XIX

THE LIFE AND DEATH STRUGGLE

THE DARKEST HOUR BEFORE THE DAWN

The Massacres of 11th February—Sunrise on the Mooi River—Weenen —Moordkraal—Blauwkrans—Bushman's River—The Fight at Van Rensburg's Laager—Marthinus Oosthuizen's Ride—Battle on the Bushman's River—Determined Zulu Onslaught—Brave Defence of Maritz's Laager—Noon—Cilliers, Malan, and Joubert to the Rescue—Exploits of Cilliers' Patrol—Renewed Zulu Assault on Maritz's Laager—Repulse of the Attacking Columns—Evening—'*Weenen*' for the Lost Ones—Brave Africander Women—Potgieter and Uys to the Rescue—Alexander and Robert Biggar—Dissensions Forgotten—Advance into Zululand—Battle of the Italeni—Death of Pieter and Dirk Cornelis Uys—Retreat of Potgieter—Abandonment of Natal by his Party—The English Expedition—Battle of Tugela—Death of Robert Biggar and his Brave Followers—Capture of Durban by Dingaan's Army—Reinforcements and New Encampments—Poverty and Distress—British Mission—Loyalty to the Soil of Africa—Proclamation by the British Government—Zulu Assault on Laager at Bushman's River—A Sortie—Foundation of Potchefstroom—The Winter of 1838 in Natal—In much Suffering and Misery—The Voices—To the Rescue—Carel Landman—Andries Pretorius.

DINGAAN and his councillors lost no time in following up the Umkungunhlovu massacre by a fierce onslaught on the encampments of the Emigrants along the Mooi, Bushman, Blauwkrans, and Tugela Rivers. Tambusa and Salela, at the head of ten regiments, ten thousand Zulu warriors in all, marched rapidly from Umkungunhlovu to the Tugela. Having crossed the stream near its junction with the Mooi River, the Zulus, at daybreak on 11th February,* surprised a small encampment of the Emigrants between the Mooi and Bushman's Rivers. Some of the waggons here stood a little to the southeast of the present village of Weenen, and others were further east still, on the banks of the Mooi River. All

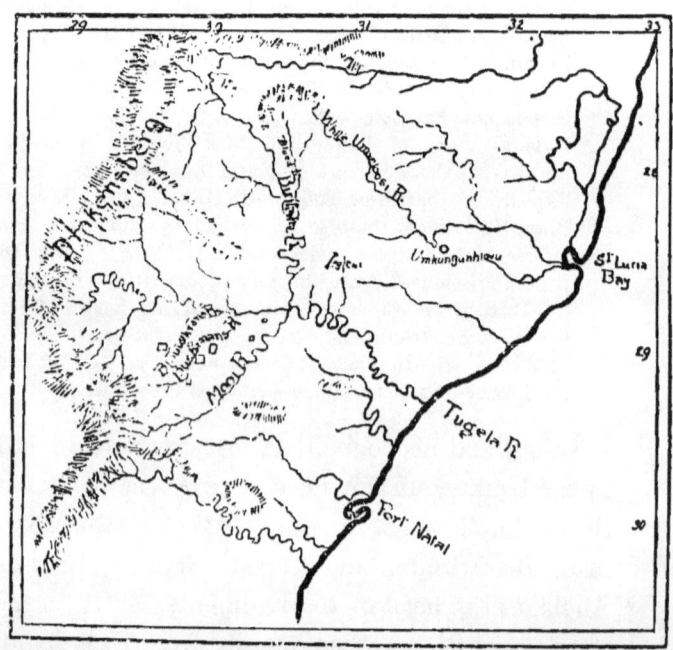

Sketch-Map to illustrate the Narrative of the Massacres of 11th February, 1838. Laagers of Emigrant Farmers on Mooi, Bushman's, and Blauwkrans Rivers, with the Position of Umkungunhlovu and of Italeni.

The Massacre of 11th February. these were surrounded in the early dawn, when the occupants were still asleep, by thousands of Zulu warriors, who, shouting their fierce battle-cry, rushed on the doomed people and butchered men, women, and children, without mercy, before they could make even an

* 17th, According to Theal.

attempt to defend themselves. Two or three lads were the only individuals who escaped. They fled to one of the other encampments on the Bushman's River, where preparations for defence were then quickly made. Large numbers of the Zulus went further up the Tugela to attack the Emigrant encampments on that stream and on the Blauwkrans River, while other attacking columns, thousands strong, threw themselves on the small laagers on the Bushman's River.

* * * * * * * *

Sunrise on the Mooi, Bushman's, and Tugela Rivers illumines a gruesome charnel-house of slaughter on the fury-swept veld. The flames from the burning waggons of the encampments light up the lineaments of the dead:—grey-haired men and young lads, their faces cold and blue, their bodies mutilated and ripped open by the sharp cutting edge of the assegai; women, with children at their breasts, lying in pools of clotted blood, their long hair dishevelled, their stony eyes turned towards heaven; and young girls and little children with their features disfigured, and their skulls broken by the murderers. There is no one left alive to weep for them.

Sunrise on the Mooi River.

As the sunlight bursts over the landscape, musket shots — the loud, reverberating roar of the heavy elephant guns—are heard higher up the Tugela. It is another death struggle. About four miles from where Colenso is now, at a spot that has since been named Moordkraal, the Bezuidenhouts are being attacked in their encampment. One or two of them have barely time to fire a few shots and bring down the foremost

Moordkraal.

Zulus, when they are overwhelmed by hundreds of the enemy; and here, also, not one, except a young lad, escapes. He, the only survivor, finds his way to the laager of the Rensburgs on the Bushman River.

<small>Blauwkrans.</small> Soon another camp, that of the Prinsloos and Bothas, on the Blauwkrans River, is overwhelmed by the rush of thousands of Zulus. Pouring over the ridge of hills, between which and the stream this camp is situated, the savages swarm down on the hapless people. At daybreak, when one of the other camps was attacked, the reports of musket shots had been heard at this laager; but it was thought that Retief and the other delegates, who were then expected from Zululand, had returned and were announcing their arrival by firing off their guns. Now the cause of the firing is explained. In attempting to fight their way through to Maritz's laager on the Bushman's River, the Prinsloos, Bothas, Botmas,* and all with them, are surrounded, and another massacre ensues. Twenty women, who have tried to conceal themselves on one of the waggons, are all stabbed to death by the Zulu assegais. A small relief column from Doornkop, Retief's laager, fight their way through to the spot, and find every man, woman, and child, in Prinsloo's encampment dead, with the exception of a boy named Rousseau, and two young girls—Johanna Catharina van der Merwe, with twenty-six, and Margaretha Catharina Prinsloo with twenty-two assegai wounds. These children are found lying among the dead, and are the only people rescued by the relievers.

<small>* Hofstede, p. 40.</small>

All the small camps along the Mooi River and on the Blauwkrans River, as well as the encampment on the Tugela, have been taken by the Zulus. Lurid flames and thick clouds of smoke mark the places where the carnage has been greatest. On the Bushman's River, a stream which flows north-eastward into the Tugela between the Mooi and the Blauwkrans Rivers, a fierce battle is in progress. On the left bank of that stream, the small laager of the Van den Bergs is soon overpowered by the enemy, and its handful of defenders all killed. The encampment of the Loggenbergs, on the right hand bank of the river, shares the same fate. But the Rensburgs—eighteen men only—stand their ground and beat off the Zulus. Soon after daybreak their camp had been aroused by the young fugitive, Daniel Bezuidenhout. He brought the tidings of the massacre of all his people in their encampment on the Tugela. "To arms!" was the cry. "The Zulus will soon be here." Instantly preparations for defence were made. Soon the warriors came with a rush. But they were met with such a withering volley, and such a well-sustained fire is kept up by the defenders, that at ten o'clock in the forenoon the Van Rensburgs still hold their position, close to a small *koppie* on the river bank, well protected on one side by a steep precipice. Now, however, their ammunition begins to fail. All hope seems gone. Death seems near. But three horsemen are seen coming across the plain. Marthinus Oosthuizen, Jacob Naude, and Abraham de Beer ride up, coming to their assistance from the laager of Maritz, five miles off. When Oosthuizen learns that they are short of

[margin: Bushman's River.]

[margin: The Fight at Van Rensburg's Laager.]

Marthinus Oosthuizen's Ride.

ammunition, he puts spurs to his horse; shoots down more than one Zulu who attempts to stop him; makes his way to a waggon some distance off on the plain; and brings back the powder and the bullets which are required, charging through a line of Zulus on his return, and escaping without injury. Then the defenders, encouraged by this bold exploit, open a terrific fire on the enemy. The attacking columns hesitate, waver, break, and are pursued over the veld by the handful of brave men.

Battle on the Bushman's River.

Still the smoke clouds roll across the plain, from the burning camps in the distance. Incessant heavy musketry firing resounds, further away, on the right bank of the Bushman's River. Maritz and his companions are making a brave stand for life. At their camp, they are surrounded by large numbers of the enemy. The waggons have been drawn up in the laager formation; for the defenders have been warned of the impending onslaught at early dawn. Thirty-three men have taken their posts inside that square, and, when Tambusa's fierce warriors form their circle round the camp and hurl their storming masses against its sides, the elephant guns belch forth their fatal thunders; large eight-ounce bullets and tremendous charges of slug-shot plough through the Zulu ranks; and hundreds of the best soldiers in the Zulu army go down. Still the attacking line presses onward. When the front ranks have fallen or given way, those following them seize the dead bodies of their companions, and hold them up to act as shields against the bullets of the Farmers, rushing

Determined Zulu Onslaught.

onward all the time to the laager. Dragging at the

wheels of the waggons and seizing the chains that lash the vehicles together, creeping underneath the shafts and stabbing at the legs and feet of the Emigrants, the Kaffirs make frantic efforts to force the position. But the thirty-three men inside the square stand firm, and pour more death-dealing volleys into the dense black masses around them. Loading and firing proceeds rapidly; for nearly every man has one or more spare guns, and the women and girls are moulding bullets, and are helping to load the muskets for their husbands and fathers. Brave Defence of Maritz's Laager.

Now the scorching hot February sun is high overhead. The smouldering fires of the encampments which were destroyed by the enemy in the early morning have nearly burnt out. The steamy mists hanging over the hilltops seem to mix with the black clouds of smoke. Occasionally, the echoing volleys of the elephant guns are heard on the distant plain, where other laagers are engaged in the death struggle, and where small bodies of Africander horsemen are galloping about, firing on the Zulus, and attempting to reinforce and to assist the small encampments which are still holding out. Mere handfuls of men perform prodigies of valour. We have already seen Oosthuizen, Naude, and De Beer saving the laager of the Van Rensburgs. Now Sarel Cilliers, the Huguenot Ironside, who in his journal has left us some account of his exploits on that memorable day, appears on the scene, and also Malan and Joubert, of the Doornkop laager, who had come with Retief from the Winterberg. Their relatives and friends had been slain with the Commandant, and stand among the cold Noon.

Cilliers, Malan, and Joubert.

sentinels of death on the Chlooma Amaboota; and now, they themselves are on the battlefield. The heroism of despair, the enthusiasm of the sacred cause for which they are fighting, the battle fury of avengers, make these men disregard danger and death, and emulate the valour of their brave ancestors the Huguenots. They see around them the innocent victims of the fierce barbarians' savagery. The slaughtered infants, the mutilated women, all the horrible sights of that dreadful day, nerve their arms and strengthen their sinews against the foe. Sarel Cilliers tells us how he, with five others, rode to the relief of the small laager of Gert Barends, on the Bushman's River. This camp had been defectively constructed for defence, the waggons being arranged in the form of a semi-circle. The attacking force of Zulus are on the point of turning the position by a flank movement, when Cilliers and his five men ride up to the relief of the handful of burghers defending it. As is his wont on such occasions, the doughty Puritan Commandant addresses to his men one of those battle orations to which he is partial, speeches characterised by pious sentiments, Spartan brevity, and soldier-like vigour. "Brethren," he exclaims, after having carefully examined the priming of his elephant *roer*, "hold God in view; let no hair on your heads be afraid; and follow me." Then, putting spurs to their horses, they charge down on the astonished Zulus, pouring in on them such a well-directed fire from the saddle that the enemy's ranks are disorganised. They are chased into the stream by the combined force now under Cilliers and Barends.

Large numbers of them are shot down, and a good many are drowned in the river. Having saved the small encampment of Barends from destruction, Sarel Cilliers and his five companions ride further up the stream. Reinforced by twelve other Farmers, they fall on a strong body of Zulus at the base of a mountain, and drive them out of the stronghold. After having occupied the hill, they discover some horses which the enemy had captured earlier in the day from Gert Barends' laager. Cilliers and his men recapture the horses, and, sending them on to the laager for riders, they thus obtain more reinforcements, and attack the Zulus with the object of retaking some cattle which the impi had also driven over the mountain. Eleven Zulus fall to the first volley which Cilliers and his men pour in on them. A fierce engagement follows. The Zulus lose large numbers of their best warriors, and, at last, give way, retiring into a cave in the side of the mountain. Cilliers' horsemen ride on in the direction in which the cattle have been driven off by the Zulus. But now they encounter more of the enemy, and soon discover that they are in the vicinity of another laager which is surrounded by the Zulus. It is the spot where the Rensburgs are making their brave stand, and another terrific encounter follows. The Zulus, taken by surprise on finding themselves attacked in the rear, fall back, fighting stubbornly, and attempting, every now and then, to surround the detachment under Cilliers. But at last they give way on all sides, and are chased, and pursued for some distance on the level plain, losing large numbers. Once more a cave in the mountain side affords them shelter from the fury of the avengers.

Meanwhile, at Maritz's laager on the river, the fight has slackened somewhat. The enemy have become discouraged by severe losses, and the attacking columns are falling back in disorder, disinclined again to face the heavy fire of the defenders. So Maritz and his men ride out into the open and pursue the Zulus. His wife and daughter have assisted bravely in the defence of the laager. Since early morning, when the Zulus first attacked the camp, these brave ladies have loaded his guns or handed his ammunition to him. Now the enemy retire in all directions from the laager.

Renewed Zulu Assault on Maritz's Laager. But soon fresh columns of Zulus appear on the Bushman's River, and attack the camp. The battle has lasted nearly an entire day. The enemy have lost heavily; but they come in such large numbers that it seems impossible to overawe them and beat them back. Once more they hurl themselves in dense masses on the devoted thirty-three men. Again the elephant guns thunder forth, and break huge gaps in the line of the savages. But their best Indunas inspire the foemen with fresh courage to make another attempt. With dismay, the besieged notice that they are running short of ammunition. Now a three-pounder, which the Emigrants have kept in reserve, is trained on the densest mass of the assaulting columns, and fired—
Repulse of the Attacking Columns. almost as a last resource. Three of the chief leaders of the attack are killed. At the same time, a deadly fire of slugs and bullets is mowing down the rank and file

of Tambusa's regiments, now dispirited, broken, and disheartened by their losses and by the fall of their three captains. The Zulu soldiers can do no more. Once more they fall back in disorder, and abandon the field to the Emigrants.

Thus passes the 11th of February, 1838. That dreadful day draws to a close. The din of battle, the loud rumbling reports of the elephant guns, and the fierce shouts of the Zulu warriors, have ceased. The conflagrations at the captured encampments are extinguished. The smoke clouds still hang over the river banks. The giant mountains of the Drakensberg tower aloft in the evening sky. *Evening.*

When the lost ones are counted, it is found that 120 men, 56 women, and 185 children, have been slain by the Zulus. The name of Weenen commemorates the sad fate of these martyrs of Natal. *Weenen for the Lost Ones.*

* * * * * * * *

After the Emigrants had ascertained the full extent of the disasters which had overtaken them, a general meeting was convened to decide what was to be done. One or two—their names have been forgotten—proposed that they should all return to the Colony and abandon Natal, as the settlement of the country was now associated with too many difficulties and dangers. When the women heard what had been suggested by these waverers, they resolved that it was the duty of all to remain in order to avenge those who had fallen. And then there was no more hesitation. It was unanimously decided to continue the struggle against Dingaan, and to punish him for the atrocities which *Brave Africander Women.*

he had committed. An appeal for help was made to the Emigrants still on the western side of the Drakensbergen, and also letters were at once despatched to the Cape Colony, asking for assistance, and giving an account of recent events and of the terrible plight in which the new settlement of Natal now found itself.

The first reinforcements came from the Klip River district of Natal (then part of Zululand), where there were other encampments—to which the Zulu attack had not penetrated—and from the passes of the Drakensberg, from which small parties of new arrivals were just then emerging into the uplands of the higher terraces. Soon the glad tidings came that Commandants Potgieter and Uys, the conquerors of Umsiligaas, were advancing by forced marches across the mountains to the assistance of their countrymen.

Potgieter and Uys to the Rescue.

The English settlers at Port Natal, also, nobly offered to assist in the campaign that was now to be commenced. One of the leading men at Durban in those days was Alexander Biggar, a merchant and general trader, whose son, George, had fallen fighting on the side of the Emigrants in the great Zulu incursion.

Alexander and Robert Biggar.

Mr. Biggar was one of those who had given his cordial support to Retief. He had believed in that great leader, and he mourned his loss almost as much as any of the Africanders. His son Robert was nominated commander of the expedition which was to advance into Zululand from the Port, while the Farmer leaders and their commando were to cross the Tugela higher up.

In a previous part of this narrative, reference has been made to the disagreements and differences that arose between Potgieter and Maritz. Beginning at the time of the first Matabele campaign, those contentions had been accentuated at a later date, and although Retief had at first succeeded in again uniting the two factions, it was well known among the Emigrants that no real peace had been established. But now, in face of the common enemy and the danger which threatened all, the parties were united in action. Their leader set them the example. Although, through the death of Retief, the command should have devolved on Maritz, he, frankly recognising the generous impulses which prompted Potgieter and Uys to come to Natal and assist their countrymen, and remembering the claims of the former to priority in rank through seniority in the field, offered no opposition to the demand of the powerful Potgieter faction that their chief should have supreme command in the new campaign. It was agreed among the leaders that Maritz should take command of the laagers remaining in Natal. It was possible that these might be again attacked by the enemy while the invading column marched into Zululand. The Zulu Chiefs were already known to be in favour of flanking movements in their tactics. The command which devolved on Maritz was, therefore, a very important one. In case of any mishap to the advancing forces, his camp would be the base on which they could fall back. His was the reserve army.

Dissensions Forgotten.

The invading force itself was composed of two

separate columns, those of Potgieter and Uys. Each leader commanded his own followers. This arrangement had worked so well in the Marico campaign against Umsiligaas, that it was not thought advisable to depart from it. The total number of men under Potgieter and Uys amounted to three hundred and forty-seven.*

On the 6th of April, the expedition under Uys and Potgieter crossed the Tugela and moved north-eastward towards Umkungunhlovu. During the first five days of the march no enemy was encountered. On 11th April they reached the Insusi valley and the Italeni or Little Itala mountain. The detachment under Uys had entered a narrow defile lying between two ranges of hills, where the *Ruigte Spruit* flows through a cleft in the rocks. Potgieter's commando was somewhat further back. No Zulus had been seen, and it was supposed to be impossible for a large force of the enemy to be in concealment at the spot. But the supposition was a fatal error, as was soon to be made manifest. When a body of Zulu warriors suddenly appeared at the far end of the ravine, for a moment faced the advancing horsemen, and then retired precipitately in the direction of Dingaan's *stad*, Uys, rising in his stirrups, and pointing in the direction of the retreating

---

* Theal: "History of South Africa." Cachet puts the number at four or five hundred at the very most.

"Take the fact of their being mounted and armed with muskets into consideration, and this expedition must still remain one of the most daring events on record, considering that Dingaan could bring into the field at least a hundred times their number of warriors trained to despise death in battle, disciplined to move in concert, and armed with the deadly stabbing assegai. The loss of their horses at any moment must have been fatal to the Commando." THEAL: "History of South Africa."

foe, called out to his burghers: " Comrades, the soldiers of the murderer are there. Let us fall on them." Then the whole column pressed forward at the charge; but, in an instant, as if by magic, the hills on both sides were covered with the black lines of an immense Zulu army, which appeared to have leaped out of the very ground. The troop at once faced round towards the entrance to the defile, but their retreat was already cut off. Large masses of Zulu warriors blocked the way. Further back still, a powerful body had thrown themselves in the line of Potgieter's advance, and, by brandishing their shields and beating on the hard oxhides, made such a din that some of the horses of the rear division became frightened, and could not be made to face the enemy. Meanwhile, Pieter Uys ordered his men to reserve their fire until they were close on the Zulus, then to fire a continuous volley into them, and to charge through the gap thus made in their ranks at the point of entrance into the defile. This manœuvre was successful. The Zulus gave way before the well-directed fire of the Farmers. As the enemy's ranks were cleft asunder by the volley, the commando, abandoning their spare horses and ammunition stores, dashed through the entrance to the defile and escaped; at least, the main body did. Uys himself, followed by about twenty others, among whom was his son, Dirk Cornelis Uys, a lad of about fourteen years of age, went to the assistance of a wounded comrade in another part of the field, and then attempted to make a detour and rejoin their companions. Riding across country with large numbers of the enemy

<small>Battle of the Italeni.</small>

gathering at all points around them, they suddenly found themselves in front of a steep precipice, on a rocky *koppie* or hill from which the river could be seen. Armed Zulus sprang at them from every side; large numbers leaped from the very base of the hill, almost from under their horses' feet. In the wild *mêlée* that ensued at this spot, seven of the twenty Africanders were killed. Uys, with the others, had been firing as rapidly as he could load. But now the flint on his gun did not seem to be as sharp as it should be, and he drew rein for a moment to quickly put an edge on it. Just then a Zulu warrior emerged from behind a rock and struck his assegai into the veteran's side. The Zulu was quickly shot down by one of Uys' men. The Commandant drew the weapon out of his own side. He was in great suffering, and the loss of blood was tremendous; but even at that moment his brave, unselfish soul thought only of those around him. Sinking and mortally wounded as he was, he lifted one of the others, whose horse had been killed, on to his own saddle; and then, looking around him and seeing hundreds of foemen close in on the survivors of his little troop, he mustered all the strength he could command, and called in a loud, clear voice, which all could hear: "Fight your way out, men; I must die." It was his last command. As he sank to the ground, his son, charging with the others, heard him and saw him fall. In that instant, the brave boy, leaping from his horse, was by his dying father's side. The fierce black warriors made a rush towards them. Three fell before young Dirk Uys' unerring aim. Then father

Death of Pieter and Dirk Cornelis Uys.

and son went down before the assegais, and all was over. The others who fell at the battle of the Italeni were Josef Kruger, Frans Labuschagne, David Malan, Jan Malan, Jacobus Malan, Louis Nel, Pieter Nel, and Theunis Nel.

Potgieter now decided to fall back on the Tugela. Discouraged and deeply grieved by the loss of their own leader, many of the followers of Uys criticised his fellow commandant's conduct rather severely, and blamed Potgieter for not coming to their assistance when the Zulus were pressing them hard. Both the nature of the ground and the great strength of the enemy, however, had made a forward movement difficult, if not impossible. By making a detour, Potgieter could possibly have executed a flank attack; but caution rather than boldness was characteristic of the tactics of this old Commandant. Anxiety for the safety of his men and grave apprehension of a more serious disaster than the forces had already suffered, which, under the circumstances, would have been fatal to the cause of the Emigrants, made him decide as he did. Potgieter had always been averse to the idea of settlement in Natal. He was now more than ever convinced of the correctness of his views on the subject. Out of sympathy for his countrymen he had come forward to help; but, so far, he had done nothing more than ascertain the strength of the enemy. Now he decided to return to his followers and to his own sphere of work north of the Vaal. He was convinced that the difficulties in the way of a settlement in Natal were too great to be overcome. There is no doubt whatever that his with-

Retreat of Potgieter.

drawal at this critical time in their history was a great loss to the Emigrants. They had already suffered so much, and the dangers of their situation were so evident, that many became seriously discouraged when Potgieter and his men re-crossed the mountains and left Natal.

Abandonment of Natal by the Potgieter Faction.

Not only the common cause, but the prestige and influence of Potgieter and his own faction, suffered by this step of the leader's. Many who were formerly not of his party had felt their hearts drawn to him when he came to their assistance in their hour of distress and sorrow. Had he chosen to remain, had he fought on with them, had he ultimately led them to victory, it is quite possible that all the different parties of the Emigrants might have united and looked upon him as their Chief. But Potgieter was not an ambitious man, and amalgamation was not his *forte*. He relied on his own followers alone, and was contented with what he had. In retiring to his own people beyond Drakensberg he showed himself the chief of a clan, not the leader of a Nation. Still, the conqueror of the Matabele, as much as any of the other pioneer captains, helped to build up the Republic in South Africa.

While the commandoes under Potgieter and Uys had been invading Zululand, the English settlers were organising their expedition against Dingaan. The Kaffir followers of John Cane and Henry Ogle had started at the beginning of the month, and, after four days' march, had captured a Zulu kraal, where a large number of cattle—seven or eight thousand in all— were taken from the enemy. A quarrel arose as to the division of the spoil, and Ogle and Cane's Kaffirs argued the matter out—with sticks—to such an extent that the expedition could proceed no further. All discipline was gone, and the leaders had to take their men back to Natal. Next, Robert Biggar took the command of some seventeen Englishmen, twenty Hottentots, and about fifteen hundred Kaffirs, three or four hundred of whom had guns. A little south of the Tugela a Zulu force was encountered, which, after a short skirmish, retreated north of the river. The Natal army followed, and found itself drawn into an ambuscade on 17th April, 1838. The fatal circle of foemen which soon closed around them numbered some seven thousand. A fiercely contested battle followed. The Zulu army made three attacks, and were beaten back with great loss on each occasion. Strongly reinforced, Dingaan's warriors again pressed forward, and, falling on the centre, which was the weakest part of the defending force, penetrated the ranks, and cut the main body in two. Each half was now surrounded by separate circles of Zulu warriors. One division of the Natal force, in attempting to retreat across the Tugela, suffered heavily, and was driven back. Three or four Englishmen, three hundred Kaffirs, and a few Hottentots, managed, however, to escape and to get to the other side of the stream. And then the remaining force, again entirely surrounded by the Zulus, stood at bay, while charge after charge was made upon them by the enemy. The carnage was frightful. The Englishmen, as well as their Kaffir allies, fought like lions, and it is supposed that some three thousand Zulus were slain

before the fight was over. Thirteen White men, viz.:
Robert Biggar, Henry Batts, C. Blanckenberg, William Bottomley, John Cane, Thomas Carden, John Campbell, Thomas Campbell, Richard Lovedale, Robert Russell, John Stubbs, Richard Wood, and William Wood, were killed, and with them fell about one thousand Natal Kaffirs. Dingaan's army marched on to Port Natal. The residents there took refuge on a vessel called the *Comet*, which was in the Bay at the time. The Zulu impi occupied Durban for nine days, killed every animal and destroyed all property there, and then went back to Dingaan's kraal.

Death of Robert Biggar and his Brave Followers.

Capture of Durban by Dingaan's Army.

After Potgieter left the encampments of the Emigrants in the basin of the Tugela and on its tributaries, Carel Pieter Landman, with a party of pioneers, advanced southwestward to the Umlaas River, where they established a laager. Commandant Landman had shortly before brought a trek of thirty families across the mountains into Natal. He and his followers had come from the Olifants Hoek, in the Uitenhage District of Cape Colony. Another party occupied a position near where Pietermaritzburg is now built; and a third body took their station at Uys Doorns, eight miles further south. The largest encampments, however, remained on the Bushman's River and on the Tugela. During the months of June, July, and August, 1838, Dingaan's armies were constantly threatening the northern laagers, where a permanent guard had to be maintained in order to prevent their being surprised by the enemy. The Kaffir scouts were conveying accurate information as

Reinforcements and New Encampments.

to all the movements of the Emigrants to Umkungunhlovu, and the armies of the Chief were continually
on the move to take advantage of any weakness or
any unguarded position. There were then in Natal
about six hundred and fifty White inhabitants capable
of bearing arms, and, with them, about three thousand
two hundred women and children. The number of
widows and orphans was large relatively to the rest of
the population. There was much poverty, for the Zulu Poverty and Distress.
armies had carried off all the cattle and live stock at
the time of the great massacre. There was no opportunity for attending to the cultivation of the soil, and
the cattle that were left could not always be sent to
suitable grazing-grounds when the enemy's marauding
bands were hovering about.

Besides Landman's trek, other parties were arriving
from the Cape Colony to reinforce their countrymen.
In the month of May, Fieldcornet Gideon Joubert,
of Colesberg, arrived in Natal on a mission from the British Mission.
Cape Town Government officials. He came to make
an attempt to induce the wanderers to return to their
former homes in the Colony. The British Government
began to realise what a loss their settlement was sustain-
ing by the emigration of large numbers of its most
industrious and most experienced Colonists; and though
it had set its face strongly against help being given to
the hardy pioneers when they called on their fellow-
countrymen to come to their assistance in founding
a new State; though it had issued proclamations for-
bidding further emigration, and threatened penalties
to all in the Colony who should lend their aid by

joining the Emigrants: it now, strangely enough, expressed itself as extremely solicitous for the welfare of the survivors of the massacre. But the Cape Government was not successful in preventing more Colonists from joining the Northern movement. Large numbers were again on the way to the passes of the Drakensberg. The disasters and the hardships which the Natal community had suffered aroused so much sympathy in the Cape Colony, that nothing could stem the tide of emigration. The tragic fate of Retief and his companions, the cruel massacres of the Blauwkrans and the Bushman's River, the heroic death of Uys and his son, were soul-stirring incidents of an eventful year. The spirit of nationality was aroused throughout the length and breadth of South Africa. Those who had, until now, hesitated to throw in their lot with the bold spirits who had risked their all in the wilderness, held back no longer. The voice of duty—not to a foreign Crown, but to the soil of Africa, and to the faithful and the brave who had already given their lives for liberty—called northwards. The cold silent sentinels stood on the hill Chlooma Amaboota, waiting, guarding the sacred document—beckoning; and on many a lonely farm near the hills around Slachtersnek, the women, clasping their children to their breasts, took the old family Bibles, and the men, grasping their guns, looked for the last time at the mountains, before leaving their homes for the unknown and terrible North.

Loyalty to the Soil of Africa.

From all the eastern districts of the Colony long lines of waggons were on the way, carrying entire families, who went to join their countrymen in Natal.

Fieldcornet Gideon Joubert failed to induce any of the Emigrants to listen to the representations of the British Government and to return to the Colony. A small and unimportant section, consisting of a few individuals only, were in favour of abandoning the enterprise of the new settlement. But, as on a former occasion, the women would not hear of any such representations. It was the duty, they said, of all to remain and inflict punishment on Dingaan for his cruelties; and the soil in which the innocent victims of the massacres lay buried must not be abandoned, however great the difficulties and dangers now encompassing the settlement. J. N. Boshoff (Clerk to the Magistrate of Graaff Reinet), who had accompanied Mr. Joubert on his mission, was so impressed by what he saw and heard, that he determined to join the Pioneers, and he afterwards attained to a responsible and a leading position among them. In the month of May, Carel Landman occupied the settlement at the Port of Natal in the name of the Association of South African Emigrants. He appointed Alexander Biggar as Landdrost of the place. Mr. Biggar's sons, George and Robert, had both been killed by the Zulus. The former had fallen at the Bushman's River, the latter in command of the army of Natal, in the battle of the 17th April, on the Tugela. L. Badenhorst, and subsequently F. Roos, were next appointed to the Landdrostship of Durban; for Alexander Biggar was despondent on account of the loss of his sons and all his property, and did not care to take the office.

In July, the British Governor at Cape Town issued a proclamation in which he announced that the Emigrants were still British subjects, and that he would, at a later date, take possession of Natal by means of a military force. In the same document he called on all the Emigrants then in Natal to return to Cape Colony, and promised them a careful consideration of all, and redress of well-founded, grievances. This was indeed a strange Government edict. As to the first-mentioned assertion —that the Emigrants were still British subjects—it seemed quite unwarrantable. After leaving the Colony, the pioneers had not gone into territory where England had authority, or to which England laid claim. The northern frontiers of Cape Colony did not then even reach all the way along the Orange River; and, as to Natal, the British Government had refused to sanction annexation on 10th November, 1834 (in answer to representations from Cape Town merchants urging that course), and again, in reply to Sir Benjamin D'Urban, by a despatch from Lord Glenelg, dated 29th March, 1836, in which it was stated that "his Majesty's Government is deeply persuaded of the inexpediency of engaging in any scheme of colonisation, or of acquiring any further enlargement of territory in Southern Africa." (*See* pp. 207, vol. i.; and 5, vol. ii.)

All the territories into which the Emigrants went were therefore, clearly, outside the British Empire. And, as, when they left the British part of South Africa, these men had announced their intention of establish-

Proclamation by the British Government.

ing a Government and a settlement of their own, it becomes difficult to see what right the English Governors had still to consider them British subjects. The Attorney-General, Mr. Oliphant—the highest law officer of the British Crown in South Africa—when appealed to in the matter, had said: "But the class of persons under consideration evidently mean to seek their fortunes in another land, and to consider themselves no longer British subjects. Would it, therefore, be prudent or just, even if it were possible, to prevent persons discontented with their condition trying to better themselves in whatever part of the world they please? The same sort of removal takes place every day from Great Britain to the United States. Is there any effectual means of arresting persons determined to run away, short of shooting them as they pass the boundary line? I apprehend not; and if so, the remedy is worse than the disease. The Government, therefore, if I am correct in my conclusions, is, and must ever remain, without the power of effectually preventing the evil—if evil it be." (*See* pp. 268—269, vol. i.)

This was clear enough. But the British Government evidently meant to go beyond the boundary line, and Major-General Napier's proclamation of July, 1838, was the prelude to the shooting which was to begin in 1842. The promise of redress of grievances came rather late in the day, considering that so many of those who had had the greatest cause of complaint against the British Government were now—dead. And it was, after all,—only a promise. The chief grievance which the Emigrants had against the English authorities was that the right to an independent existence was denied the new Settlement.

In August, 1838, Dingaan's army was once more south of the Tugela. A furious onslaught was made on the laager on Bushman's River. There were here a large number of women and children, and the Zulu Chief's ever active and vigilant scouts had taken reports of the weak defensive position, and of the unpreparedness for attack at this encampment, to Umkungunhlovu. Maritz was ill at the time, and the laager stood under command of Joachim Prinsloo and Jacobus Potgieter. Besides the women and children, there was a large number of wounded in the camp, and the force which could be mustered to resist the assault was a small one. Early in the morning of 13th August the battle commenced. Anna Elizabeth Steenekamp, a niece of Pieter Retief's, has left a narrative of the encounter (published in the Dutch magazine, *Elpis*, in 1860). "The Kaffir hordes, thousands upon thousands, stretched as far as the eye could reach. It was terrible to see. I cannot describe their numbers; for one would think that all Heathendom had assembled to destroy us."

The battle lasted for two days. The Zulus made repeated attempts to take the camp by assault; but, during both days, they clung persistently to their usual tactics of forming their columns in a circle before rushing onwards; and the defenders, having by this time acquired considerable skill in the best methods of fighting Dingaan's regiments, directed their fire almost entirely at the front extremities of the wings which were thrown out from the Zulu centre to form the circle. Before each onslaught, as the main body of the centre and reserve columns sat down on the plain opposite the laager, the horns or wings, which were thrown forward to encircle the camp, sustained such a concentrated fire, that large numbers of those in front (at the points of the wings) were shot down. Knowing that the centre square would not move before the circle had been completed by the tips of the horns uniting, when the ring of black warriors would rush to the assault, the Farmers made it their main endeavour to shatter the extremities of the circling columns, to "shoot away the tips of the horns," as they termed it. So well did they succeed, that the wings of the Zulu battle-formation were continually thrown into disorder and confusion by the enormous losses which they sustained. The three-pounder cannon, also, again did good service. It was fired, occasionally, into the densest parts of the Zulu columns when they made their most determined onslaughts. At last, after two days' constant fighting, and after having lost very heavily, the enemy became discouraged and gave up the attempt. Only one of the defenders, a Farmer named Vlotman, lost his life in the fight. A large number of cattle, however, was again captured by the Zulus. In order to attempt to recover them, the Farmers sallied forth from the camp, and pursued the retiring army. Only some of those who engaged in this pursuit of the enemy were on horseback, for there were not horses left to mount all. Exhausted with two days' hard fighting, tired out from want of sleep, the hardy citizen-soldiers yet managed

A Sortie

to keep up such a spirited chase, that more of the Zulus were shot, and a good many of them driven into the river, where they were drowned. But the Zulu forces were too numerous to permit of the cattle being retaken, and the small body of Farmers had to return to their laager without succeeding in their main object.

Potgieter and his party, after leaving Natal and re-crossing the mountains, had proceeded to the Sand River. Afterwards they crossed the Vaal, and established themselves on its tributary the Mooi. Here, in November, 1838, they founded the town of Potchefstroom (Potgieter-Chef-Stroom)—the first township built in the Transvaal. The Potgieter party had then (until September, 1840) a Government separate and distinct from that of the main body of the Emigrants, who were shaping out their own career in Natal and Zululand. Potchefstroom was the capital of the country which embraced not only the Transvaal, acquired by conquest from the Matabele, but also the north-western half of the present Orange Free State, purchased by Potgieter from the Barolong Chief Makwana. The eastern and south-eastern part of the country which is now the Free State Republic, came then more under the sphere of influence of the Natal leaders.

Foundation of Potchefstroom.

The Winter of 1838 in Natal.

The winter of 1838 was a time of great distress and suffering—one of the darkest periods in the history of the emigration. The cattle had been nearly all carried off by the Zulus. The wounded had suffered much from exposure and want, and from the absence of medical comforts and treatment. Sickness, in the form of fever—caused by the constant exposure to great hardships and fatigue, along with the deficiency of good, wholesome food, and, in many cases, by the drinking of impure water—had broken out in several of the laagers. Maritz himself was seriously ill, and his life was soon despaired of. With some of the camps full of widows and orphans; with the wounded men in want of hospital accommodation; with poverty and sickness adding to their sufferings; with the enemy always upon them; two of their trusted leaders, Retief and Uys, dead, and another, Maritz, dying; Potgieter not with them to help in their day of greatest distress; the English Government threatening them with annexation: —it seemed as if their struggle was hopeless. *In Much Suffering and Misery.*

But their hearts did not fail. They believed in the justice of their cause. They heeded neither the promises nor the threats of the British Government proclamations. They had appealed to their countrymen to come to their assistance. They knew that that appeal would not be in vain. The way was far. Roads there were next to none in those days. But the voices from Slachters- *The Voices.* nek mountain, and from the Chlooma Amaboota in Zululand, were loud; and onwards—nearer, over the plains of the Orange River and through the passes of the Drakensbergen—came those who had heard the mandate and the call—the mandate of the martyred fathers: the call of the murdered sons.

Carel Landman was now acting temporarily as Com- *To the Rescue.* mandant in place of Maritz. He and those who came with him from Olifants Hoek had brought a valuable accession of strength to the ranks of the Emigrants, and more aid was on the way. Stores and medicines were sent by sympathisers in the Cape Colony; and, in November, Andries Pretorius arrived in Natal, bringing with him some influential burghers of the district of Graaff Reinet. He had previously, shortly before Retief went to Zululand, made a visit to the settlement, in order to ascertain for himself the condition of the country. He now returned to throw in his lot with that of his countrymen.

Andries Pretorius.

Andries Willem Jacobus Pretorius, Fieldcornet in one of the divisions of Graaff Reinet district, traced his descent from Johannes Pretorius, first Secretary to the Orphan Chamber in Cape Town at the time of its establishment (in 1674). In the Cape Town archives, Johannes Pretorius is subsequently mentioned as one of the most notable burghers in 1691, under the Government of Simon van der Stell. He was the son of a clergyman at Goeree, in the South of Holland, had been a student at Leiden University, and, afterwards, Secretary to the Council of the Government of the Mauritius. In 1691, he is mentioned in the archives as having a wife and children. The Dutch author, Pieter de Neyn, in his "Lusthof der Huwelijken," published at Amsterdam in 1697, states that the wife of Johannes Pretorius had, when a young girl, with the help of one or two other ladies, saved the life of a little Hottentot child. The narrative is also contained in the archives in the Library at Cape Town.

It was in 1668, when Commander Jacob van Borghorst was Governor. Near the fort of Good Hope, which was then the only white settlement in South Africa, a party of Hottentots were burying a woman of the tribe—who had died, leaving a little infant. According to the barbarous custom of the nation, they were about to inter the living baby with its dead mother. The ladies begged and prayed so hard for the life of the little child, that the savages spared it. It was taken to the Castle, and adopted by the Colonists. One of the women who interceded for the little savage, and saved it from a cruel death, was she who afterwards married Johannes Pretorius. From her, therefore, the founder of the South African Republic was descended. The sons and grandsons of Johannes Pretorius became ranch-owners on the frontiers in the early days of the Cape Settlement.

The Frontiersmen of Graaff Reinet district were always noted for their sturdy spirit of independence. It was in this district that Andries Pretorius was born and brought up. There were then very few opportunities in the outlying country regions for the children of the Colonists to acquire any but the most elementary education. The country being very thinly populated, the farms and cattle-ranches were situated at immense distances apart. Towns and villages were few, and of small size. The literature of the people consisted of the illustrated family Bibles and a few standard historical works. But although their education was necessarily neglected, owing to the circumstances of the country and the time in which they lived, the Frontier Farmers of those days were neither narrow-minded nor behind the age in their views as to politics and government. It has been said that Andries Pretorius represented the Seventeenth rather than the Nineteenth century.* The accomplished English writer who makes this statement has, by his work and his researches, done more than any man living to make known to the world the history of the dominion of the White race in South Africa, and his estimate of the character of Pretorius is more impartial than that of most authors of British nationality. It will be well, however, while here taking note of this estimate, as coming from an authority on South African History, to leave for a later page, when we have before us his career as warrior and statesman, and when his life's work can be reviewed, the consideration of the personality of the great Frontiersman.

Born near Graaff Reinet in November, 1798, he was just forty years of age when he settled in Natal. He was then a man of considerable wealth and influence. Like most South Africans who lived on the frontiers, he had acquired considerable experience of Kaffir warfare in the then recent hostilities with the Amakosas in the Cape Colony. His reputation as a military leader was already favourably known among the Emigrants. His brothers Bart and Louw Pretorius, who came with him, were also well-known as skilful commandants. Carel Landman, who now had the command of the Emigrants in place of Maritz, as well as Joachim Prinsloo, Jacobus Potgieter, and other leaders, recognised in Andries Pretorius the man who was wanted to lead the people.

* "His knowledge and his opinions, as well as his virtues and his failings, were those of the seventeenth, not of the nineteenth, century."—THEAL: "South Africa," vol. iv. p. 149.

On the 15th of October, Gerrit Maritz, after suffering much pain with great fortitude and patient resignation, had breathed his last in the laager on Bushman's River. Barely two years had passed since he first came among them in their camps near Thaba 'N Chu. In that relatively short space of time, however, by his skill and valour in the campaign against the Matabele; by his loyal support, first, of Pieter Retief, and, afterwards, of Potgieter and Uys as Commandants in Natal; by his constant and faithful services; by his patient sufferings and death: he had so endeared his memory to the Emigrants, that they and their descendants have enshrined it in the beautiful capital of Natal, which bears his honoured name coupled with that of the other martyr-hero who also gave his life for the young Republic. By his death-bed his sorrow-stricken companions and friends, bearing in affectionate remembrance his great services to his countrymen, and his self-denying devotion to their cause, had wept disconsolate tears of grief. Despair had almost over-mastered the stoutest hearts in their dark hour of distress and affliction.

But a brighter day was dawning.

PART III

THE REPUBLIC OF NATAL

CHAPTER XX

THE MARCH OF THE AVENGERS

THE WIN-COMMANDO

Andries Pretorius appointed Commandant-General—The Muster on the Tugela — Reconnoitring—Numbers, Armament, and Commissariat of the Force—Religious Observances—The Leaders—Precautions—Line of March—Strategy of Pretorius—The Diary of the Secretary to the Krygsraad—March up the Tugela—Pretorius speaks to his Army—Crossing the Tugela—The Vow—Crossing the Buffalo—Scouting and Skirmishing—Setting Zulu Prisoners Free—Message to Dingaan—Advance up the Bloed River—Skirmish of 14th December—Further Advance up the River—Enemy in Front—Laager Formed—The Night Patrol—Circle of Light—Dingaan's Whirlwind—Battle of Bloed River—Tambusa's Assault—Salela Joins—Charge of Bart Pretorius on Flank of Assaulting Columns—Horsemen Driven back on Laager—Second Charge of Bart Pretorius on Zulu Flank repulsed—North and East Faces of Square cleared by Volunteers under Sarel Cilliers—Third Charge of Horsemen under Bart Pretorius—Assaulting Column Cleft in Two—Artillery Fire and Charge of Andries Pretorius—Pursuit of Zulus—Salela's Impi Driven into the River: Great Slaughter—Andries Pretorius Wounded—March to Umkungunhlovu — Dingaan's Stad in Flames—The Cold Sentinels on the Chlooma Amaboota—Horse Patrol on the White Umveloosi—Hans de Lange saves the Column—Battle of the Plain of the White Umveloosi—Burning Kaffir Kraals—The Return March—Fight near New Year's Spruit—Capture of Zulu Cattle—Close of the Campaign—The Dark Clouds Dispersed.

ON the 28th of November, 1838, at a meeting attended by delegates from all the different encampments, Andries Pretorius was appointed Commandant-General, and preparations were at once commenced for resuming the campaign against Dingaan.

This expedition, known in their history as the *Wincommando*, formed a turning point in the career of the Emigrants in Natal. At the beginning of December a camp was formed on the banks of the Tugela, which was then in flood. Reconnoitring parties, under Commandant Stephanus Erasmus, were despatched up the river. But rain and mist often obscured the view, and the night patrols had to exercise great caution to avoid falling into ambuscades. The commando assembled under Pretorius at the point of rendezvous, and Carel Landman was moving upwards from the Umlazi with another detachment. When the entire force had concentrated, it was found to number four hundred and seven white men and fifty-nine coloured servants, waggon-drivers, and herdsmen. The column carried its stores and ammunition in fifty-seven waggons drawn by oxen, and was fairly well provided with horses. These had been sent in considerable numbers from beyond the mountains and from the Cape Colony. The Farmers were well armed, with elephant guns; and a good supply of bullets and *loopers* (slugs) had been cast in the various encampments and sent on with the stores. The commando also took three small pieces of ordnance—a small brass cannon, which belonged to Andries Pretorius, and two three-pounders which had already seen service in the defence of the laager on the Bushman's River. One of them was at a much later date (at the time of the War of Independence in 1880-81) known as *ou Grietjie*, and used with effect against the British camp at Potchefstroom by the Free State artillerist Pelser.

The provisions taken by the expedition consisted mainly of camp biscuits, *biltong* (sun-dried antelopes' meat or beef), coffee, and tobacco. Fresh meat had to be procured by capturing cattle from the enemy. Subsisting on this simple fare, the pioneers of 1838 broke the power of Dingaan, and fought their way to dominion in Natal and in Zululand.

The march was commenced on the 3rd of December. Firmly believing in the justice of their cause, and confident that Providence would assist them in their struggle to avenge the death of the unfortunate victims of the great massacre, the Voortrekker warriors were sincere and fervent in their religious devotions. Many of their leaders set them that example of unfeigned piety which strengthened and encouraged them in the fray. Religious observances were never omitted at the evening encampments. There was much fervent praying, and the psalms and hymns of the Dutch Reformed Church service were frequently sung at these meetings. There was no hypocrisy in all this. It was the unanimous opinion of all the Emigrants that the campaign could not be successful without the help of Heaven. <small>Religious Observances.</small>

The principal officers of the expeditionary force were Andries Pretorius, Commandant-General; Carel Pieter Landman, second Commandant; Pieter Daniel Jacobs (second member of the Krygsraad or War Council), whose brother Jan (familiarly known to his associates as Jan Hermanus) also served in this commando, and afterwards distinguished himself in the hostilities against the British in Natal and at Boomplaats; Gerrit Jacobus <small>The Leaders.</small>

Potgieter; Johannes de Lange (nicknamed Hans Dons); Stephanus Erasmus; Bart Pretorius, who commanded a detachment at the battle of Blood River; and Alexander Biggar, who led a contingent of Natal natives, and was killed at the battle of the White Umvcloosi.

Approaching the upper waters of the Tugela, where, in the vicinity of the Drakensberg range, the river was more easily fordable (for the Lower Tugela could not be crossed at that season of the year), the little army moved cautiously onward, constantly keeping scouts well in advance. At the encampments the waggons were invariably drawn up in laager formation, and numerous patrols were posted at some distance outside the camp to guard against surprise by the enemy. The route now followed by the commando was different from that which had been taken by the flying columns under Potgieter and Uys in the early part of the year. They had crossed the Tugela much lower down the stream, and then made a direct advance to the northeast, moving almost in a straight line on Umkungunhlovu. Pretorius, after crossing the Umzinyati or Buffalo River, pushed northwards in the fork of country lying between the Buffalo and the stream now known as the Blood River. His object was to choose his own battle-ground and to be near a river. Had he not been attacked on the Blood River, he would have made his way to the head waters of the White Umveloosi, and then moved down along the banks of that stream to the Zulu capital. By following this course he would always be near a river, and could so place his laager as to have it protected on at least one side by the

Precautions.

Line of March.

stream. Natal itself was well guarded from a Zulu invasion by the swollen torrent of the Tugela, and Pretorius knew that, while the burghers were advancing into Zululand, the armies of Dingaan would not attempt an invasion by way of the Upper Tugela.

J. G. Bantjes, the Secretary to the Krygsraad, kept a diary of the expedition. *Diary of the Secretary.*

On Monday, 3rd December, the united columns of Pretorius and Landman moved up the Tugela. The advance was continued on the 4th (Tuesday). Commandant Hans de Lange, with three experienced scouts, was reconnoitring in advance. On the 5th, two letters reached the Emigrant encampment from Cape Colony. One was from Christiaan Hatting, and the other from the Rev. G. W. A. van der Lingen of the Paarl. Pretorius read to the assembled commando his replies to the letters, and then delivered a short address to the burghers. *March up the Tugela.*

He pointed out to them the necessity of union and concord, discipline, and obedience to their officers, in order to ensure victory. He did not conceal from them the disparity in numbers between their own force and that of the enemy; and yet his words impressed them favourably, and inspired them with confidence. "Fellow countrymen," he said, "rely on your God, the Lord of Hosts. He can, and will help you. In that faith you will find your strength. The shades of your murdered relatives and friends, hovering around your path, will bless you in your heroic undertaking." And now, still standing on the gun-carriage from which he had spoken, he called up the other Commandants *Pretorius speaks to his Army.*

and then the Fieldcornets, addressing each one of them separately. His words were hearty and cheerful; but his bearing was characterised by earnestness and seriousness, as befitted the occasion. He spoke of the cause, the issue at stake, and the great responsibility devolving on himself and on each of his fellow-officers. The lives of women and children, the safety of the entire community in Natal, depended on them. They were to set an example to their men. Resolute action was wanted against the savage enemy; valour on the battlefield, but mercy to the helpless and the weak; no women and children on the side of the enemy were to be harmed. "No soldier born under the light of the gospel," said Pretorius, "may wage war against helpless women and children."

At night, Commandant Hans de Lange returned to camp with his scouts. They brought with them a Kaffir over six feet in height, whom they had taken prisoner in a skirmish with the enemy in which De Lange himself had slain three Zulus. They had also captured fourteen cattle and eleven sheep, which they drove into the laager. According to Commandant De Lange's report, the column was close to a large Zulu kraal—that of the chief Tobe. Early on the morning of the 6th of December (Thursday), Pretorius, leaving a guard of about twenty men in the laager, made a dash on this kraal with between three hundred and eighty and three hundred and ninety men on horseback. The place was, however, found deserted by the enemy. On the 7th the Tugela was crossed, and Commandant Jacobus Uys joined the commando

Danskraal, a few miles north-east of the present town of Ladysmith, was reached on the same day. It was resolved that the entire army should take a vow to God, that, if He granted them victory, they would build a Church and set aside a thanksgiving day to commemorate the event. Cilliers says in his Diary that Andries Pretorius first spoke to him about this solemn vow, and asked him at Danskraal to address the commando on the subject. This he did. It was then decided to advance at once on Umkungunhlovu, and the first part of the line of march was nearly as the road now goes from Ladysmith to Dundee. On the 8th, the Sundays River was crossed, near where now the farm of Roodepoort is, and on the same day the march was continued to near the Platberg on the Blyde River. Here the night halt was made, and the next day (Sunday) the little army remained in camp. The grass was found in very good condition, and horses and men rested and refreshed themselves by the river side. The Vow to God.

On that Sunday morning, Andries Pretorius called Commandant Landman and the aged P. Joubert, with Sarel Cilliers, to his tent, in order to take their opinion on the subject of the ceremonies to be observed in connection with the ratifying and confirmation of the solemn vow to God. Religious services were then performed in three tents set apart for the purpose. Early on Monday morning the march was resumed. On that day (the 10th), and also on the 11th, numerous smoke signals were observed on the hills. As the grass along the line of march was very thick, the veld was set on fire, so that boulders and ravines could be seen more easily from a distance and ambuscades might be readily detected. On the 11th, the Buffalo River was crossed at the ford now called Landman's Drift. As soon as the column was well through the river, Zulu smoke signals were noticed on all the hills in front. An encampment was, therefore, formed, and scouts were sent out in all directions to ascertain the nature of the country, and the whereabouts of strong bodies of the enemy.

One of the patrols came into collision with a small party of Zulus at some distance from the camp, and a skirmish ensued. Nine Zulus fell. There were no casualties on the side of the burghers. On the same day, Mr. Parker, an Englishman from Durban, who had come with Alexander Biggar to take part in the expedition, killed a Zulu spy who rushed at him from a thick clump of grass. On the 12th December another Kaffir spy was shot by one of the scouts, and Parker, who was out reconnoitring with a party of Natal Kaffirs, came upon a small Zulu kraal, where they captured some women and children and one man. As the prisoners were being brought into camp, the Zulu warrior made a rush at Parker, and pulled him from his horse. Falling on the Englishman's double-barrel gun, the Zulu, attempting to get possession of the weapon, was severely wounded in the arm and shoulders, and died soon after.

Pretorius set the women and children at liberty as soon as they were brought into camp. He gave them a white flag with his name on it. He instructed them to have this flag sent on to Dingaan, their Chief, and also a message to the effect that the Emigrants had come to wage war against the Zulu King; but that, should he desire it, they were still prepared to come to terms of peace with him, on condition of his at once delivering up the guns, horses, and other property, which his armies had taken from the Farmers' encampments and at Umkungunhlovu at the time of the massacre. The messengers were to state, also, that the choice of peace or war now rested with the Chief of Zululand, and that, in case he chose war, Pretorius and his followers were ready to continue hostilities for ten years, if necessary. The white flag, Pretorius said, would be a sacred emblem of peace. They, the women themselves, or even a warrior of their nation, could return with it and bring a message back, for they would not be injured by the Emigrants; and, whatever might be the issue of the war, no women or children would be harmed by the white people.

Message to Dingaan.

The Zulu women were loud in their praises of Pretorius. "Dingaan," they said, "never forgives even defenceless women or innocent children. He often kills them for pastime." (Hofstede: "Geschiedenis van den Oranje Vrijstaat," p. 47.)

The little invading army now cautiously continued its onward march. On the 13th there was another skirmish, and three Zulu warriors were killed by a patrol. A body of the enemy, with a large number of cattle, was observed on a neighbouring mountain. Three more Zulus were shot in a skirmish close to this hill. Very early on the morning of the 14th,

A Skirmish.

one hundred and twenty men advanced on horseback and attacked the Kaffirs, who fled after losing about eight in killed. The advance was continued up the right bank of that tributary of the Buffalo which is now called the Blood River.

On Saturday, the 15th of December, in the forenoon, the commando was pushing onwards, with the scouts well in advance as usual. To the left was the mountain Gelato, now called Vechtkop—a high hill with a steep summit—and some distance in the rear were some other high mountain ridges. The river was to the right of the column. In front stretched a plain for a considerable distance, its level expanse broken only in one or two places, where there were small *koppies*. But further on in front, to the left, the country became mountainous. Here the enemy were found in strong force by the scouts, whose report was at once sent in.

Enemy in Front.

The exact number of the Zulus could not be ascertained; but the column was immediately brought to a halt, and Pretorius ordered the waggons to be drawn up in laager formation at a spot where there was a deep reach or pool of the river, and, at right angles to this, facing the camp on the north side, a dry *donga* or ravine with a very steep bank (more than fourteen feet high) towards the laager.

Laager Formed.

The encampment was thus well protected, there being only two open sides on which the Zulu attack could be made. That fiery evangelist, Sarel Cilliers, was in favour of at once attacking the Zulus on the mountain. But Pretorius would not hear of this.

Situation of the Battlefield.

The Impetuous Ironside.

Further reports had come into the camp. The enemy could be distinctly seen by the patrol. There was a steep path leading up the mountain, and large numbers of Zulus were observed in two wide and steep ravines on either side of the path. The Zulu force which had at first been seen was intended to act as a snare. The larger body was lying in ambush in the ravines. Cilliers requested Pretorius to allow him—with fifty men—to advance on the enemy, engage them in battle, and then fall back on the plain, where the main commando was to come to his assistance. The Chief-Commandant was, however, firm in refusing his sanction to all the Ironside's plans of battle. It was now late in the afternoon—too late, Pretorius said, to attempt anything against the enemy. The next day would be time enough. Then Cilliers could go. Sarel Cilliers himself tells us all this in his quaintly-worded *Diary*. The next day was Sunday. Pretorius had chosen his own battle-ground, where he knew the enemy would attack him in the night or early in the morning. Cilliers says he felt vexed, but frankly admits that Pretorius was quite right. *Pretorius restrains him.*

Strong wooden gates, fastened by firm iron bolts and rivets, were now used to close the spaces between the wheels of the waggons, and also the openings between the different waggons, so that the enemy would not be able to creep into the laager when they made their assault. A small night patrol was stationed on a koppie some little distance from the camp, to keep an eye on the Zulus, and, when it became dark, several lanterns, attached to long bamboo whip-sticks, were lit and hung up over the laager. The weird appearance created by this circle of lights, as seen from a distance, worked on the superstitious fears of the Zulus, who believed that the white invaders had secured some powerful magic. At daybreak, however, the patrols fell back on the camp and gave the alarm.

The Circle of Light.

Immediately after, the onslaught commenced. The impis were commanded by Tambusa and Salela, and numbered altogether, according to a rough estimate, some ten or twelve thousand men. While Salela's division took up a position facing the camp on the other side of the river, that under command of Tambusa massed its attacking columns on the plain to the north-west of the laager. Large numbers were observed, in the grey dawn, creeping out of inequalities and depressions in the ground. Then their general struck some resounding blows on his hard ox-hide shield, while his deep bass voice thundered forth the commands for a general assault.

Dingaan's Whirlwind.

Once more Dingaan's whirlwind burst on the Emigrants struggling for life.

Tambusa's Assault.

A furious rush was made on the two open sides of the square by large numbers of the enemy, representing five of the Zulu King's best regiments. They fell back after considerable losses; but again came up to attack, bravely facing the very heavy fire which was poured in on them. Four times the assault was repeated, and on each occasion the Zulus had to fall back after severe loss. On the other side of the river, immediately opposite the camp, Salela's impi had sat down, watching the fight which was in progress.

IN SOUTH AFRICA   97

Pretorius ordered a herald to ask them why they were sitting still. "What are you doing?" was the next question. "I have come here to fight. Why don't you attack me?" When no answer was returned, and while the battle was still raging on the two other faces of the square, the Commandant directed one of his cannon at the dense mass of Zulu warriors sitting on the river bank, and fired. At the first shot, they

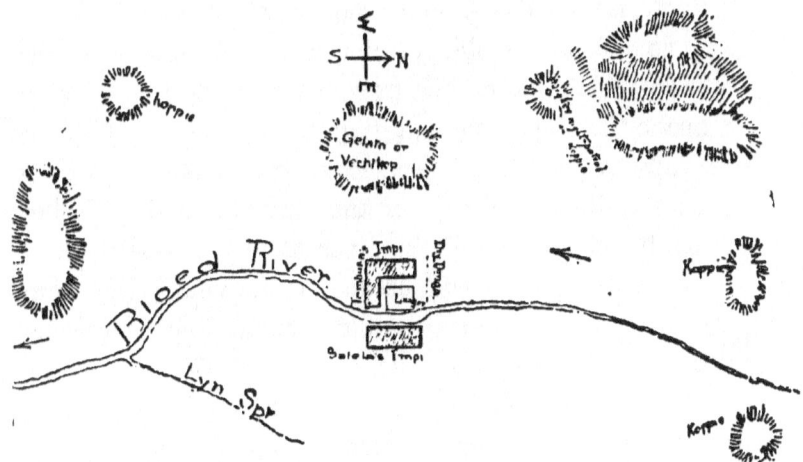

Sketch Plan of the Bloed River Battlefield.

sprang to their feet. When the second gun was fired, they uttered a furious roar and at once commenced crossing the stream higher up, to join in the battle. Salela Joins. "The more of them there are around us," said Pretorius, when Commandant Jan Jacobs remonstrated with him for bringing down on them this additional force of the enemy, "the greater execution will our bullets do amongst them, and the sooner will the battle be over. Besides, I wish to avoid being attacked by them, afterwards, when our ammunition is exhausted."

VOL. II.   G

For a full hour after that, fierce onslaughts were made on the camp by the united Zulu impis. "Then they closed around us," says one of the old Voortrekker Commandants. "We could not run out our artillery. For a full hour, we had to fire and load our muskets as fast as we could. We fired chiefly slug shot. Although nearly every one of us had two or three guns, the barrels had then become hot with constant firing." (Oral narrative of Commandant J. H. Visser).

Narrative of J. H. Visser.

To add to the danger of the defenders, some of the oxen, which had on the previous evening been brought inside the laager so that they should not fall into the hands of the Zulus, became so frightened by the incessant din and tumult of the assault that they dashed madly against one of the lines of waggons, attempting to break through and escape to the veld. Had they done so, the Zulu army would certainly have succeeded in rushing in by the opening made. But the danger was soon averted by the capture of the stampeded cattle inside the encampment.

Stampede of Cattle.

Once again the Zulu captains were heard urging their men forward to the charge; but the attacking columns had met with such a warm reception that, although they kept up the fight very pluckily, the fury of their onslaughts began to abate somewhat. Bart Pretorius, at the head of a body of horsemen, was now ordered to charge and try to cut the Zulu army in two. Galloping forward from one face of the square, and firing huge charges of slugs from the saddle into the densest masses of the enemy, the horsemen attempted to work their way round the flank of the

First Charge of Bart Pretorius.

Zulu columns, attack them from the outside, and then break through them while the laager would be pouring in heavy volleys from the other side. By this bold manœuvre, Bart Pretorius endeavoured to put the entire Zulu force between two fires. For a time he and his men succeeded, by means of their destructive volleys of *loopers* and by their skilful horsemanship, in pressing back the black masses before them, and in gradually working their way round one flank of the attacking columns; but the Zulus closed in again, and the horsemen, in their turn, had to fall back. A second charge was more sustained; and the enemy lost heavily, and yielded more than at first. But, once more, the warriors pressed forward and closed up their ranks. Second Charge of Horse.

Meanwhile, some Zulus, who had crept round to that side of the square facing the river, lay down on the water's edge, covering themselves with their ox-hide shields; but a destructive musketry fire swept them off, and many were drowned in the river. At the same time a considerable number of the enemy had crept into the dry donga on the north side of the square. The high steep bank facing the camp prevented them getting out on that side, and rushing the laager, as they had intended. They were attacked by Sarel Cilliers and eighty volunteers, who went outside the laager and fired on them from the edge of the steep bank. The Kaffirs made a rush to escape from the *sloot*. As they clambered up the opposite bank, they received several volleys from all the north side of the square. Their losses at this place alone amounted to about four hundred. North and East Faces of Square Cleared by Volunteers.

Then Bart Pretorius, with a larger number of horsemen, made his third charge from the western face of the square, and was successful in cutting the entire Zulu impi in two. Instantly, the guns were run out and a heavy artillery fire directed on the disorganised mass. They wavered, and then, after the battle had lasted two full hours, Andries Pretorius, putting himself at the head of about three hundred men, rushed out upon them. The pursuing column divided itself, and each section now charged down on a separate body of Zulus, who fled across the plain in opposite directions. The division of the Zulu army under Salela, three or four thousand strong, which had had less fighting than the main body under Tambusa, fared badly. They did not attempt to make a stand; but were driven helter-skelter over the level *veld* by a body of horsemen, about one hundred and fifty in number, with whom was the impetuous Sarel Cilliers, who tells us in his quaint phraseology that the Kaffirs soon lay as "thick on the ground as pumpkins on a fertile plot of garden land." The one hundred and fifty Farmers with whom Cilliers rode had divided themselves into two columns. Each of these bore down on one extremity of the mass of disorganised and confused Zulu warriors at a gallop, firing scattering volleys of the terrible charges of slug-shot from their long *roers*, and driving Salela's routed army towards the river. At the point where the stream was reached there was a deep pool,* such as South African rivers have at

---

* These long reaches of deep water are known by the Dutch name of *zeekoegat* (plural form, *zeekoegaten*), being supposed to have at one time constituted the haunts of the Hippo.

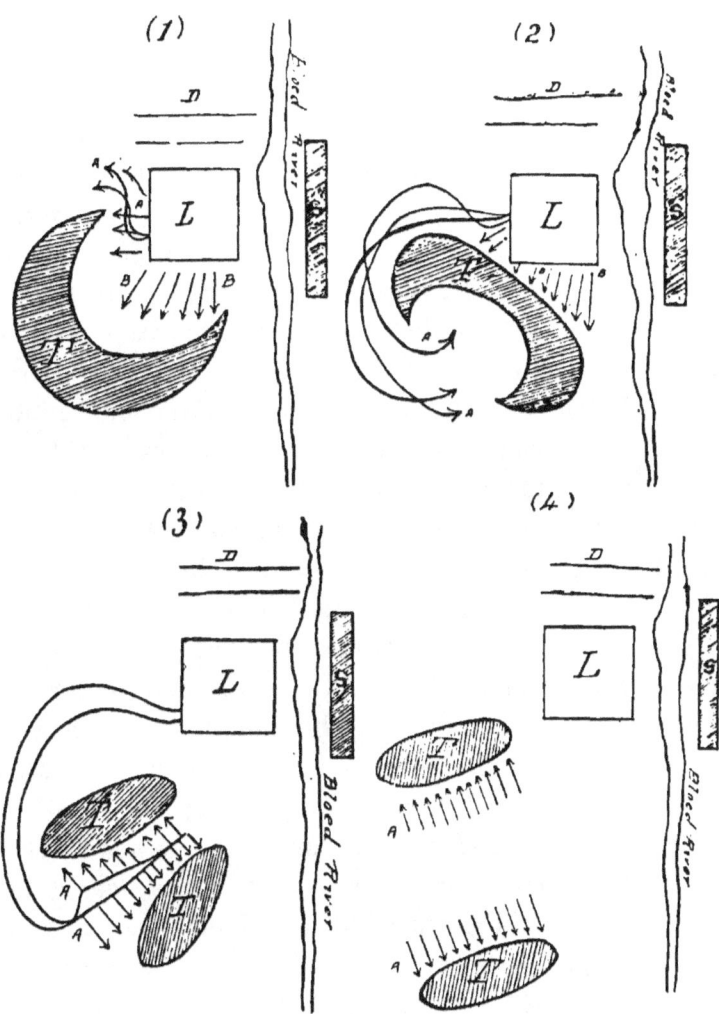

Diagrams to illustrate how Bart Pretorius and his Horsemen cut the Zulu Army in two at the Battle of the Bloed River:—

1. Charge round Zulu flank. Volleys from two faces of the Laager Square.
2. Horsemen attack the Zulu Army in the rear.
3. The Zulu Impi cut in two.
4. Disorganised masses, driven across the plain in opposite directions.

L. Laager.
A.A. Lines of attack of horsemen under Bart Pretorius.
B.B. Line of fire from sides of Square.
S. Position of Zulus under Salela in the early stages of the Battle.
T. Tambusa and Salela's united Impis.
D. Dry Donga.

various points along their course. Rushes and reeds grew along the river bank in this locality. Large numbers of Zulus were, in their headlong flight, precipitated into deep water, and, being bad swimmers, were drowned. A very great many were shot. Where the reeds and rushes grew thickest, hundreds sat down in the water and at the water's edge, attempting to find cover and make a fresh stand. But the avengers of Retief and of the murdered women and children of the Weenen massacre were close upon them. The thunders of the elephant guns echoed on the river banks in the still, clear morning air (it was only about nine o'clock), and few indeed of Dingaan's warriors made their escape from that fatal spot. The stream was soon stained red with Zulu blood, from which circumstance it derives its present name. Andries Pretorius and his horsemen had now spread their columns out in every direction over the plain, in pursuit of Tambusa's flying legions. Nowhere did these Zulus attempt to stand. It was a headlong rout. More men had come out from the laager. Louw and Bart Pretorius, Jan and Pieter Jacobs, Gert Potgieter, Hans de Lange, and other officers, led separate bodies of the Emigrants in the pursuit, which was kept up a great way across the plain. Andries Pretorius himself, when at some distance from the camp, was in the act of riding close up to one of the flying Zulu warriors, attempting to take him prisoner in order to send a message to Dingaan, when the Zulu, turning round suddenly, brandished his shield and struck a loud blow on the hard ox-hide. The horse

Salela's Impi Driven into the River.

Great Slaughter of Zulus.

which Pretorius rode, taking fright, sprang to one side. Gun in hand, he immediately leapt from his saddle; but, in the same instant, the Zulu made a spring towards him. His musket missing fire, Pretorius had to parry the stabbing assegai, which struck him in the wrist. Then he closed with the Zulu warrior, and threw him on the ground. As they lay struggling, one of the burghers, Jan Rudolph, who was near, galloped up, and, seeing the assegai which stuck in the Commandant's arm, grasped the weapon, pulled it out of the wound, and then killed the Zulu with it. But the sharp cutting edge of the assegai had severed the radial artery, and Pretorius lost a good deal of blood before the rough surgery of the camp arrested the flow.

Andries Pretorius Wounded.

The battle and pursuit had lasted five hours.

The remnants of Dingaan's armies, broken, discomfited, routed, and thoroughly disheartened, only saved themselves from further destruction by headlong flight, and because the victors—men and horses—were too much exhausted to keep up the pursuit and continue the slaughter. The Emigrants estimated that they had killed between three thousand and three thousand five hundred Zulus. The Zulus themselves, however, have given the number of those who fell on their side as considerably greater.

The power of Dingaan's dominion and the terror of his name were gone.

Pretorius now decided to at once attack the Zulu Chief in his capital, before he had time to rally his forces and recover from the great defeat of his main army. On the 17th, the laager was pushed forward towards the upper basin of the White Umveloosi. While the waggons, always accompanied by a strong guard, and ever ready to take up a defensive position in case of necessity, were advancing down the banks of the river, a flying column, consisting of an effectively organised horse commando, moved rapidly on Umkungunhlovu, which was reached on the 21st December.

Dingaan's Stad in Flames. Dense clouds of smoke rose from the kraal as the commando approached it. Dingaan and his defeated soldiers had, before retiring to the neighbouring bush and deep ravines, set fire to the huts, which were now ablaze. Commandants Jacobus Uys and Sarel Cilliers were among the first to enter the burning town. Soon

The Cold Sentinels of the Chlooma Amaboota. the avengers stood on the Chlooma Amaboota, the frowning hill overlooking the precipice at the back of the kraal. Here they found the bodies of the victims of the massacre of February. In the dry, rarefied atmosphere of this part of Zululand no putrefaction had taken place. The remains of Retief and his companions, untouched by either vultures or wild animals, were mummified and crumbling into dust. Impaled on stakes driven into the ground, there, with their chief, stood the sixty-five silent, cold, sentinels, the tried and faithful men—faithful even in death—guarding the inheritance which their indomitable leader had obtained for the Republic. Many of those taking part in the commando under Pretorius were kinsmen and near relatives of the men who had been murdered with Retief, and whose bodies were now recognised by the clothes which they had worn. The remains

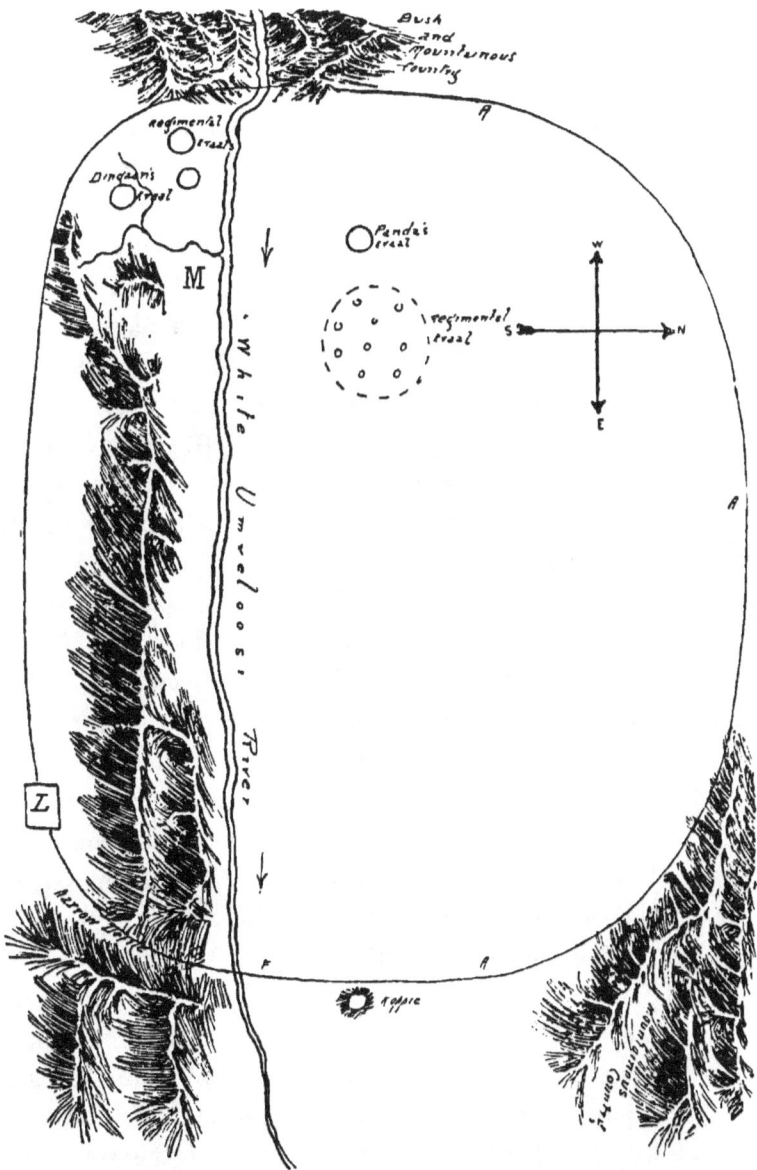

Sketch Plan of the Battle of the White Umveloosi.

M. Hill and Precipice of Chlooma Amaboota, where Retief and his followers were murdered.
   L. Laager of the Emigrants.
   F.F. Drifts or fords.
   A.A.A. Line of advance of Column under Hans de Lange.
        (*After a pencil drawing by Oud Commandant J. H. Visser.*)

of Pieter Retief himself were easily distinguished by a satin vest, and by a small leather despatch bag which hung suspended from one shoulder, and in which was found—in perfect preservation—the treaty, signed by Dingaan, and ceding to the Emigrants and their descendants all the country lying between the Tugela and Umzimvubu rivers. This document was found by Evert Potgieter, and handed to Pretorius.

The solemnity of the occasion, with its tragic surroundings, deeply impressed on all those who were present the intensely dramatic circumstances associated with this rescue of the title-deeds of the infant Emigrant Commonwealth.

The remains of Retief and his companions were interred in one large grave at the spot (not far from Dingaan's kraal) where the laager stood, and the camp was then moved south-eastward to a point on the southern slope of a mountain—one of the elevations in a range of hills stretching almost parallel with the river. To the north of the stream a broad level plain extends towards another mountainous ridge, which separates the watersheds of the White and Black Umveloosi.

<small>Horse Patrol of the White Umveloosi.</small> On the morning of 30th December,* a horse commando of about two hundred and fifty or three hundred men started from the camp, and proceeded in a north-easterly direction towards the river. The scouts had brought in a report that a considerable number of cattle had been seen to the north of the river, where the enemy were known to be in force. Andries Pretorius himself had suffered a good deal from the

* Diary: Sarel Cilliers.

wound received on the 16th, and the Krygsraad had given its decision against his leading the expedition or taking part in it. He, therefore, remained in the laager.

Carel Landman acted as patrol-captain, and under him served Hans de Lange as second in command. Early in the morning, before the patrol started, Pretorius cautioned Landman to beware of falling into an ambuscade, and advised him to move forward warily, and with horsemen scouting well in advance and on the flanks of the column, so that the stealthy approach of Zulu impis might be at once detected. The Emigrants had now learned by experience what a skilful foe they had to contend against, and were, therefore, well on their guard. The route by which the commando approached the river was a mountain defile gradually sloping downward and narrowing towards the northeast, where the ford lay. On the north side of the stream was a *mielie* plantation, and, a little further on, an isolated rocky koppie on the open plain. Landman and De Lange, with their little commando, had traversed the mountain pass, and were approaching the banks of the stream, when they saw, on the plains to the north, what they at first supposed to be large herds of Zulu cattle. Then the curious fact was noticed that the different herds were of distinct colours—black, white, red, black-and-white, etc. The mystery was soon explained.

The river was crossed, and then the burghers found a pretty large *mielie* plantation in front of them. Some armed Zulus were also observed, but they were few in numbers. Such an extensive view of the plains to the north as had been obtained from the higher ground in the mountain defile was not then available. But, on glancing round towards the rear, some of the horsemen were struck with amazement at what they saw. "Look!" they shouted to the others; and there, cutting off the retreat, as if by magic, so suddenly had they appeared on the scene, thousands upon thousands of Dingaan's warriors lined the hills on both sides of the ravine, as well as the slopes of the defile through which the column had just passed. As at Italeni, a Zulu army appeared suddenly to have sprung out of the ground. The great leaders of Dingaan's armies, determined to retrieve the fortunes of their Chief and their race on the field of battle, had been successful in executing as masterly and skilful a piece of strategy as is to be found in the records of the warlike achievements of their nation. Their thoroughly trained scouts had kept them well informed of all the movements of Pretorius and his followers on the south side of the river. When the expedition under Landman had started, and while it was moving north-eastward towards the river, large numbers of Zulus, who, under cover of the hills, had crossed to the southern banks of the White Umveloosi quite unobserved, were advancing round the mountains so as gradually to mass their columns in the line of march of the commando, but well to the rear, so as to keep out of sight.

The Zulu regiments on the southern side of the river now formed roughly a semi-circle which completely prevented all possibility of retreat to the small

Emigrant force. To the north of the river, large masses of Zulus were converging towards the ford where the Farmers had crossed the stream. But in that direction the field was still open—though only relatively so—for, to close up the way and complete the formation of the fatal circle, a thin line of Zulu warriors was already forming. A general skirmish ensued, and had lasted nearly half-an-hour, when Commandants Landman and De Lange quickly consulted as to what was to be done. Landman's plan was to advance straight on the rocky hill in front of them, and there give battle. There was a ridge of stones and boulders running round the koppie. With the ridge as cover, he intended his commando to hold the Zulus at bay. Hans de Lange swore roundly when he heard this proposal. "*Verdom!*" said he, "look at the Kaffirs. How many of them do you think there are? How many can we kill, and for what length of time can our powder and lead last us against such an immense number? It is certain death for us to go on that hill. Forward, men, forward! He who loves me follows me." * <small>Hans de Lange Saves the Column.</small>

---

* This impromptu battle oration is a curious—but quite characteristic —admixture of convincing, logical argument and rapid decision, followed by instant action and assumption of responsibility, with a final flourish of the ever popular Biblical phraseology—probably to tone down the somewhat incongruous and incompatible introductory expletive Cambronneism. As given in the text, it is a literal translation, word for word, from the narrative dictated to the author by Senior Commandant J. H. Visser of Schoonspruit, near Potchefstroom, on 25th May, 1881. The entire account of the battle as here given is from the same source. Sarel Cilliers, the pious and decorous Ironside, also fought in the battle of the White Umvcloosi, and must have been shocked to hear the swearing. He says nothing about it in his Diary;

Spurring forward their horses, the burghers, led by De Lange, charged down on the thin line of Zulus which was already beginning to block the way towards the north. Past the rocky koppie, where Landman had intended to make a stand, they dashed at a

Battle of White Umveloosi Plain.

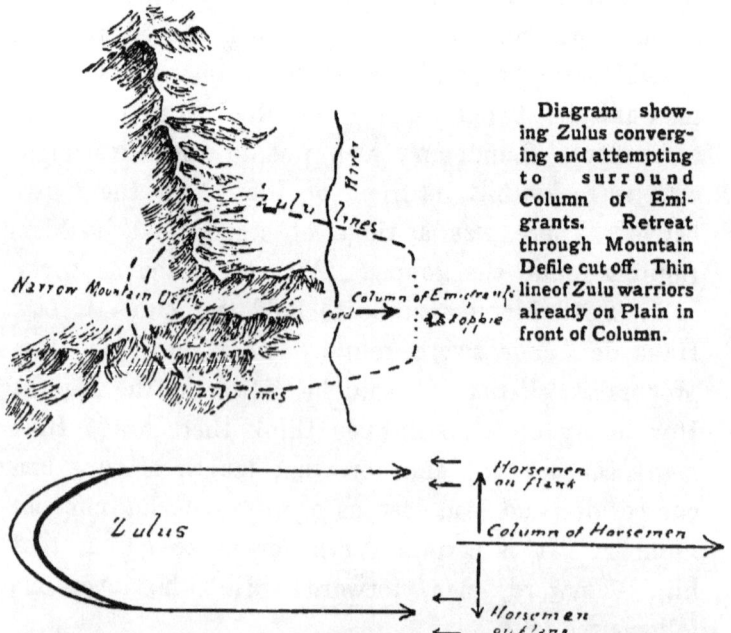

Diagram showing Zulus converging and attempting to surround Column of Emigrants. Retreat through Mountain Defile cut off. Thin line of Zulu warriors already on Plain in front of Column.

Diagram showing Column of Horsemen advancing over Plain and keeping back the Zulu Front Ranks.

gallop, and, firing from the saddle at the Kaffirs in front of them, they rode straight for the north—right into the heart of the enemy's country. Without them-

but narrates how Commandant De Lange ordered every one to mount and charge the enemy in extended line, and how this manœuvre was successful in extricating them from a dangerous position. J. H. Visser, in his narrative, says: "Were it not for Hans Dons (the nickname by which Commandant De Lange was known), we had all been killed that day."

selves losing a single man or horse, and after inflicting heavy loss on the enemy, they emerged on to the open plain. Not a moment too soon. Long black lines were already seen converging from the east and from the west, attempting to surround them. Onward, like black serpents gliding over the plain, came the extended ranks of the Zulu regiments; but the horsemen rushed on at a gallop where the country was still open. About twenty-five men or so, however, were, when clear of the Zulu wings, detached from each flank of the flying column. These charged eastward and westward to delay the enemy's advance. Reining up their horses when close to the foremost Zulus, they fired into the extremities or points of the lines, and then rapidly galloped northward towards their own main column, reloading as they retired, and, when ready with fresh charges of slug-shot, again wheeling round to keep back the Zulus, whose pursuing lines were now following close on the heels of the patrol. By this manœuvre, constantly repeated, while all the time the little body of horsemen were cantering further and further northward, the burghers managed to inflict considerable loss on the Zulus, and at the same time to prevent the enemy from doing any harm whatever. For two hours this retreating fight was continued. The horses were kept at a canter most of the time, and were beginning to be somewhat tired, for it was a hot day. As may be seen by referring to the illustration on p. 105, the advance had, so far, been in almost a straight line to the north, away from the White Umveloosi river. The enemy were now well to the rear. Straight in front of the column, and barring further advance northward, was a high mountain with steep rocky slopes and deep glens and gorges. This mountain was one of the chain of hills separating the basin of the White from that of the Black Umvcloosi, further to the north. At the foot of this *kop* the Farmers turned their horses' heads to the west, and pushed across the veld in that direction, *i.e.*, parallel with the mountain range, between which and the White Umveloosi all the plain was covered with the long black rows of the advancing Zulu regiments. The latter, also, had now changed their line of advance and were moving westward. Some of them, by taking short cuts across the level plain, had succeeded in getting close up to the horsemen; but the foremost Zulus again encountered a stubborn resistance, and lost heavily from the well-directed musketry fire. For fully two hours more the horsemen rode in almost a straight line towards the west. During all this time their skirmishers, galloping out towards the left rear, were engaging the enemy and keeping back advance parties of Zulu warriors who threatened the line of march. The entire body of the Zulu army was now also advancing towards the west. By constantly falling back before the main body of Dingaan's battalions, while their own mounted skirmishers in the rear and on the left flank were inflicting heavy losses on the enemy, the Africanders were making a wide detour across the plain. When the advance towards the west had continued for over two hours, the horses' heads were

A Running Fight.

turned first to the south-west and then to the south.
The object of this move was to reach the river and
recross it at a point much higher up the stream than
where the Zulu force had first been encountered.
Between the two points, that at which the battle
had commenced in the morning, and that towards
which the commando was now moving, the White
Umveloosi River was easily fordable all the way. The
water was shallow enough. There were no *zeekoegaten*
or deep reaches, and the banks were low. The only
danger was from quicksands. These, however, had
not been met with at the drift where the crossing
was effected in the morning, and it was deemed
inadvisable to proceed further westward and attempt
to recross higher up the stream than the ford towards
which the burghers were riding. Indeed, that would
have been impossible, for, more to the west, the country
became mountainous. The river banks were steep
and rocky. There was also a good deal of bush
further up the stream, and the small body of horsemen would have run great risk of falling into an
ambuscade had they ventured into this hilly country.
The Emigrants, therefore, rode in almost a straight
line to the south. For two hours more they cantered
their weary horses over the veld, while columns of
Zulu warriors were moving westward, attempting to
cut off their retreat. Like immense black trailing
serpents,* the impis moved across the level plain,
directing their course at right angles to that of the

---

* "*Soos groot swarte syl slange.*" (Oral narrative of J. H. Visser as given to the author.)

white horsemen. It was now a race as to who should reach the river's crossing first. The heat was intense. The panting horses were utterly exhausted by their long six hours' gallop; and yet everything now depended on their exertions. Close on their hind quarters pressed the fleet-footed Zulu soldiers who were still keeping up the pursuit, and, nearer and nearer—every moment threatening to bar the way to the river — crept the points of the long black lines which were moving forward from the east.

<small>At the Ford.</small> At last the river was reached. As the horses dashed forward into the stream, some Zulus who had crept up the banks of the river—to intercept the column—rushed at them in the water, brandishing the stabbing assegai. Hardly had a few yards of the drift been crossed, when several of the horses sank up to their shoulders in quicksands. The Zulus threw themselves on the struggling mass of men and horses in the river, and a fierce hand-to-hand combat followed. While many of the savages were shot down in the water, others rushed forward to take their places; for the plain up to the water's edge was now covered with large numbers of warriors swarming to the assault. Soon there were several riderless horses. Alexander

<small>Death of Alexander Biggar.</small> Biggar, whose two sons had already given their lives in the struggle for the foundation of the Republic, was slain, and five others* also fell in the fierce onslaught of the Zulus.

* Jan Oosthuizen, Marthinus Goossen, Gerrit van Staden, Barend Bester, and Nicolaas le Roux. Some half dozen Natal Kaffirs, who had followed Biggar in the campaign, were also killed at the drift.

Bart Pretorius had a narrow escape. Having had his horse killed under him, he was fighting on foot in the water, attempting as best he could to get through to the opposite river bank. But he saw Zulus closing in around him on every side, and most of his companions already a good distance off. Striking down several of his stalwart foemen with the butt end of his gun, and successfully parrying more than one deadly stroke of the broad-bladed stabbing assegai, he fought his way to where a riderless horse was wading through the stream. Then, leaping into the saddle, and dashing past the astonished Zulus, he was soon in safety on the other side of the river. *Narrow Escape of Bart Pretorius.*

On the southern bank of the White Umveloosi the commando again adopted the formation to which they had adhered in their six hours' ride across the plains north of the river. For the Zulus, now in thousands on the other side of the drift, had already commenced to cross the stream. While the main body of the horsemen were advancing—as rapidly as their jaded steeds could travel—towards the laager from which they had started in the morning, a rear guard of from twenty-five to fifty in number was told off to keep the enemy back. About half way between the camp and the river a small reinforcement, which had been sent forward by Andries Pretorius, came up and assisted in covering the retreat. When the Zulus finally fell back, the retreating commando were in sight of the laager. Seven hours had elapsed since the battle began in the *mielie* plantation at the lower drift of the Umveloosi. During all that time the *The Laager Reached.*

small body of two hundred and fifty men on horseback, in constant danger of being cut off and surrounded by Zulu regiments numbering between seven and ten thousand men, had kept up a running fight against large detachments of a brave and determined enemy. A line describing a semi-circle, over the plain to the north of the Umveloosi, shows the route followed by the commando in its ride from the lower river crossing, where the battle began, to the upper drift or ford, where Alexander Biggar and the five others were killed by the Zulus. All along this line there had been almost constant fighting, and, when at last the river was reached, it was not a moment too soon. Large numbers of Zulus would have cut off their retreat had the Farmers been a quarter of an hour later in arriving at the drift; for while the horsemen were making their wide detour over the open veld, Zulu regiments — thousands strong — were moving parallel with the river to intercept them. The various movements executed by the opposing forces on the plain to the north of the Umveloosi River during a period of more than six hours can be diagrammatically represented by a bow-shaped figure. The extended black lines of Dingaan's warriors moving parallel with the river form the string, while the course which the horsemen followed in their long ride forms the arc of the bow. But at almost every step along this arc-shaped course there was fighting going on; for large numbers of the enemy were in close pursuit, and had to be kept back. The Zulus fought bravely, and put their own losses at considerably over a thousand.

Such is a brief description of the battle of the White Umveloosi, the first engagement in the open which the Emigrants had fought against the armies of Dingaan since Uys had met his death. The presence of mind and sound judgment of Commandant Hans de Lange had saved the commando from utter annihilation; to this result the hardihood and power of endurance of their horses had in no small measure helped to contribute.

Carel Landman, the Commandant who took the place of Pretorius in this expedition across the river, was a favourite officer of the Emigrants. He was well advanced in years, and not so active as some of the younger leaders; but he was as brave a man as any among them. If he lacked any of the qualities of a commander, it was prudence. As was the case with the division under Pieter Uys at the battle of Italeni, his commando had fallen into a trap set for them by the Zulus; and this had happened because, in moving north-eastward towards the river, the troop was not sufficiently protected by scouts thrown forward on either side of their advance, as Andries Pretorius had advised when he handed over the command to Landman in the morning.*

On 31st December what was left of Dingaan's capital was burned and razed to the ground. The

* "Landman, set jou spioene wyd uit an weerskaute van die patrollie" ("Landman, place your scouts well forward on both sides of the patrol"), were the words used by Pretorius.

"Carel Landman had bevel. Hy was 'n goeije ou man, wat nooit gevaar kon sien nie, daar hy van gedagte was dat almal soo'n goeije hart als hy self had." ("Carel Landman was in command. He was a good old man, who could never see danger, because he took it for granted that others were as well disposed and kind-hearted as he was himself"). (Oral narrative of J. H. Visser.)

two large regimental kraals near Umkungunhlovu were also destroyed by fire. The return march to Natal was commenced on New Year's Day. In the early morning of 2nd January, before daybreak, a horse patrol started from New Year's Spruit, and, after riding some considerable distance eastward through mountainous country, succeeded in surprising a detachment of a Zulu regiment which was guarding some five thousand of the King's cattle.

Less than a month had passed since the small force of the Emigrant Farmers in Natal had entered into the solemn covenant in their camp on the Sundays River, and had commenced the campaign against Dingaan in order to avenge the death of Retief and his companions, and of those men, women, and children who had been massacred in the encampments on the Bushman's, Mooi, and Blauwkrans rivers. In less than a month, the mighty military hosts of the great Zulu Chief had been routed with a loss of several thousands; Umkungunhlovu, Dingaan's capital, and the two great regimental kraals near it, had been captured and burnt to the ground; and half of Zululand—all the country to the south of the White Umveloosi River —was in the power of the handful of bold invaders.

Close of the Campaign.

The expedition of the preceding April, ending in disaster, had but served to accentuate the sorrows and to emphasise the forlorn condition of those who had survived the treacherous and cruel massacres of February. The tragic death of Uys and his son with their followers, the withdrawal of Potgieter and his adherents, had come as further afflictions to those who—on the blood-stained soil of Natal—had wept by the lonely graves of their murdered relatives, then unavenged. The first campaign against the ruthless enemy had ended in humiliating defeat for them. Another of their leaders had been struck down, and yet another, from whom they had expected much, had abandoned them to their fate. The dark clouds of grief, which had hung over the new settlement since the death of Retief, had been made still blacker by the failure of the first campaign under Potgieter. But now all this was changed. Andries Pretorius, the new leader, by his skilful conduct of the second expedition against Dingaan, had secured victory to their standards, re-established confidence in the ranks of the Emigrants, and completely broken the power of the Zulu King. In the camps beyond the Tugela, tidings of the great triumph in Zululand, and of the capture of Umkungunhlovu, were brought by Kaffir runners. It was evident to the Emigrants that a great military leader had appeared among them.

Dark Clouds Dispersed.

CHAPTER XXI

FIRST PLOT AND PLAN OF CAPE EMPIRE-EXTENDERS FOILED

THE NAPIER-CHARTERS RAID

Governor Napier's Plan—Annexation Urged from Cape Town—Downing Street Refuses its Sanction—Sympathy with the Emigrants in Cape Colony—Sir George Napier "takes the Bit between his Teeth"—Major Charters sent to Seize Port Natal—Instructions from Cape Town—Closing of the Harbour of Natal—Arbitrary Buccaneering—*Onze Groote God zeggen wij toen Dank*—A Test Case—The New Townships in Natal—Condition of the People in the Laagers — Evidence of Major Charters—Brave Women—Negotiations with Dingaan, who sends Spies instead of Delegates—The Burghers on Guard against his Treachery—Volksraad instructs Pretorius to Demand Restoration of Stores and Ammunition—Correspondence—Volksraad Proclamation—Downing Street Despatch—Check to Cape Town Rubramania—Failure of First Raid.

Seizure of Port Natal by Governor Napier.

AT this crisis of their fate it seemed as if the Voortrekkers would soon, more than ever before, require a good commander. As Pretorius and his officers recrossed the Buffalo River, intelligence was brought to them from the Natal laagers that English troops had occupied the Port of Durban; seized stores and ammunition belonging to the Emigrant settlement; and put a stop to all sea traffic except in the case of such vessels as had a license from the Governor at Cape Town, Sir George Napier. This step had been taken by Sir George Napier entirely on his own responsibility. The Glenelg administration in England

HISTORY OF THE REPUBLIC 121

had not so far shown itself at all in favour of extending British dominion in South Africa. Governor Napier's predecessor at the Cape, Sir Benjamin D'Urban, had, in December, 1835, recommended the annexation of Natal, and in January, 1834, the same course had been urged on Downing Street by the petition forwarded from Cape Town after the public meeting at the Commercial Exchange. On both occasions the Home authorities had refused to sanction any extension of the territories of the Crown in South Africa. (*See* pp. 207, vol. i.; 5, 72, vol. ii.) *[margin: Annexation Urged from Cape Town.]*

"In the opinion of Earl Glenelg extension of the Colonial territory implied not alone extension of responsibility and increase of military expenditure, but injustice towards native tribes. Knowing nothing of the condition of the Bantu of the interior, the Secretary of State and the English people believed that the emigrant farmers were in collision with peaceful and inoffensive clans of aborigines, and did not imagine that the Zulus and the Matabele were the most cruel foes the aborigines ever had. These erroneous impressions were strengthened by the violent language of Captain Stockenstrom and the Rev. Dr. Philip concerning the dealings of the emigrants with the blacks, which, though it seemed to South Africans to be the phraseology of vindictiveness, appeared to Earl Glenelg as the outpouring of indignation against the perpetrators of wrong. *[margin: Downing Street Refuses its Sanction.]*

"How could further emigration be prevented, and the farmers who had left the Cape Colony be compelled to return? Captain Stockenstrom urged that

Port Natal should be occupied by troops, so as to cut off supplies of ammunition, and thus leave the emigrants only the alternative of retreat or death. His representations on this subject show as plainly as his evidence before the Commons Committee that at this unhappy period of his life his chief object was to please the Secretary of State. Thus he recommended Earl Glenelg to occupy Port Natal as 'the first step towards further arrangements for arresting a system of encroachment, usurpation, oppression, and bloodshed, which, though familiar in the history of South Africa, was even there unparalleled in atrocity and extent.' Lord Glenelg could not see that language such as this conveyed utterly erroneous impressions, but he declined to act as advised."—THEAL.

Sympathy with the Emigrants.

Ever since his accession to the Governorship, Sir George Napier at Cape Town had had abundant evidence— as had his predecessor Sir Benjamin D'Urban—of the widespread sympathy with the Emigrants which existed throughout the country districts of the Colony, and more especially on the frontiers. He had seen many of the frontier districts being gradually depleted of their best inhabitants, who were leaving their homes to join in the movement which was to build up the Republic in South Africa. The reverses and disasters which had overtaken the pioneers of Natal and Zululand had but served to swell the stream of those who were on the roads leading north-eastward across the Orange River and toward the Drakensbergen. It was known to the Governor that the English settlers in Natal, spurned and repulsed by the mother-country, had thrown in their lot with those who were founding a new State, and that a township under the Government of the Emigrants had already been established on the Bay of Natal, towards which port trade and commerce were being attracted. The English merchants and shopkeepers of Cape Town became afraid of losing their trade monopoly with the interior. Is it strange that they should have hated Retief and Pretorius, whose policy was to enrich South Africa by giving it another harbour?

As to the attitude of the authorities at Government House towards the Emigrants, it was consistent enough. As servants of the British Crown they did all they could to prevent the formation of a new settlement, where, —owing to the action of the Home officials in refusing to sanction any scheme of extension of territory or any annexation—the British flag would not be acknowledged. True, the policy of England in South Africa at the time was that of the dog in the manger. But Sir George Napier and the Cape Town merchants determined to show that they, at least, were not responsible for this. In May, 1838, a Government mission had been sent to the Emigrants in order to persuade them to return and abandon the settlement in Natal (*see* p. 69). This had failed, and had been followed in July by a proclamation again advising the Emigrants to return to the Old Colony, refusing British sanction to the establishment of any independent Republic, and threatening military occupation of Port Natal. And now the Governor, pressed by the inhabitants of Cape Town, had resolved to carry out this threat, even without the sanction of the Home Government.

Accordingly, in November, 1838, a small expedition, consisting of a company of the 72nd Highlanders and a detachment of artillery, left Port Elizabeth for Natal in the chartered transport *Helen*. The officer in command was Major Sam Charters, R.A., the Governor's military secretary. Stores for the expedition were conveyed in the coasting schooner *Mary*, and the interpreter was Shepstone, who, forty years later, became the famous would-be Boer-Extinguisher, Sir Theophilus.

Closing of the Harbour of Natal.

Major Charters' instructions were to occupy the Bay of Natal, but not to annex any territory * (in order not to offend Downing Street); to seize all arms and warlike stores; to disarm, and, if necesssary, apprehend or expel any individuals whom he might consider dangerous; and to close the harbour against all trade not expressly sanctioned from Cape Town. Peaceful trading vessels sailing under flags of foreign nations were to be prevented from entering the Port. The landing of cargoes, even on the neighbouring coasts, and all commerce, unless licensed at Cape Town, were to be stopped; and, where necessary, force of arms was to be used by the British officer to carry out his instructions.

It seems hardly conceivable to us at the present day that such arbitrary proceedings and such a direct violation of the rights and privileges of other nations could be resorted to by British officials,†

---

* "In a proclamation the Governor announced that the occupation of Port Natal was temporary and purely military, not partaking in any degree of the nature of colonisation or annexation to the British dominions."—THEAL.

† Written before the Jameson Raid, this sentence now requires qualification.

more especially when we consider that Sir George Napier was acting without the sanction of Lord Glenelg. There is, however, no doubt that these were the orders given to Major Charters. They were all publicly made known in a proclamation issued by the Governor.

On the 4th of December, the Major landed at Durban without opposition, and proclaimed martial law in the town and for two miles inland. Three guns were landed and mounted in commanding positions, and while an encampment for the troops was being constructed, a message was sent up country to warn the Emigrants against undertaking any expedition against the Zulus. But the Burgher army under Pretorius was already well on its way towards Zululand when the messengers reached the nearest Africander laager. Sarel Cilliers says that when he was returning from Zululand with the commando under Pretorius, they were startled, after their last fight with the Zulus near New Year's Spruit on 2nd January, " by a Proclamation which the British Government sent us, in which we were threatened that, should we go into Dingaan's country, armed help would be given to Dingaan against us."

Arbitrary Buccaneering.

It is not difficult to understand that the simple farmer warriors felt incensed and bitter against England. They had left the British dominions in South Africa, and, at great sacrifice, settled in a land where England had no authority and could claim none—a country which the British Government had refused to annex, and expressly declared to be outside its rule and its responsibilities. Here, without provocation on their

part, they had been cruelly attacked by a ruthless and
barbaric foe; their beloved leader and all with him
treacherously murdered; their women and children and
their old men—the helpless and defenceless—brutally
massacred. For an entire year they had carried on a
war of self-defence against a powerful savage nation.
Many of them shoeless and in threadbare clothes;
others famishing with hunger: overwhelmed by disaster,
out-numbered by the enemy, maligned and slandered in
Europe; this handful of African pioneers had persevered
in their heroic struggle for independence. They had
bravely defended their surviving women and children
while Dingaan hurled his countless battalions of savage
warriors, and the British Governor his inhuman proclamations, on their sorrow-stricken laagers. Even
their countrymen in the old Colony had been forbidden
by the authorities to come to their assistance. When
their supplies of ammunition had run short—when fell
disease had attacked them in their camps—it was again
the British Government which had interfered and prevented succour being brought to them by those who
sympathised with them in the South. And, after
having endured unheard-of privations and sufferings;
after having dauntlessly persevered in what at one
time seemed a hopeless struggle; when the day
of victory was at last dawning on their standard,
and the savage foeman was receiving some slight
castigation for the enormities and atrocities which his
regiments had committed:—again British interference and a British proclamation.[a] "*Maar onze groote
God zeggen wij toen dank,*" exclaims Cilliers. "*De slag*

[a] "*Onze Groote God zeggen wij toen Dank.*"

was geleverd." ("But we thanked our Lord God. The battle had been fought.")

When Major Charters landed at Durban, and during the time that the campaign in Zululand was in progress, the main encampments of the Emigrants were on the Upper Umgeni. The township of Pietermaritzburg had not yet been formally established, but there were several laagers where the capital of Natal now is. A good many small buildings had already been erected, and the place was known as Pieter Mauritsburg, in memory of Pieter Maurits Retief, the fallen leader. There were also encampments of the Emigrants on the Bay of Natal and on the Umlaas River. The Volksraad then consisted of twenty-four members, and met every three months. All appointments were made by this assembly, which, therefore, acted not only as a legislative but also as an executive body. The members of the Volksraad were chosen every year by the people.

Immediately after the return of the commando under Pretorius, the Volksraad instructed Carel Landman to proceed to the Bay and request Major Charters to give up the ammunition and stores which the English officer had seized. The latter declared himself willing to accede to the request on condition of the leaders of the Emigrants agreeing to bind themselves only to use the arms and ammunition in self-defence, and not again to cross the Tugela into Zululand—in other words, not to follow up the victory they had gained over Dingaan. After due consideration, the Emigrant leaders decided not to agree to these conditions. They stated that they were a free people; that they had a perfect right to carry on war against the Zulus; that the ammunition was their lawful property, and ought to be given up unconditionally. Major Charters, however, took a different view of the matter, and retained the stores and ammunition.

The British troops had now constructed an encampment of huts enclosed by stockades and earthworks. This camp was called Fort Victoria. The three guns, mounted on sandhills, commanded all the approaches to the spot. A large stone building near the Point was converted into a magazine and store-room. When all these arrangements had been completed, Major Charters returned overland to Cape Town, leaving Captain Jervis, of the 72nd Highlanders, in command. Meanwhile Governor Napier was pressing the Home authorities for their sanction to the seizure and annexation of all Natal; but Lord Glenelg persistently refused.

A Test Case. A Farmer being charged with assault, Captain Jervis summoned him to appear and stand his trial. This summons was issued under the provisions of that strange enactment, the Cape of Good Hope Punishment Bill. The Farmer refused to appear, stating that he was a subject of an independent State, and responsible for his actions only to the Landdrost holding a commission from the Volksraad. Captain Jervis, canny Scot as he was, now asked for further instructions from the Governor, who thought it unwise to proceed further in the matter. "Thus," says Theal, "began and ended the attempt to exercise judicial authority over the emigrants at Natal, for in no other instance was the slightest effort made to interfere with their civil government. In the absence of instructions from the Secretary of State, which were repeatedly solicited, but in vain, the Governor could do nothing more than inform them on every opportunity that they were still regarded as British subjects, and officially ignore their Volksraad and courts of law, while all the time they were acting as an independent people."

In January, 1839, the Volksraad took steps for the establishment of a township at Durban. A resolution to the same effect had already been passed by the English settlers on the Bay, in 1835. Now streets were laid out and the limits of the town were fixed. The village of Weenen was built at a later date. In March, 1839, Pietermaritzburg was established as a township, the old name of Pieter Mauritsburg being changed in order to do honour to the memory of Gerrit Maritz as well as that of Retief. This town was made the capital of the settlement, and here the Volksraad now held its meetings. But the great majority of the Emigrants still lived in laagers and camps scattered along the Tugela, Klip River, Bushman's River, and Umgeni. The country had so far been too unsettled to permit of the occupation of many farms. The few that were established were near some of the great laagers. There was much poverty among the people, and the closing of the Port by the English had not improved matters in this respect. Major Charters in travelling overland to Cape Town, passed through the districts where many of the encampments were, and he has left us a picture of the condition in which he found the inhabitants.

New Townships.

"A few of them were tolerably comfortable, but, generally speaking, there existed every indication of squalid poverty and wretchedness; and it was deplorable to see many families who, a short time previously, had been living in ease and comfort in the Colony, now reduced to poverty and misery. They bore up against these calamities with wonderful firmness, however, and, with very few exceptions, showed no inclination to return. They considered themselves as unjustly and hardly treated by the Colonial Government while under its jurisdiction, and all they now desired from it was to leave them to their own resources, and not molest them again.

"This spirit of dislike to the English sway was remarkably dominant amongst the women. Most of these, who formerly had lived in affluence, but were now in comparative want and subject to all the inconveniences accompanying the insecure state in which they were existing, having lost, moreover, their husbands and brothers by the savages, still rejected with scorn the idea of returning to the Colony. If any of the men began to droop, or lose courage, they urged them on to fresh exertions and kept alive the spirit of resistance within them." *

Captain Jervis, who was left in charge of the troops by Major Charters, also seems to have been favourably disposed towards the Emigrants, and did his best, in the beginning of 1839, to make Dingaan agree to peace. He sent a messenger to the Zulu King,

* Major Charters' report, as quoted in Norris Newman's "With the Boers in the Transvaal and Orange Free State, in 1880-1."

inviting him to delegate some of his chiefs with authorisation to discuss terms and conditions. The indunas soon made their appearance in Natal, bringing with them over three hundred horses. These animals had been taken from the Emigrants during the previous year; and were now returned by Dingaan, doubtless by way of showing his sincerity.

The Zulu delegates, after meeting Pretorius and other Emigrant leaders in the presence of Captain Jervis near the English fort, returned to Zululand in order to convey to their Chief the conditions under which the Farmers would agree to peace. These were:— *Negotiations with Dingaan.*

(1) Confirmation by Dingaan of cession of territory made to Retief. (2) Restoration as far as possible of all cattle, sheep, horses, guns, and other property taken from the Emigrants, and, where this was impossible, indemnity for losses. (3) No Zulus in future to cross the Tugela into Natal, and no white Emigrants to cross the same river into Zululand, and parties so transgressing to be shot.

Dingaan's answer was forwarded to Captain Jervis at the Bay, and was to the effect that the other property belonging to the Emigrants would be given back to them if they would send for it. Commandant Badenhorst, on receiving intelligence of this message from Captain Jervis, had it taken on to Pietermaritzburg, where the Volksraad at once issued instructions to Commandant-General Pretorius, who, with a commando of three hundred and thirty burghers, formed a laager at the junction of the Mooi with the Tugela, and then sent William Cowie, J. A. van Niekerk, and J. P. Roscher to interview Dingaan and receive from him the property of the Emigrants. Not far removed from the site of Umkungunhlovu the commission came to Dingaan's new head kraal. Surrounded by large numbers of his warriors and attended by his chief indunas, he received the messengers of Pretorius, with whom he pretended to be very desirous of concluding peace. Being kept well informed of the movements of the Emigrant leader by his own scouts, fearing the destruction of his new kraal, and remembering that already nearly ten thousand of his warriors had fallen during a year's hostilities with the white strangers, he took care to send to the laager some 300 cattle, 400 sheep, 52 muskets, and 43 saddles. He at the same time expressed to the commissioners his regret at large numbers of the captured cattle and sheep having died, and many of the guns having been lost. Pretorius and the Farmers with him were not deceived. They understood that the savage Chief was temporising and quietly preparing to resume hostilities at a more favourable moment. They resolved to be more on their guard than ever against that treachery on the part of Dingaan of which they had already had such terrible experience. Zulu indunas of high rank were now expected at the laager, Dingaan having stated that he would send these chiefs to arrange with Pretorius as to the proposed treaty of peace. At the appointed time (13th May, 1839), two minor chiefs only made their appearance. They were received, however, as delegates, declared that they were authorised by the King to accept the conditions of peace already laid down, and, promising that chiefs of higher rank should come to confirm their signatures, affixed crosses to the document placed before them. Pretorius told them what the estimate was as to the number of cattle still due as indemnity, and agreed to accept ivory in part payment.

The indunas who should have ratified the treaty did not arrive. But at the end of June two other delegates reached Pietermaritzburg. They stated that they came from Dingaan, and that they were authorised to confirm the treaty. They brought neither cattle nor any of the other property of the Emigrants with them. Nor did they bring even a part of the promised indemnity in ivory. Moreover, they were not chiefs at all. It had now become more than evident that Dingaan, while pretending to be anxious for peace, was treacherously preparing for further fighting. The leaders of the Emigrants therefore sent word to the Zulu King that, unless the indunas authorised by him to agree to the terms of peace arrived within twelve days, no more delegates would be received and Pretorius would march into Zululand to resume the campaign. The only effect produced by this peremptory message was the arrival at Maritzburg—at different times—of so-called delegates from Dingaan, who were in reality spies.* {Spies instead of Delegates.}

* "On several occasions afterwards messengers arrived, but they did nothing else than deliver compliments, make promises, and apologise for mistakes, until it became evident that Dingaan's only object was to ascertain whether the farmers kept in laager or were dispersing over the country." THEAL: "History of South Africa," vol. iv. p. 158.

The history of the interruption of these negotiations through Dingaan's treachery and double-dealing is important as bearing on the shooting of the spies Tambusa and Combezana at a later date. The Voortrekkers still living agree in stating that Dingaan was distinctly warned through his messengers that should he send any more pseudo-delegates, they would be dealt with as spies—and shot.

Burghers on Guard against Treachery.

Meanwhile, Pretorius had been instructed by the Volksraad to ask Captain Jervis for the ammunition and stores which Major Charters had seized in the previous year. The British officer, however, did not see his way to agreeing to this request unless Pretorius would promise that neither the arms nor the ammunition should be used in aggressive warfare against the Zulus; and, of course, this promise could not be given.

Volksraad Instructs Pretorius to Demand Restoration of Stores, etc.

The long continued occupation of the Bay of Natal was causing considerable uneasiness to the Volksraad and Executive of the Emigrants. Although Major Charters and Captain Jervis had made themselves personally very popular with all who had come in contact with them, and although the most friendly relations existed between the British officers and the Africander leaders, the latter could not be indifferent to the gravity of a situation which, at any moment, might become more strained and even critical. Rumours found their way to the Emigrant encampments and to Pietermaritzburg, that the Cape Town Government intended shortly to land large numbers of Scotch and English Colonists in the country—in order to bring about a peaceful incorporation with the British Empire. To be prepared for any forward movement that might be intended, a burgher guard of forty or fifty men was permanently stationed near Captain Jervis' encampment; and Pretorius wrote a despatch to the English officer, pointing out to him the serious consequences which such a step as the rumoured immigration scheme would bring about. On the 11th November the Volksraad issued a proclamation in the following terms:— Correspondence.

"Should foreign emigrants land in the Bay of Natal without having previously obtained the Volksraad's consent, such emigrants will be regarded as enemies of the State. In case the British Colonists are landed under the protection of such a strong military force as to make resistance impossible, then we shall retreat to the woods, mountains, and ravines, which surround the Bay on all sides, and there—in separate small parties, each one acting on his own responsibility—follow the example of the oppressed Spaniards, and, actuated by the same principles as the adherents of Don Carlos, neither ask for nor give quarter until we have recovered what is lawfully ours." Volksraad Proclamation.

But Cape Town and Sir George Napier were not yet to have their way. Under date of 30th April, 1839, there had been sent from Downing Street a despatch, in which the Earl of Normanby, Lord Glenelg's successor at the Colonial Office, informed the Governor that there was to be no attempt at further extension of the British Empire in South Africa. Captain Jervis, therefore, received orders to return to the Cape with Downing Street Despatch.

<small>Check to Cape Rubramania.</small> his expedition. The arms, ammunition, and stores which had been seized were now given up to Pretorius unconditionally, and, on 24th December, the gallant Captain and his soldiers set sail from Natal, leaving the harbour and the new settlement once more free. On the 25th, the Emigrants hoisted their flag over the fort which Captain Jervis had built, and proclaimed the re-establishment of the Government of the South African Association of Port Natal at the Bay. Salutes of artillery were fired from the cannons which had done service against the Zulus on the Bushman's River, and there were public rejoicings at Durban and at Pietermaritzburg.

CHAPTER XXII

THE CONQUEST OF ZULULAND

WEENEN AVENGED

Sufferings of the People—Dingaan Prepares for War and sends Spies—Pretorius Receives Instructions from the Volksraad to Invade Zululand—Panda, the *Bon Vivant* of the Umveloosi—Becomes Conspirator—Revolution in Zululand—Sapusa Defeats Dingaan—Panda Retires over the Tugela—Interview with Volksraad—Landdrost Roos and Heemraad S. van Breda Proclaim Panda King of the Zulus in Alliance with the Republic—Campaign against Dingaan—Forces in the Field—Instructions to Commandants—Line of March—Arrest of Tambusa and Combezana—Precautions against Treachery—Nongalaza's Skill as a Leader—Defeat of Salela and Dingaan—Trial and Execution of Tambusa and Combezana—Punishing the Murderers—A "Boer Crime"—Flight of Dingaan over the Pongola—The Laager on the Black Umveloosi—Panda Proclaimed King—Pretorius Speaks to the Zulus—The Sermon on the Rock—Proclamation of 14th February—Sovereignty of the Republic over Zululand—Death of Dingaan.

WHILE the English expeditionary force had been stationed on the Bay, the closing of the harbour had interfered considerably with trade in the new settlement. The cutting off of their supplies of provisions led to great distress and want in several of the Emigrant encampments. To add to their sufferings, measles broke out among the children, assumed a very virulent type, and carried off large numbers. Of the adults, also, many were ill with fever, and there was much poverty. Even the best families did not escape the effect of the great losses which they had sustained in the war against the Zulus, and of the heartless aggression of the British officials at Cape Town. To mention only one instance among many: Anna Steenecamp—a cousin of the murdered Commandant-General Retief—while tending her sick children and grandchildren, had to endure the heat by day and the cold by night without other shelter than that afforded by a waggon tent, and had barely enough food to keep herself alive. Stores for the sick and medical comforts had been sent to the settlement by sympathising friends in the Cape Colony; but the vessel containing these hospital necessaries was refused admission to the harbour of Natal by the agents of the British Government.*

Sufferings of the People.

The widows and orphans of those who had fallen would now have to be provided for out of the indemnity which Dingaan had bound himself to pay. But months passed, and neither this nor the large number of cattle which the Zulus had captured, and which their Chief had also agreed to return to the Emigrants, was forthcoming. Zulu spies had been seen in the neighbourhood of many of the Emigrant encampments, and it became more evident every day that, while the settlers were suffering from poverty and sickness, their powerful enemy was preparing for another onslaught. Realising that their very existence as a nation was again at stake, and believing that the surest method of defence lies in attack, Pretorius and the Volksraad at once made preparations for invading Zululand before Dingaan's indunas again brought their regiments

Dingaan Prepares for War.

* Stuart: "Hollandsche Afrikanen"; and "Zuid Afrikaan" (Cape Town).

south of the Tugela. Messengers were therefore sent to the King's kraal on the White Umveloosi River to inform Dingaan and his councillors that, as they had not carried out the stipulations of the treaty to which they had bound themselves, as they were sending spies into Natal, and as they were known to be preparing for war while pretending to desire peace, the Volksraad refused to negotiate with them any longer, and that Pretorius would lead another commando against them, to punish them for their treachery and for the atrocities which they had committed, and to exact from them the indemnity that was due to the Emigrants.

Meanwhile, important events were transpiring in Zululand. Umpanda or Panda was Dingaan's elder brother, who should, by right, have ruled the country after the death of Chaka, but was too effeminate, too fond of ease and luxury, to assert his claims to dominion. He had taken part in Chaka's ill-fated expedition against the Sosangaan Kaffirs of Delagoa Bay. When he returned with the remnants of the army, he found his elder brother slain and the throne of Zululand usurped by the assassin. Retiring to a kraal situated between the White and Black Umveloosi rivers, he entirely withdrew himself from all interference with the affairs of State or of the army, and, surrounded by boon companions and by women, spent his days and nights in debauchery and dissipation. This was, perhaps, as much diplomacy as inclination on Panda's part. Dingaan had, so far, encouraged him in dallying and toying with women. While many of the ablest councillors and bravest warriors, the men who

[margin: Pretorius Instructed to Invade Zululand.]

[margin: The Bon-Vivant of the Umveloosi.]

had helped Chaka to build up their country's power and greatness, were put to death by Dingaan, who feared them, Panda was spared. It was thought that he was without ambition, and never likely to exchange the life of licentious indulgence which he was leading for that of either the military chieftain or the statesman. During a time of murders and massacres innumerable, perpetrated by Dingaan and his councillors Tambusa and Salela, after the assassination of Chaka, when every chief suspected of being dangerous to the new ruler was slain, the elder son of Sensengakona was safe amongst his concubines, because the usurper supposed him to be perfectly harmless and without influence in that warlike land. But, as year after year went by, and Dingaan's iniquitous atrocities went on increasing, numbers of the disaffected in Zululand, and among them some indunas of high rank who still regretted the fall of Chaka, found their way stealthily and in secret—so as not to arouse Dingaan's suspicions—to Panda's kraal, north of the White Umveloosi, and began to arrange plans to bring about a revolution. Among the women at Panda's *stad* were many of the daughters and widows of adherents of Chaka—chiefs who had been put to death by order of Dingaan. These women became active conspirators; and, soon, all the south of Zululand was ready to rise in arms against the tyrant. The indunas Nongalaza, Sotobe (formerly Chaka's ambassador to Cape Town), and Sapusa were, with Panda and three or four other chiefs, the principal plotters. Their plans were to bring about the fall of Dingaan by forming an alliance with the Emigrants under Pretorius. But, before they could complete their deliberations and carry out their project, Dingaan, whose suspicions had been aroused, and whose spies had not been idle, fell upon Sapusa's kraal with four regiments. The tide of victory was, however, turning against the tyrant. In the battle that ensued Dingaan lost a very large number of his best men. According to Panda's statement,* half of Dingaan's fighting force were slain. Hurrying up two more regiments to the scene of the engagement, the Zulu King at the same time sent messengers to order his brother to come to his assistance. But Panda saw the trap, and refused to move. All the south of Zululand was now in revolt against the usurper King, who, concentrating his army north of the Black Umveloosi, and taking with him all his women and cattle, sent Salela to Panda's head kraal to attempt to gain over some of the minor chiefs and their followers. This mission also failed, and Panda with Nongalaza, Sotobe, Sapusa, and other indunas, collecting all their adherents, moved towards the Tugela. They then sent messengers to the Landdrost of Durban, asking for the help and alliance of the Emigrants. On the 14th September these ambassadors reached the Bay, and, soon after, Panda and the other chiefs, crossing the Tugela, had an interview with Commandant Hans de Lange, who was guarding the frontier with a small patrol of burghers. Suspicious of further treachery on the part

Sapusa Defeats Dingaan.

Panda crosses the Tugela

---

* Report of interview between members of Volksraad and Panda, 15th October, 1839. Hofstede: "Geschiedenis van den Oranje Vrijstaat."

of the Zulus, the Emigrant leaders were at first disinclined to entertain Panda's offers of alliance, and disregarded his request for protection against his brother. As, however, large numbers of Zulus, with their women and cattle, continued to cross to the southern banks of the Tugela, and as Panda and his indunas persisted in their efforts to obtain assistance from the burghers, it became evident that the Zulu nation was now divided into two hostile camps, and that the downfall of Dingaan was at hand. On the 15th October, 1839, Panda was admitted to an interview with the members of the Volksraad at Pietermaritzburg, where it was agreed that he should be acknowledged as King of the Zulus, that he should for the present be allowed to remain in the country between the Tugela and Umvoti, but should, with his followers, remove to Zululand after the war was concluded, and should then assume the rulership of that country as a vassal of the Republic. Landdrost F. Roos with the Heemraad Servaas van Breda, Commandant Fourie, Fieldcornet Jan Meyer, Dr. Krause, and Messrs. Delegorgue,* Morwood, and G. Kemp were deputed by the Raad to proclaim Panda's accession to the chieftainship of the emigrant Zulus. This was done on 27th October. Surrounded by his chief indunas and councillors, Panda promised to be the faithful vassal and ally of the white Emigrants, not to engage in hostilities with any neighbouring tribes without the

---

* Adulphe Delegorgue, author of " Voyage dans l'Afrique Australe, notamment dans le territoire de Natal, etc., exécuté durant les années 1838—1844."

Volksraad's consent, and always to spare the lives of women and children in war.*

An artillery salute was fired when the Volksraad's proclamation had been read, and, on the termination of the ceremony, Panda sent a present of one hundred and one cattle to the members of the commission, for distribution among the families who had suffered losses from Zulu depredations in the war with Dingaan.

In the months of November and December, 1839, Pretorius and his Commandants were engaged in active preparations for the coming campaign. A commando of two hundred and sixty-five men was laagered on the Tugela. This was joined in January, 1840, by some seventy burghers from the country to the west of the mountains (now the Orange Free State). These men were under Commandant Andries Spies, and came as volunteers to take part in the campaign. Further reinforcements raised the total number of burghers under Pretorius to about four hundred. Panda's fighting forces, under command of the Zulu indunas Nongalaza and Sapusa, numbered altogether between four and six thousand. A native contingent under the minor chiefs Matawaan and Joob—some six hundred strong—also joined the expedition. Dingaan's available forces still amounted to ten thousand men. On January 4th, 1840, the Volksraad instructed Pretorius to march into Zululand, and demand from Dingaan the forty thousand

<small>Forces in the Field.</small>

* Report of Volksraad Commissioners S. v. Breda and F. Roos, dated November, 1839.

cattle which he had agreed to pay and failed to deliver. The Commandant-General's instructions were contained in a written document consisting of twenty-two articles, which had been drawn up for his guidance in the conduct of hostilities. These instructions bear evidence that the Emigrants had resolved to carry on with humanity the war which had been forced upon them, and that, notwithstanding the great provocation which they had received when their leader and his companions were treacherously murdered and their women and children cruelly massacred, they were guided by loftier and nobler motives than the thirst for revenge. A point on which great stress was laid was that the chief officers of the native allies should take their orders from Pretorius and his Commandants, who were to see that no harm befell any women and children or unarmed men on the side of the enemy. The Zulu auxiliary forces were to be prevented from committing any excesses, and compelled to conform to civilised methods of warfare by sparing the helpless and the weak.

Instructions to Commandants.

On the 14th January all was in readiness for the commencement of the campaign. While Nongalaza was sending scouts to the northern side of the Tugela, to penetrate Zululand in all directions and to bring back reports as to the movements of the enemy, Pretorius, with his commando, marched along the south side of the Upper Tugela, in the direction of the modern village of Colenso, to the spot from where the campaign of 1838 had been commenced and Zululand entered; for the country to the north of the

Upper Tugela was not then part of the settlement of Natal—it was included in the land still under the sway of Dingaan. The line of march from the Upper Tugela was the same as in the first campaign; but it was a double line, for, parallel with the commando under Pretorius, moved the army of Nongalaza's Zulus— between four and six thousand strong. While Panda's followers were thus kept some distance from the fighting force of the Emigrants, the Chief himself remained with Pretorius, whose officers retained complete control of the Zulu allies, and who was in reality the Commander-in-Chief of both armies. Every precaution was thus taken to guard against treachery; for their previous experience had taught the Emigrants that precautions were necessary, and the good faith of Panda and his adherents had yet to be proved.

Shortly after the campaign had commenced, two Zulus suddenly made their appearance one day at the encampment of the Emigrants, and announced themselves as emissaries of Dingaan. The one was evidently an induna of high rank, and proved to be the commander Tambusa, one of Dingaan's chief counsellors. The other was a warrior named Combezana. They were immediately arrested as spies. Previous ambas- *Arrest of Tambusa.* sadors of Dingaan had shown themselves to be spies. On a former occasion the Chief had been warned that no more embassies would be received, and that no further negotiations could be entered into with him and his counsellors,—accomplices in the murder of Retief and the women and children, and likewise culpable through breaking faith with

Pretorius in not carrying out the provisions of the treaty to which they had agreed in May, 1839. Now Tambusa himself, the chief of these counsellors, had come as an ambassador. When arrested and accused of being a spy, he unhesitatingly admitted that such was the case, and that he and Combezana had instructions from Dingaan to obtain all possible information as to the preparations and dispositions of the Emigrants for the coming campaign.

While the columns were moving forward, Pretorius took care to protect his men against being surprised by the enemy. A fixed laager was made every day, and garrisoned by a small detachment. Each laager was constructed of improvised earthworks protected by huge hedges of the thorny branches of the acacia tree, behind which the defenders could defy a strong Zulu force. On this entrenchment the commando could fall back in case of a check, or even in the event of a reverse. The column did not move forward at the same rate of speed as in the first campaign. The banks of the Upper Tugela were left on 21st January, and the Buffalo River was not crossed before 29th January. There was considerable difficulty in getting the waggons across this stream, for heavy rains had fallen in the mountains, and the current of the swollen river was strong in some parts of the drift or ford, while in others the water was so deep that the oxen had to swim. On the evening of 29th January the camp was formed on the banks of the Bloed River, at the spot where, on the 16th December, 1838, Dingaan's forces had been defeated.

Then the commando proceeded down the valley of the White Umveloosi to Dingaan's new head kraal near to Umkungunhlovu. This was reached on 31st January, and found deserted by the enemy.

Nongalaza's scouts had not been idle. Reports were now coming in from the country to the north of the Black Umveloosi as to the whereabouts of Dingaan's fighting force. Panda's general was distinguishing himself as a great military leader. The Zulus under his command had several skirmishes with the enemy, and took several prisoners. By order of Pretorius, the lives of these prisoners were spared, and they were set at liberty. On 30th January, a great battle was fought between the regiments under Nongalaza and a superior force of Dingaan's men under the induna Salela. Shortly after the engagement had commenced, one of Dingaan's regiments deserted and joined Nongalaza. The Black and White Shields, the two most famous of Dingaan's cohorts, stood their ground, and were almost annihilated. Salela himself and many other chiefs were slain, and Panda's army gained a great victory, although they also had lost heavily. *Battle Between Armies under Nongalaza and Salela.*

On the 31st of January, Pretorius had his head quarters at Dingaan's new kraal, not far from Umkungunhlovu—the place where Retief and his followers had been murdered. Tambusa, one of the murderers, was still under arrest as a spy, and was now brought to trial before the *Krygsraad* or Court Martial. He and Combezana were both condemned to death as spies, and Tambusa was also found guilty, on the evidence of Panda and other Zulu leaders, of having *Trial of Tambusa.*

instigated Dingaan to commit the murder and to order the massacres on the Bushman's River. After Tambusa had confessed that the evidence brought against him was true, both were shot. They met their fate with all the stoicism and the fortitude of Zulu warriors. When admonished to pray to God for forgiveness before the death sentence was executed, Tambusa answered that he had but one master—Dingaan—and that it was his duty to remain faithful to his own Chief to the last. "The Great Chief," he said, "before whom the white men say I shall have to appear hereafter, cannot find fault with me for this."

In his "Lectures on the Emigrant Farmers," Cloete says that this campaign against the Zulus was conducted with as much skill and bravery as humanity, that the burghers showed mercy to the women and children and to all non-combatants, and that the only stain on their cause and their fame was the execution of Tambusa and Combezana, who should have been regarded as ambassadors of Dingaan. All English historians of South African events who deal with the matter take the same view. Even Theal, one of the few impartial British writers, says (vol iv. p 163): "This act of Mr. Pretorius—for the chief blame must rest upon him—was a great mistake as well as a great crime. It gave those who were jealous of his influence an opportunity to attack him, which they at once availed themselves of. In the Volksraad he was accused of having exceeded the authority entrusted to him by creating a tribunal with power of life and death. His partisans, however, were so strong that, after a time, the charge was allowed to drop."

The impartial reader must form his own opinion. The facts are before him. To claim the sanctity of an ambassador for a treacherous murderer and a spy is absurd. Tambusa and Combezana had been arrested as spies at a time which was a turning point in the career of the Emigrants in Natal, and after Dingaan had been warned that no more delegates would be received. Moreover, Tambusa had himself admitted that he came as a spy. The mere handful of white men constituting the entire fighting force of the Voortrekkers were threatened by a powerful and treacherous enemy bent on their destruction, and had, at the same time, to be on their guard against an army of Zulu allies, who, on the least sign of weakness, might be expected to go over in large numbers to the foe. The greatest precautions, the most constant watchfulness, the most determined and undaunted firmness had, under these circumstances, to be exercised by the leader of the expedition to ensure its success. As the commando had advanced into the heart of Zululand, more and more evidence had accumulated to show that Dingaan was bent on war, that his pretended overtures for peace were a farce. All the conditions to which he had agreed in the treaty of 13th May were not only evaded, but entirely ignored by this Chief, from whose treachery and duplicity the Emigrants had already suffered so much. When the White Umveloosi—the scene of the cruel murder of Retief and his companions—was reached, it had further become clear to Pretorius that Tambusa was not only a spy, but also one of the chief instigators and planners of that murder, and of the massacre of women and children in the camps on Bushman's River.*

<small>Flight of Dingaan.</small>

Dingaan, with the remnants of his army which were still faithful to him in his adversity, was now in full flight northward, to the Swaziland frontier. Pretorius, with a commando of two hundred and fifty horsemen, followed in hot pursuit, while Nongalaza and Sapusa's Zulus, making wide detours in north-westerly and north-easterly directions, attempted to intercept the fallen tyrant at the Pongola river. The country through which the commando travelled was mountainous, and there were numerous caves, forming natural fortresses, into which small bands of the enemy were sometimes driven, and where they were

---

* "We have all resided in the vicinity of the Zulu capital, where Tambusa lived; every action of his is known to us; and we are prepared solemnly to swear, in the face of that Omniscient God of whom you (white men) have spoken to us, in the face of the Sun, of yourselves, and of the world, that Dingaan never orders any great deed of bloodshed without first obtaining the express consent of Tambusa as one of his Privy Councillors ('als een van zijne geheime Raden'). Tambusa always proposed to his King to cause this or that kraal of Zulus—women and children, as well as men—to be massacred for some trivial fault or misdemeanour. The suggestion was always approved by the King and Salela."

"It was the same Tambusa who urged the King to murder your Governor Retief and his men, as well as the women and children of your nation." (Diary of P. H. Zietsman in *Report to Volksraad*, dated 24th February, 1840. Evidence of Panda and his Captains before the *Krygsraad*).

"He (Tambusa) was a great instrument in the shedding of innocent blood; he instigated Dingaan to have P. Retief murdered, threatening, in case his wish were not gratified, with all his people to secede from Dingaan; he was himself at the head of the Zulu army when your defenceless pregnant women, and even infants at the breast, had to fall as hapless victims before the blood-stained weapons of the murderers." (Declaration of the Zulu Chief Matawaan, as quoted by Zietsman in his Diary; *Volksraad Report*, 24th February, 1840).

lost sight of. On the 6th of February, the anniversary of the death of Retief, Pretorius and his horsemen were approaching the Pongola river, which they reached on the 8th. There they ascertained that Dingaan had crossed the stream, and was a fugitive in Swaziland. Sickness breaking out among the horses of the expedition, Pretorius decided to return to Natal, and left it to Nongalaza to follow up the pursuit of Dingaan.

On the evening of 9th February the horsemen again reached the place where, on the upper waters of the Black Umveloosi, the waggons of the main laager had been left. The camp was situated about twenty-five miles south-east of the present town of Vryheid. There, on the following day, 10th February, 1840, Dingaan was declared deposed, and Panda proclaimed King of Zululand.

Ranged round a huge rock boulder—some twenty feet long by fourteen broad—were the indunas and delegates from the different districts of Zululand, and the entire burgher force under their Commandants and Fieldcornets. On the summit of the rock stood Pretorius, with Panda by his side. Turning towards the Chief, the Commandant-General addressed him as follows: "Chief and ally, according to the state- Pretorius Speaks to the Zulus. ments of representatives of all the tribes of Zululand, you appear to be entitled to the Kingship of the country. Dingaan has fled into the territory of another nation, and, if he should ever fall into our hands, we shall inflict capital punishment on him for the horrible crimes he has committed against our people. I now deem it right, in the name of the Volksraad of our South African Association, to appoint you King or Chief of the Zulus,—the people under your rule as well as those who, fleeing from Dingaan, may put themselves under your protection, and those whom we may be able to place under your government. I also have instructions to acknowledge you as our great ally, and to treat your enemies as ours. You will not be allowed to make war upon any nation without our consent, and we shall on all occasions help you against your foes." *

Then the two pieces of artillery in the laager fired a salute of twenty-one shots; and, while the echoes were reverberating in the mountains, Panda, turning to his Chiefs and followers, called out in a loud voice: "Pretorius is father of Zululand!" This, the first declaration of the new Zulu King, signified his announcement of the sovereignty of the Republic over Zululand.

And then Pretorius addressed the Zulus.

"Whose blood has made Panda King, and destroyed Dingaan's power?"

Instantly thousands of arms were extended towards the rock where he stood, and stentorian voices echoed: "His blood!" — the Zulus remembering that the General had been wounded in the battle of 16th December, 1838.

"No, Chiefs! No, Zulu warriors!" replied Pretorius; "you err. It was the blood of the women and children

* P. H. Zietsman: "Diary of the Campaign in Zululand": *Report to Volksraad.*

murdered by Dingaan. It is a law of all white people that the nation which kills women and children must be destroyed. Panda and his people must now know that as long as this rock remains they will not be allowed to kill a single woman or child, even in war. White nations do not act in that way. Only men must fight. Only against men must you make war. Let this matter not pass from your memory. As long as this rock stands here, our alliance will exist and remain in force. When this rock exists no longer—when it has fallen to dust—then, also, our treaty ceases." *

The Sermon on the Rock.

All the missionaries who ever went to Zululand—to preach the Gospel of Peace—have perhaps been as zealous and earnest men as are to be found in their calling; but it is questionable whether their united sermons and exhortations did as much to teach Chaka's race the true spirit of Christianity as these words from the rock. The Zulus are a nation of warriors. When the great founder of their military power was in his death agony, he foretold the advent of the white Conqueror who would vanquish their armies and humble their King. The indunas and chief representatives of the nation now stood in the presence of that Conqueror. His word was law to them. He now repeated the message he had sent them at the commencement of the first campaign against Dingaan; and once more taught them the lesson which he had made them learn all through the second campaign, when Nongalaza was leading them against

* Literal translation from J. H. Visser's oral narrative. (Schoonspruit, 26th May, 1881).

Salela's impis: "*Show mercy to the helpless and defenceless. Spare the women and children.*" The chiefs and the warriors now heard the same words from his own lips. Nongalaza and his regiments had already proved their obedience to this command of Pretorius by their conduct all through the war. In not a single instance had they been guilty of taking the life of a woman or child, or of committing any atrocities whatever.* And now the Conqueror's exhortations were repeated in every corner of Zululand: "*In future no more women or children are to be put to death.*"

While the Government of the Emigrants in Natal lasted, Panda and his chiefs remained faithful to the terms of their agreement with Pretorius. As soon as the Africander Republic was conquered by England and British rule established in Natal, there was a reversal to the old order of things on the White Umveloosi; and then the groans of the helpless victims, and the thousands of fugitives flying across the Tugela, announced to the African world that the sermon from the rock had been forgotten in Zululand—because the warrior-preacher had been vanquished.

On 13th February the Emigrant commando left their laager on the Black Umveloosi. The waggons moved in a westerly direction. That night the camp was formed at the foot of a high mountain, some six miles from the starting-point and mid-way between the Black and White Umveloosi Rivers. Here, on the following day, Pretorius issued his proclamation, by which the Republic assumed the

* *Report to Volksraad*: 24th February, 1840.

sovereignty of Zululand, the territories of which country were in future to be ruled in such a way as to ensure the safety of the adjacent white settlement. The wording of this important State document was as follows : *

"Whereas the Volksraad of the South African Association, by reason of the unprovoked hostilities which the Zulu King, Dingaan, or the Zulu nation— without previous declaration of war—began against the said Association, has been obliged to incur expenses to the amount of one hundred and twenty-two thousand six hundred Ryksdaalders † for hire of horses and waggons, besides other expenses for this and the two previous commandoes,

"And whereas the Zulu King, according to all appearances and reports, has crossed the Pongola River (the frontier), his remaining people being in concealment in numerous bands, so that there is no one to whom I can apply for payment of these and previous expenses,

"Be it, therefore, hereby known that I proclaim and announce, in the name of the said Volksraad of the South African Association, that I take possession of all the country between the Tugela and Umvcloosi Umjama or Black River, by way of compensation for the above-named one hundred and twenty-two thousand six hundred Ryksdaalders; that our boundary will for the future be from the sea along the Black Umveloosi, where it flows through

Proclamation of Republic's Sovereignty over Zululand.

* *Report to Volksraad* : 24th February, 1840.
† 122,600 Rs. = £9195. (The Cape-Dutch Ryksdaalder = 1s. 6d.)

the Double Mountains (near its source), and then along the Randberg, in a similar direction to the Drakensberg, the St. Lucia Bay being included in our territories, as well as all coasts and harbours which have already been discovered, or will be discovered in future, between the mouths of the Umzimvubu and Black Umveloosi Rivers.

"These lands and sea-coasts shall, however, be considered as possessions of the Association, distinct from those which the late Mr. Retief acquired from the Zulu nation.

"God save the Volksraad.

"Given over my signature in my camp on the Umveloosi Umjama or Black River, on this 14th day of February, in the year of our Lord one thousand eight hundred and forty.

"(Signed) A. W. PRETORIUS, *Chief Commandant.*

"H. J. LOMBAARD
"JAC. POTGIETER
"ANDR. SPIES
"MARTHINUS SCHEEPERS
} *Commandants.*"

Thus, at the end of twenty-four days after the commencement of Pretorius' second campaign against Dingaan,* the regiments of the great Zulu Chief were

---

* The advance into what was then the Zulu country began on the 21st January, when the commando, under Pretorius, left the banks of the Upper Tugela, and marched towards the Buffalo River. The war was virtually ended by the defeat of Dingaan's united forces under Salela by Nongalaza on 30th January. The campaign, then, may be said to have lasted only ten days. Besides the great battle on the 30th, there was no other fight of any importance. All other engage-

defeated, destroyed and scattered, all Zululand was conquered, and a new ruler — in vassalage to the Republic — was installed on the White Umvcloosi. All this was done without the loss of a single man on the side of the Emigrants. The dream of Retief was more than realised; for his countrymen now possessed not only Natal, but the entire sea-coast from the mouth of the Umzimvubu to the St. Lucia Bay.

While the expedition was on the return march to Natal, intelligence was brought to Pretorius by some of his Zulu scouts, that Nongalaza, having crossed the Pongola into the southern part of Swaziland, had followed the fugitive Dingaan northward until he came to a new kraal established in that country by the defeated despot. Here Dingaan's mother, and the few followers who had remained faithful to him in his misfortune, had surrendered to Panda's general. Their Chief himself had, some days previously, fallen by the hand of an assassin — a Swazi warrior, who had formerly served in the Zulu army.

The victorious commando was again approaching the banks of the Upper Tugela; and soon the tidings were carried to Pietermaritzburg, and to the laagers on the Bushman's River, where the widows and orphans of the fallen Voortrekkers were waiting. After two

ments were mere skirmishes. The small army under Pretorius himself was never attacked, because the forward movement was conducted in such a masterly way, and in such thorough preparedness for the fierce foeman's onslaughts, that Dingaan's indunas, declining to risk another defeat similar to that in the previous year, made up their minds to attempt to crush Nongalaza first. In that attempt Salela not only failed, but was himself overwhelmed and crushed through the defection of large numbers of his own followers.

years' struggle the Zulu Chief's power was shattered. Dingaan, Tambusa, and Salela—the murderers of Retief—had paid the penalty of their treachery; and the triumph of the Emigrants' arms was complete and decisive. Salvoes of musketry announced the return of the conquerors; and there was much rejoicing in the encampments of the burghers when full details of the success of the expedition became generally known.

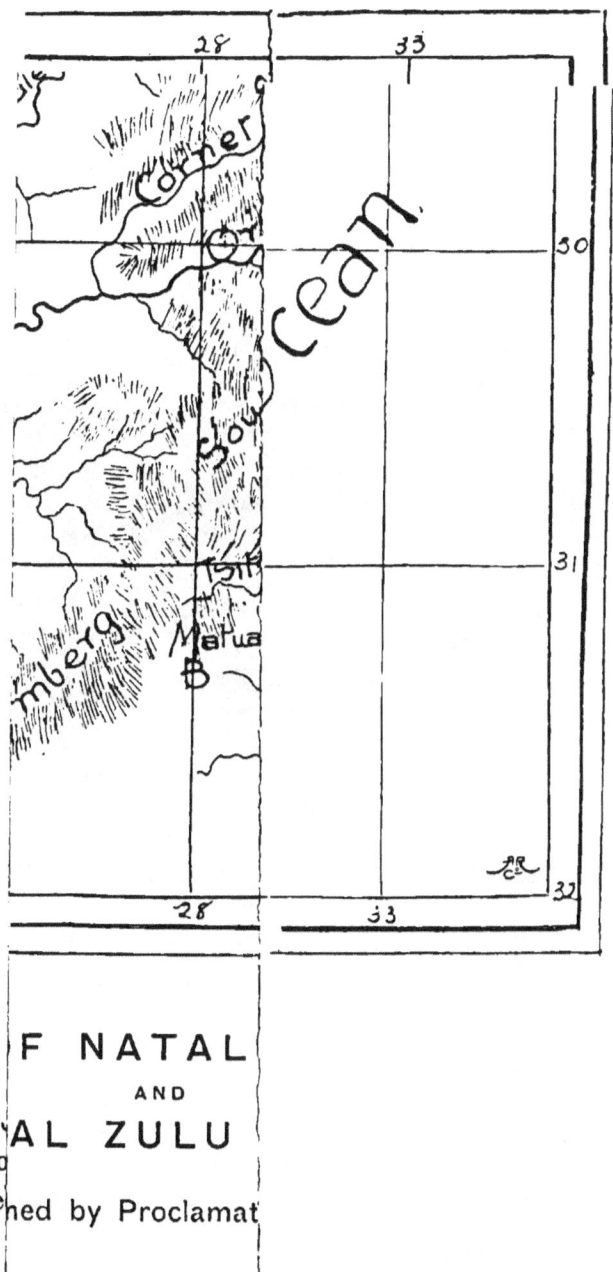

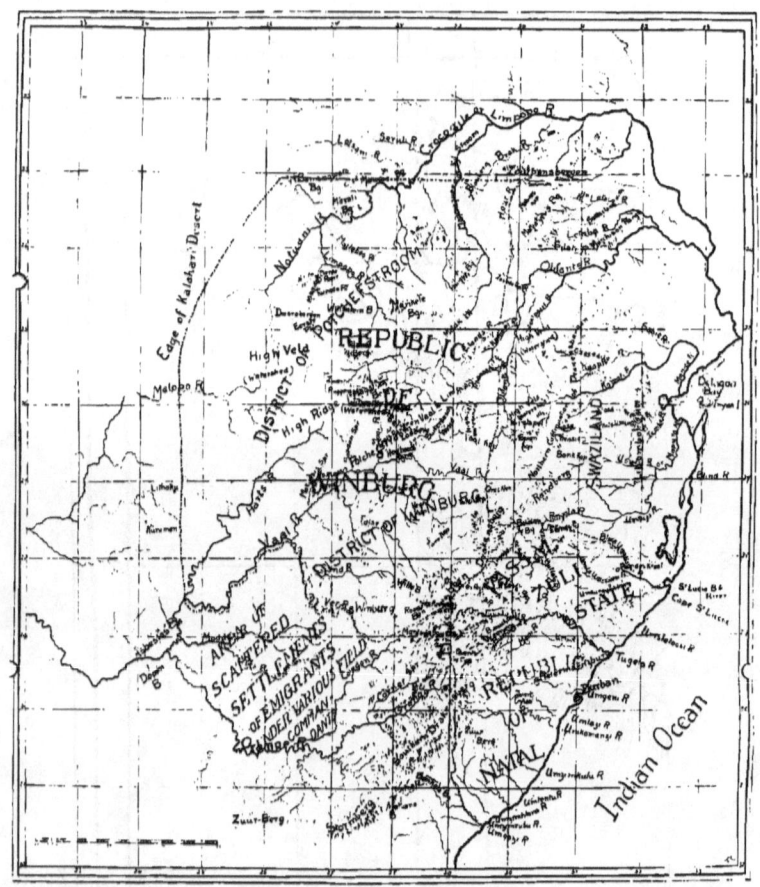

REPUBLICS OF NATAL AND WINBURG
AND
VASSAL ZULU STATE.

Boundaries approximate only, as roughly defined by Proclamations of Hendrik Potgieter and Andries Pretorius.

CHAPTER XXIII

THE FEDERATED REPUBLIC

THE VELD WHICH THE VOORTREKKERS FOUGHT FOR AND WON

Establishment of Republican Governments North of the Orange River—The Republic of Winburg—The Settlements between the Orange and Vet Rivers—The District of Potchefstroom—Settlement North of the Vaal—Boundaries and Extent of the old Potchefstroom District—Townships—Government—Franchise, etc.—Republic of Natal—Boundaries—Townships—Government—Revenue—Noble Missionary Clergymen—First Attempt at Federal Union—Comparison between the old Homeland and the New Country—What British Rule had done for the Former—What the Republic had done for the Latter—Benefits to the Natives—Saved from Destruction—Prosperity of New Settlements—The Harbour—Cape Town's Jealousy.

HOSTILITIES with the natives having ceased, it remained for the Emigrants to make arrangements for permanently carrying on the government of the territories which they had acquired by treaty and by conquest.

To the north of the Orange River there was the country (between the Vet and Vaal) which Potgieter had purchased from Makwana. This region, corresponding in area to what is now about half the Orange Free State, was then known as the district of Winburg, and formed, with Potchefstroom, a Republic, ruled by a Volksraad of twelve members and by a Chief Commandant (Andries Hendrik Potgieter). The rest of the country which afterwards became the Free State Republic, the land to the south of the Vet River and lying between that stream and the Orange, was partly occupied by scattered sections of Emigrants under the leadership of different Commandants. These small settlements were independent of the Republic of Winburg, and had primitive governments of their own. In the localities where they established themselves, along the Lower Vaal and Caledon, on the Orange and on the Modder and Riet Rivers, the Pioneers who founded these outlying colonies entered into arrangements with various native and half-breed tribes (Korannas and Griquas). These agreements were generally of the nature of permanent or temporary cessions of territory to the Emigrants. The establishment of these different settlements to the south of the Vet River, outside the limits of the district of Winburg, was a further departure from Retief's policy of centralisation—which Potgieter and his followers had been the first to ignore when they separated themselves from the main body of the Emigrants, and decided in favour of a Government distinct from that to be formed to the east of the Drakensbergen.

The Old Potchefstroom District.

North of the Vaal River was the territory of Mooi River or Potchefstroom, the country conquered from the Matabele. Its boundaries were very different from those of the present district of that name. It represented the Transvaal of those days. Its western frontier was the edge of the Kalahari Desert, or, in other words, a line running between the 24th and 25th parallels of East longitude. On the south was the Vaal River. The eastern boundary line was roughly as follows :—From a point on the Vaal River near the present town of Standerton, northwards to Rhenoster Poort, and from there on to the Zoutpansberg Range. The natural physical features of the country—the mountains and rivers—along this eastern frontier were the Olifants River from its source to the junction of the Zebedelas River; then the Zebedelas River to the Strydpoort Berg; and from there along the Strydpoort, Houtbosch Berg, Matyatyes Berg, and Spelonken Berg, to the Zoutpansberg Range.* The northern boundary was (approximately) the Zoutpansberg, Makatoe Berg, and Bamangwato Berg. None of these frontiers were accurately defined, and in 1840 there were already many farms further to the east than the 30th parallel of East longitude.

Boundaries.

The district of Potchefstroom, bounded as above described, formed with the district of Winburg (the country lying between the Vet and Vaal Rivers) the Republic of Winburg, in which there were then two

* The old district of Potchefstroom, therefore, included all the modern Transvaal, with the exception of Lydenburg, Pieter Retief, Ermelo, Standerton (a portion), Wakkerstroom, Utrecht, Vryheid, and large parts of Zoutpansberg and Middelburg districts. It also included the territories afterwards occupied by Sechele's Bakwana and by Montsiwa's Barolongs. All the country subsequently known as Goshen and Stellaland belonged to it. Potgieter's policy was to keep open the road to the interior of Africa, in order to safeguard the subsequent northward expansion of the Republic. Pretorius also attached great importance to this matter, and the sum and substance of the treaty of Sand River, by which Great Britain guaranteed the independence of the South African Republic (Transvaal) in 1852, was that there should be no British territory to the north of the Vaal. After Majuba, however, English diplomacy succeeded in detaching from the Transvaal that large portion—along the western border—which was afterwards to be utilised for the British advance to the north, and which then became British Bechuanaland.

townships, that of Winburg, the capital, near the Vet River, and that of Mooiriviersdorp or Potchefstroom, on the Mooi River. The State Volksraad consisted of twelve members. There was a Court of Landdrost and Heemraden, and the principal burgher officials were the Chief Commandant, Andries Hendrik Potgieter, and the Commandants and Fieldcornets under him. Every white inhabitant had the franchise, and all white emigrants who settled in the country received a free grant of land for a farm. There were no taxes, and the officials were unsalaried.

East of Drakensberg were the Republic of Natal and the subject Zulu State under Panda. The first formed a triangular area, bounded, on the east, by the Indian Ocean; on the west, by the Umzimvubu River and Drakensberg range; and, on the north, by the Tugela River. The Zulu State was a quadrangular-shaped territory, bounded, on the south, by the Tugela River; on the north, by the Black Umveloosi; on the east, by the Indian Ocean; and, on the west, by the Drakensberg. In the Republic the townships were Pietermaritzburg, on a tributary of the Umgeni; Durban, on the Bay of Natal; and Weenen, near the Bushman's River, a tributary of the Tugela. This last-named township was founded in 1840. In divisional relationship to each of these towns, respectively, were the districts of Pietermaritzburg, Port Natal, and Weenen.

The Volksraad of Natal, which met at Pietermaritzburg, the capital, four times every year, consisted of twenty-four members. It combined both legislative and executive functions. For the Chairman of each session acted as President* or head of the Government for the next three months, and the other members of the executive during that time were the Commandant-General and the representatives of the *Commissie Raad*. These representatives were members of Volksraad, chosen (with the chairman) to form the Executive for three months. All appointments were made by the Volksraad.

Elections took place yearly, and were managed as follows:—Each burgher handed in to the Fieldcornet of his *wyk* or ward a paper, signed by himself and having over his signature the name of the representative whom he wished to be elected. The twenty-four members of Volksraad for the next year were those who had received the highest number of votes. There were Courts of Landdrost and Heemraden, as in the Republic of Winburg. Elections.

There was no direct taxation, with the exception of a land tax (eighteen shillings per year on farms not over three thousand *morgen*. On farms larger than three thousand *morgen* a higher tax was paid). The revenue was derived from this tax; from transfer charges, which Government obtained on purchases of land; from port dues, paid by ships in the harbour; from duties levied on wines, spirits, and imported tobacco; and from *ad valorem* duties on timber, wooden materials, and general merchandise. Revenue.

As was the case on the other side of the mountains (in the Republic of Winburg) free grants of land were

---

* There was as yet no separate office of State President. Nor was there a Vice-President.

given to all white emigrants who settled in the country. The franchise, also, was free and unrestricted to all white inhabitants. The Commandant-General or Chief-Commandant, the Commandants, the Fieldcornets, and the members of the Volksraad, had no salaries whatever. The Landdrosts, the Secretary to the Volksraad, the Port Officers, and the clergyman of Pietermaritzburg, were in receipt of small stipends.

The clergyman — the Rev. Daniel Lindley — was one of the American missionaries whom the Farmers under Maritz and Potgieter had found at Mosega in 1837. In the winter of 1839 he settled in Natal, and, finding that the Emigrants had established congregations in all three of their townships, but could prevail on no minister of the Dutch Reformed Church of the Cape to come and reside among them, took upon himself the duties of their clergyman. He lived at Pietermaritzburg, and travelled from there, not only to Durban and Weenen, but also on the other side of the mountains, to Winburg and Potchefstroom, to preach to the members of all the five congregations, to visit their sick, and to do what he could to educate their children. The name of this noble, self-denying man is still remembered with affection and held in high esteem in Natal, the Orange Free State, and the Transvaal. Erasmus Smit, the missionary teacher who, in 1837, had been made chaplain by Pieter Retief, was in receipt of a small pension, as his health had broken down. He, also, will be remembered as one who shared their sufferings and hardships with the Voortrekkers, when, among all the many clergymen of the Dutch Reformed Church in the Cape Colony, not one could be found to brave the privations and the dangers of the wilderness, and to speak words of comfort, encouragement, and consolation to some ten thousand of their own congregations.

Many of the Emigrants saw the advisability of union between the two Republics, and in September, 1840, Potgieter and Pretorius entered into an agreement by which the members of the Raad of Winburg were also acknowledged as members of the Volksraad of the Republic of Natal. The Volksraad of Winburg, however, retained for itself complete local autonomy in the country to the west of the Drakensbergen, and the alliance was followed by no permanent tangible results. For Potgieter's adherents do not seem to have availed themselves of their right to take part in the deliberations of the Volksraad of Pietermaritzburg. Nor could they have done so without much difficulty and inconvenience, considering the expense, trouble, and hardships of travel in those days. Their twelve representatives would have been under the necessity of constantly journeying backwards and forwards through the mountain passes, in order to attend the sessions of the Natal Volksraad every three months. The alliance was of a vague, indefinite, and impracticable nature, and brought about no effective union. In reality, there was nothing whatever to prevent such union, excepting factious differences between the leaders of the two parties; and it soon became apparent that the time was badly

Closer Union.

The Volksraad.

chosen for allowing such differences to stand in the way of a step which was absolutely necessary for the common cause.

Extent of Federated Republic.

The territory which was under Republican rule now reached from the Orange River, in the south, to the Zoutpansberg, in the north, and from the Indian Ocean, on the east, to the border of the Kalahari Desert, in the west. Its seaboard extended from the mouth of the St. John's River (Umzimvubu) to the St. Lucia Bay.

The Old Country and the New.

In four years' time the Emigrants had transformed the wilderness into what would soon have grown into a flourishing state. The Voortrekkers had created a country of their own, about as large as that which they had left and which still owned the sway of England. The new land was more beautiful and more valuable than the old. The old country had taken one hundred and eighty-eight years—nearly two centuries—to grow to the size it then was, and to attain to the condition in which it then existed. And

Condition of the Cape Colony in 1840.

what was that condition? Its frontiers ruined, depopulated, abandoned to barbarians; its inhabitants discontented and unhappy; its commerce, its prosperity, vanishing; its Government vacillating, unpopular and incapable; life and property unsafe, murder and pillage going unpunished in its dominions.*

* By the terms of the Stockenstrom treaties of 1836, no farmer could claim compensation from Government for losses sustained from Kaffir depredations unless he employed armed herdsmen to guard his flocks and herds. The British Government thus admitted its incapacity to protect the property of its white subjects. During four years (1836-1840) forty-nine of those unfortunate herdsmen were murdered by the Kaffirs. And this was at a time when there was

And how was it at that time in the new land which the Emigrants had created, to which they had brought their flocks, and in which they had built their homes? From the banks of the Orange River to the Zoutpansberg range, from the shores of the Indian Ocean to the great Kalahari Desert, there was not a single native tribe which defied the power of the Pioneers. The great military despotisms which had sought to destroy them had been humbled and shattered. The Matabele had fled far to the north. The hostile Zulu Power was broken. Its place had been taken by a friendly subject State. There was no further danger from hostile native tribes. Towns and villages were being built both east and west of the Drakensberg mountains. Flourishing farms and homesteads had been established in the basins of the Umgeni, Umvoti, Umlaasi, and on the Upper Tugela tributaries, as well as along the Vaal, Mooi, and Vet rivers. Large numbers of stock farmers continued to leave the British Colony, because they saw better prospects for themselves and their children in the new territories occupied by the Emigrants,

Condition of the Republic.

---

supposed to be peace. In September, 1840, the Governor. Sir George Napier, who had come to South Africa a believer in Lord Glenelg's views, wrote to the authorities in England, urging on them the necessity of taking steps to ensure the safety and security of the frontiers, pointing out that, after four years' trial, the treaties which had been concluded with the Kaffirs had proved utterly inadequate to meet the requirements of the country. Something, he said, would have to be done at once, as there seemed every probability " of the plundered, harassed, and justly irritated farmers taking the law into their own hands and suddenly entering the Kaffir country with commandoes, to retake their cattle by force, if not to revenge by bloodshed all their wrongs."

Another great Kaffir war was already certain.

where life and property were safe—thanks to the energy and perseverance of the Voortrekkers—and where the further development and progress of the country were not, as in the Colony, menaced by hostile natives and unwise legislation. Peace and prosperity were assured, not only for white settlers, but for the numerous native tribes which previously had been subjected and oppressed by the Zulu and Matabele Powers.

<small>Peace and Prosperity Assured.</small>

Then, as now, the Republicans had many enemies at Cape Town, where missionary and merchant politicians and the so-called negrophile party were doing their utmost to persuade the British authorities to annex Natal. The Empire-extenders were active. Their views were that the Emigrants had carried on unjust and aggressive wars against the Matabele and Zulu nations, and that England should not allow the establishment of an independent white Government in South Africa. They found support from many writers and orators in Great Britain. But, while the faddists and the self-styled philanthropists in England were reviling and libelling the South African frontier farmer, holding him up to public censure as an unattractive type of cruelty and savagery, a very remarkable movement was in progress among the natives to the east of the Drakensbergen and to the north of the Vaal River.

The scattered remnants of conquered nations which were hiding in the forests and mountains, where they had sought refuge from the spears of Dingaan's and Umsiligaas' warriors, soon recognised that the establishment of the Emigrants' Government meant safety and security for themselves. They returned to the regions where they had formerly dwelt in Natal and in the Transvaal, and where the white men had now taken the place of the savage rulers whose marauding raids formerly depopulated the land. Many of those who had been driven south-westward out of Natal, by the tribes which fled before the advance of Chaka's armies, now returned from the country beyond the Umzimvubu. From Zululand, where the different contending factions had exercised a disturbing influence, many refugees came to Natal. From the central and southern part of the present Orange Free State, the Barolongs, who had previously lived in dread of the Matabele Power, removed to the south-western Transvaal region. In the west of the old district of Potchefstroom, also, tribes which had formerly fled into the Kalahari Desert now settled. Thus, great streams of native immigration were pouring into the territories of the newly-established Republics, where the aborigines found protection and safety. And, while the missionaries of Cape Town were telling the people of England that Pretorius and Potgieter and their followers were the oppressors and exterminators of the native races, those natives themselves regarded the Voortrekker Commandants as deliverers, under whose rule they came to place themselves in thousands and tens of thousands. *The Republic the Protector of the Natives.*

Very few, if any, events in the history of South Africa ever benefited the aborigines so much as the Great Emigration movement to the North, and the conquest by the Emigrants of the Zulu and Matabele systems. The remnants of tribes which had been swept *How the Great Emigration Benefited the Aborigines.*

from the land by Umsiligaas' impis returned to their old homes, and, receiving considerable accession of strength from the tide of black immigration now flowing in, re-peopled the once desolate regions. Where the native population had been barely a few hundreds, and these starving and in hiding among the rocks and in the forests, there were now thousands of prosperous Kaffirs planting their own crops and herding their own cattle. Flourishing kraals and maize gardens soon took the place of the many ruined native villages in the southern and western Transvaal. The huts were rebuilt. The cattle grazed in security on the lands where the Matabele war-cry was no longer heard. The birth of the Republic saved from annihilation all the numerous tribes which had been conquered by the Zulu and Matabele nations. Under the protection of the Government of the Emigrants, the races which had been threatened with extinction found safety and security. They were no longer subject to being chased and hunted like deer, to be stabbed and clubbed for mere sport by the raiding parties of their savage foes. Their lives were under the protection of European laws and institutions. Their property was their own. Their crops and their cattle were no longer interfered with. They were not even required to pay taxes or rent for the land on which they built their kraals, planted their crops, and grazed their herds and flocks. Within a very few years after the establishment of the Emigrant Government, the aborigines had attained to a degree of prosperity unknown to them since the days preceding the Zulu and

Matabele conquests—when they were governed by their own chiefs. During the few years that the Republic of Natal was in existence, the native population increased at an enormous rate. In 1837 and 1838, when Retief and the Emigrant Farmers under his leadership came into the country, they found in it a black population which, at the very outside, numbered ten thousand men, women, and children. Indeed, it seems probable that there could not have been many more than five thousand; for we know that that was the total number of natives whom Dingaan had placed under the chieftaincies of Farewell and Cane. These white chiefs were then the only rulers in the land, and the number of natives who wandered about in the forests without acknowledging the authority of these headmen under Dingaan must have been small and insignificant; for the armies of the Zulu King had frequently raided the land, and driven away nearly all its former inhabitants. When, in November, 1843, at the fall of the Republic and the annexation of Natal, the British Commissioner Cloete gave an estimate of the number of black inhabitants, the figures were between eighty thousand and one hundred thousand, at the very lowest. Even if we subtract from this total some fifty thousand, representing the Zulu refugees who had then but recently fled into the country for protection, the fact still remains that in the four years during which the Emigrant Farmers governed the country, the native population of Natal had become fully quadrupled in numbers.

Native Population of Natal, etc.

While this remarkable and extraordinary influx of

Kaffirs into Natal and the Transvaal was in progress, the white inhabitants of the Republics also were increasing in numbers; for the tide of the Great Emigration from the Cape Colony northward showed no signs whatever of abatement till after 1840. It has been estimated that, between the years 1836 and 1840, some ten thousand Colonists crossed the Orange River, to take up their abode in the new countries which were then being founded. The vast majority of these were frontier farmers with their families. But, as soon as the country had become settled, and hostilities with the natives had ceased, traders and shop-keepers also found their way to the new territories, where they established themselves in the townships and villages. More substantial houses than the dwellings which had first been erected at Winburg and Potchefstroom were built at both these places. Pietermaritzburg, also, grew rapidly, and this town, and the little village of Weenen were already the centres of flourishing, although somewhat primitive, agricultural districts.

At Durban some Cape Town merchants built quite an important trading establishment. The town was growing rapidly in size, and both here and at Pietermaritzburg recent arrivals from Cape Colony had settled in considerable numbers. In August, 1841, the harbour was entered by the American ship *Levant*, with a cargo of merchandise for the Emigrants. This vessel was the first harbinger of the opening up of a new commercial pathway to the interior of Africa. Its arrival in Port Natal caused a flutter in the dove-cots of those enterprising and enthusiastic Empire-extenders, the Cape Town shop-keepers. They had the ear of Government House, and it was arranged that British dominion and the Queen's authority could not tolerate a free harbour in South Africa. Then, as now, a so-called South African Association was formed—in London. To suppress the Africanders, and to paint the map red, were the objects of that agitation, as of to-day's.

Prosperity and Progress for South Africa by Means of British Bayonets.

CHAPTER XXIV

THE SMITH RAID

ANOTHER PLOT AND PLAN

MAJOR-GENERAL SIR GEORGE NAPIER, K.C.B., MISSIONARY JENKINS, AND KAFFIR FAKU, PUT THEIR HEADS TOGETHER

The Plot—The Cape Town Merchant—The British Government—The Uitlander—The Missionary—The Governor's Message to Faku—Ncapayi—Mr. Jenkins with the Pondos—The Troops on the Frontier—The Letter of Invitation—Correspondence between Sir George Napier and the Volksraad of Natal—Despatches from Downing Street—The Governor's Proclamation of 2nd December, 1841—Captain Smith's Movements—Henry Ogle's Spies—The Volksraad Protest—Unpreparedness for War—Clever Missionary—The True Protectors of the Aborigines—The *Brazilië*—Alarm of Cape Town Merchants—Smellenkamp—The Old Fatherland—Two Pictures—Magnificent, but not Diplomatic—Treaty of Commerce—Arrest of Smellenkamp.

The Cape Town Merchant.

FIRST in the field was the Cape Town merchant. Sincere and honest enough in his protestations of loyalty and attachment to the British Crown, he was, at the same time, sufficiently shrewd and far-seeing to understand that Natal—made an English Colony by force of arms, and with a discontented white population—would be a far less dangerous commercial rival to the Cape than the prosperous free Republic, which would grow up on the Indian Ocean's shores, were the Emigrants to be left unmolested and unassailed by Britain.

In close alliance with the Cape Town merchant, was

the British nobleman. Younger sons could find preferment and promotion when an expeditionary force was sent to Natal to extinguish the "*Boer*"; or could obtain civil appointments in the new Colony—after the war.

It was in 1840 that the British Secretary of State for the Colonies allowed himself to be persuaded, by the British-born South African Association and their aristocratic backers in London, to sanction the annexation scheme which the Cape Governor had been urging for some time. This sanction, however, was conditional on the expense being limited. Downing Street was not prepared to embark on a costly military expedition. It was, therefore, stipulated that the Emigrants should be dealt with in a conciliatory spirit. First, there was to be an occupation of the Bay of Natal by a British force. Then, in the event of no determined resistance by force of arms, the Emigrant Farmers were to be allowed a sort of limited autonomy under a President and Legislative Council chosen by the Cape Governor. This wonderful scheme of aggrandisement was elaborated and explained in two despatches, dated 18th June and 5th September. The contents of these important State papers were, of course, not made public until long afterwards, when they appeared in the Parliamentary Blue-Books. Meanwhile, the other agents in the plot set to work. They were the Uitlander and the Missionary. *The Scheme Elaborated.* *Despatches.*

The Uitlanders in the Republic of Natal were the Cape Colonists and English traders who had arrived in the country and settled in the towns after the Emigrant Farmers had broken the power of the Zulus and *The Uitlander.*

made the land safe and habitable. They enjoyed equal civil and political rights with the original founders of the Republic. But a pastoral State, where the highest officials were content to serve without salary, did not suit the tastes of the new arrivals; and their remedy was—to call in the British Government. Henry Ogle and some of the other English settlers who had been chiefs in Dingaan's time, and who now also had a grievance—one solitary grievance—in the diminution of their own importance and dignity, took an active part among those who attempted to bring about a change in the rulers of the country.

Let us pause, to glance, for a moment only, at some of the chief actors on the stage of History—more than half a century later than the Napier-Jenkins-Faku-Smith Jameson Raid.

Exaggerated self-esteem is a leading characteristic of many Cape Colonists. Nearly every one of the financiers, lawyers, and parsons from the South, who recently led the Uitlander hosts and beat the Uitlander drums north of the Vaal, had a real grievance—a very real one, and, therefore, one not included in Mr. Charles Leonard's list—against Paul Kruger. The grand old Statesman of South Africa had had the execrable taste not to abdicate and make way for each and every one of those superior persons to become President of the South African Republic.

Their self-esteem having been thus grievously wounded, these modern Knights of the Rueful Countenance mounted the shadowy and somewhat shady Rosinantes of the Johannesburg grievances, and ran full tilt at the innocent windmills of conservatism in a pastoral State. The wind-bag Sancho Panzas of Cape Town and London announced to the world that these windmills were the castled strongholds of the tyrant.

The opera-bouffe revolution was advertised as the sacred cause of reform. The union of South Africa was to be brought about by force of arms. Recruits were plentiful—at a pound a day—and " heroes " were imported. But when it became apparent that the Cape Town wire-pullers of the agitation meant to seize the Republic for the English, then it was also seen that the Uitlander had not forgotten how poverty and distress had been his hard lot in Natal after he had helped to call in the British Government to annex that country ; how prosperity had not followed the change of rule east of Drakensberg ; and how the extinction of the Republic had brought retrogression instead of progress into the land. Knowing the history of South Africa, and remembering all this, the Cape Colonists among the Uitlanders also remembered that they were Africanders, and refused to assist in handing over the soil which was the heritage of the Voortrekkers to the greedy Rhodesian Empire-builders and the Imperial schemers of Downing Street.

In Natal, the Uitlander of yore was poor and tried to better his condition by the help of British bayonets. He found out his mistake when it was too late ; but his sons have not forgotten the lesson taught by the history of those days.

In 1840, the missionary was a power in the land, not only in South Africa, where he ranked as an equal with the chiefs in the numerous independent native territories, but also in Downing Street, where the friends and supporters of the Rev. Dr. Philip exercised almost unlimited power in the councils of the Government.

The southern boundary of the Republic of Natal was the Umzimvubu or St. John's River. For several miles inland from its mouth, this stream cuts its way to the ocean through high precipitous banks of rock—steep and rugged cliffs: in some parts covered with dense vegetation, in others bleak and bare; gigantic masses of stone walls. More inland from this picturesque region of the *Gates of the St. John*, the course of the river is through a broad and fertile valley. This valley was the home of the Pondo nation at the time when the Emigrants were crossing the Drakensberg into Natal. Chaka's wars and the devastations caused by the numerous fugitive tribes which came from Natal had dispossessed that people of the land which they had formerly occupied to the north of the Umzimvubu. At one time one of the main divisions of the Abantu race, the Pondos, under their chief Faku, had become reduced to a comparatively insignificant and weak tribe. Their principal kraals were on the Umgazi, and none of these were then to be found to the north of the St. John's river.

Nearer to the Drakensberg, on the upper and inland part of the Umzimvubu, dwelt the Baca tribe. They also had come from the north. Fleeing before the assegais of Chaka's regiments, they had established themselves in the mountainous country along the Tsitsa and Tina tributaries of the Upper Umzimvubu, and

Pondoland.

The Pondos.

The Bacas.

there made themselves a terror to the surrounding nations by their depredations and robber raids. Their chief was called Ncapayi.

In the Pondo country there were at that time several English missionaries. They were, most of them, earnest, zealous, and well-meaning men, actuated by what they themselves and their admirers regarded as high and noble motives. *The Missionaries.*

Unfortunately, however, their zeal was not confined to civilising and christianising the heathen; for they were all keen politicians, and their policy was the same as that of the Rev. Dr. Philip—to champion the cause of Native rulers and Native states against those whose motto was—South Africa a White Man's Country. Consequently, they differed from the American and from many of the English Wesleyan missionaries in being bitterly opposed to the Emigrant Farmers and their Republic.

In 1838, Faku and his people, having received details of the contest which was then in progress between Dingaan's legions and the Emigrants, and having made up their minds that the Zulu power, which they had always dreaded, would now be broken, removed from their kraals on the Umgazi to the country north of the Umzimvubu.

In the following year, a Mr. Jenkins, one of the missionaries whose wife was such an enthusiastic partisan of the Pondo chiefs that she was afterwards known as the "Queen of Pondoland," visited Faku at his new residence on the Umzimhlava, and conveyed to the chief a message from the Governor at Cape Town. *The Pondos. Missionary Jenkins takes a Message.*

The Kaffir ruler was told that all the country as far northward as the banks of the Umzimkulu river—in other words, a great deal more than had ever been owned and lost in war by his ancestors—was to belong to him and his people; that the British Governor guaranteed the possession of all this land to him; and that, if molested or disturbed in the occupation of the new territory, he was to apply to Cape Town for protection.

To the historian it is of the greatest importance to determine whether any such construction could be put upon the language which the Governor used when sending this message. Theal says it could not. In relation, however, to the effect desired by the plotters in London and Cape Town, it really mattered very little whether the words were actually those which the messenger of the Gospel of Peace delivered to the Kaffir Chief. British diplomacy in South Africa knew, then, as well as now, how to convey a hint and how to choose its messengers. Mr. Jenkins seems to have interpreted Sir George Napier's instructions quite as cleverly as Mr. Lionel Phillips recently understood Sir Henry Loch's veiled suggestions.

The Bacas. Faku and the Pondos had been hitherto on very friendly terms with the Emigrant Farmers. They had often suffered from the depredations and cattle-thieving raids of Ncapayi. They had asked permission of the Government at Maritzburg to be allowed to make war on the Bacas, and to ally themselves with the neighbouring clan of Fodo for this purpose. When, towards the end of 1840, the Bacas carried off some cattle belonging to Farmers in Natal, Pretorius determined to punish the raiders, and was authorised by the Volksraad to lead a commando into the valley of the Upper Umzimvubu. Two hundred and sixty burghers, under him and Commandant Lombaard, assisted by some of Fodo's native auxiliaries, attacked Ncapayi's stronghold, took it, and broke up the robber clan. By this expedition the Emigrants not only protected the interests of their own settlers in the Republic, but also rendered a great service to Faku and his people, who had suffered much from the Bacas, and who had but recently applied for assistance. The missionaries, however, thought otherwise. From the 1st to the 5th of January, 1841, three of them were in conference at Faku's new kraal on the Umzimhlava, within the territory of the Republic of Natal. A letter was drawn up to the British Governor of Cape Colony, *who, as it happened, was then not at his usual residence in Cape Town, but on the eastern frontiers of the Colony, and therefore conveniently near.* British troops were also at hand. The document set forth that all the country between the Umzimvubu and Umzimkulu—all the southern part of the Republic, in fact—belonged to Faku, that the Pondos dreaded being attacked by the Emigrant Farmers, and asked for British protection. It was put before the Chief, whose mark was duly affixed. Two minor Pondo captains also made crosses on the paper. The Revs. Thomas Jenkins, Samuel Palmer, and William Garner signed *as witnesses*. Having sent off this letter on the 5th of January, Faku's advisers travelled south-

<small>Expedition against Ncapayi.</small>

<small>The Missionaries and Faku.</small>

<small>Missionary Jenkins and his Mission.</small>

westward with the Chief and all his followers. Having again crossed the Umzimvubu, they proceeded to the old Pondo kraal on the Umgazi.

To this point British troops were already on the march from the south. The plot was succeeding admirably for the Empire-extenders.

In the Volksraad at Pietermaritzburg there was more enterprise than statesmanship, and more talk than wisdom. In September, 1840, it had been resolved to enter into correspondence with the British Government, in order to obtain an acknowledgment of the independence of the Republic. Under date Pietermaritzburg, 4th September, 1840, the Secretary to the Volksraad, J. J. Burger, wrote to Sir George Napier, proposing to send Commissioners to Cape Town, with the view of arranging the future relationship of the new State towards the Colony and the British Empire. The Governor was requested to represent to the Queen's Ministry that the Emigrants desired a recognition of their complete independence and autonomy. But the letter was ambiguously worded, and actually became a formidable weapon in the hands of the Governor and those who sought the downfall of the Republic.

Correspondence.

The words "*erkenning van onze onafhankelijkheid met de rechten van Britsche onderdanen*" ("acknowledgment of our independence, with the same rights as British subjects," or "with the rights of British subjects"), were afterwards referred to, by the apologists for England's action, as a justification for Sir George Napier's military movements and Empire-extension arrangements.

IN SOUTH AFRICA 183

The meaning really intended to be conveyed by the writer of the sentence quoted was that the Emigrants desired complete independence from England, under the continued Government of the Republic, with an arrangement by which reciprocal commercial and customs relations should exist between their State and the British Colony, so as to secure to subjects of the Republic the same trade privileges as British subjects enjoyed. A subsequent despatch explained all this in detail. Sir George Napier sent his reply to the first letter in November, but in June he had already received discretionary authority from England to take military possession of the Bay of Natal. *Instructions from England.*

On the 14th of January, 1841, the Volksraad, in answer to a request of the Governor, formulated the terms and conditions of the agreement which was desired with England:—

The independence of the Republic of Natal was to be acknowledged by Britain. In case of war between England and other countries, the Republic was to be neutral, and no aid of any kind was to be given by the Emigrants to the enemies of the Queen's Government. Further, in case of any native war in South Africa, outside the borders of Natal, free passage was to be allowed to British troops, and permission to traverse the territory of the Republic. Reciprocal customs duties were to be established in Natal at the same rates as in the British Colony, but wines and spirits to be taxed differently and at higher rates. No war was to be undertaken against the Kaffir nations southward of Natal without notice having previously been given to *Conditions of Treaty proposed by Volksraad.*

the Government of the Cape Colony, and any such war to be entered into by the Emigrants only in self-defence. Civilisation and Christianising of the natives to be encouraged, and no slavery to be allowed by the Republic.

Such were the terms of the alliance proposed by the Volksraad, the members of which now began to suspect that they had made a great mistake in asking at all for England's recognition of their independence. For something of what was going on in Pondoland and at Cape Town, though by no means everything, soon became known. Sir George Napier had already received the Jenkins-Faku letter of 5th January, and the troops were moving. No reply was sent to the Volksraad's despatch of 14th January, until June. But meanwhile, on 28th January, 1841, Captains Smith and Warden, with two companies of the 27th regiment of the line, fifty Cape Mounted Rifles, and a small detachment (consisting of two officers and twelve men) of the artillery and engineers, had started from Fort Peddie, on the eastern colonial frontier, with about fifty waggons. Their destination was the Pondo head kraal on the Umgazi, where Faku and the missionaries now were.

<small>Captain Smith's Force.</small>

The correspondence which had been commenced by the Volksraad, instead of averting absorption and annexation by England, in reality favoured and helped the plans of the plotters. Besides, there were other weapons against the Republic which the diplomatic British Governor did not neglect to make use of. In the expedition against Ncapayi, the burghers under Commandant Lombaard, after the robber-clan had been scattered and driven from their kraal on the Tsitsa, had found several Baca children wandering about on the veld, without food. Instead of allowing these little Kaffirs to starve and die of hunger in a fruitless attempt to reach the encampments of their tribe, the farmer commando had taken them back to Pietermaritzburg, given them food, and provided for them by apprenticing them to white settlers in Natal. This, according to the philanthropists, was slavery.

The same system of apprenticing is still in vogue in every British Colony in South Africa. After every native war, captive children are thus dealt with. It is a far better and more humane method than the alternative one of leaving the deserted and homeless native waifs to die of famine, or be killed by wild beasts, and, therefore, it is still countenanced and even practised by British officials. Where the "*Boer*" was concerned it was, of course, inexcusable; and so it was made a further pretext for his country being seized by the self-righteous Government of the Cape, which itself, only quite recently, resorted to apprenticeship on a far larger scale, and under much less justifiable circumstances, in the case of the vanquished and famishing Bechuanas. *Apprenticeship of Native Children.*

Another excuse was found, or supposed to be found, in a resolution of the Volksraad (in August, 1841), to form a large native Location in the south—between the rivers Umtamvuna and Umzimvubu—where the great numbers of refugees from beyond the Tugela, who had been flocking into Natal ever since the Emigrants had established their Republic, were in future to reside. The Cape Government argued that this collection of large *The Southern Location.*

186   HISTORY OF THE REPUBLIC

numbers of natives in the southern part of the Republic would create disturbances on the *adjacent* (! !) Colonial frontiers, where the tribes would become involved in war, and get restless and unruly.

Sir George Napier.

On the 10th of June, Sir George Napier had sent his answer to the Volksraad's letter of 14th January. The Government of the Queen could not acknowledge as being independent some of her own subjects who had left the Colony and settled in Natal. If the Emigrant Farmers were willing to receive a British military force into their country, then all commercial privileges enjoyed by British colonists would be guaranteed by England, but no further negotiations could be carried on unless the sovereignty of England was recognised. Such was the reply. Then, over the signature of Joachim Prinsloo, President of the Volksraad, and Jacobus J. Burger, Secretary, and under date 11th October, 1841, the following rejoinder was sent * from Pietermaritzburg.

Volksraad's Despatch.

"YOUR EXCELLENCY,—We are of opinion that both her Majesty and yourself are misinformed concerning us, our claim to independence, and the right which we have to the country now in course of occupation by us. We are by birth Dutch-Africanders (Hollandsche Afrikanen). Immediately after we had left Her Majesty's territory in South Africa, we published our declaration of independence, and from that time until this day we have acted as an independent nation, governed ourselves according to our own laws, and, consequently, ceased

---

* A portion only of the despatch is here quoted.

to be British subjects. We have obtained by lawful means the land now inhabited by us, and it has never at any time been a British Colony or province. Notwithstanding Your Excellency's repeated declarations that we are British subjects and colonists, we must affirm that, by the laws of all civilised nations, we are neither the one nor the other. Furthermore, we must courteously decline to accept Her Majesty's military forces. We are at peace with all nations, and require no protection."

A despatch from Downing Street, bearing date 21st August, now also reached the Governor, authorising and ordering him to occupy the harbour of Natal. On 2nd December, 1841, he issued a proclamation announcing the intention of the Queen's Government to refuse to acknowledge the independence of Natal, and claimed justification for proceeding to send British troops to occupy the country. The district between the Umzimvubu and Umtamvuna rivers was referred to in this proclamation as part of Faku's territory, and the resolution of the Volksraad declaring this district a native Location was termed an unjust and illegal proceeding from which there was reason to fear that warfare and bloodshed would follow. *Sir George Napier's Proclamation of 2nd December, 1841.*

To reinforce Captain Smith's troops in Pondoland, Captain Lonsdale marched towards the Umgazi river. He took with him a hundred and twenty-five infantry, Cape rifles, engineers, and artillery, with two guns. Sir George Napier, like Sir Bartle Frere at a later *Captain Lonsdale's Force.*

date, firmly believed in the helpfulness of artillery when arguing with Africander Republicans.

Henry Ogle, who was then living about thirty miles from Durban, made himself useful to Captain Smith, as a spy. The Uitlander residents of Durban promised their assistance, and despatched secret messages to the English officer, assuring him of their help, and offering him a hearty welcome. Captain Smith himself sent several messages by way of preparation. Letters and messages were all conveyed to and from Durban by Kaffir runners in the service of Ogle. Meanwhile, Captain Smith awaited the arrival of his reinforcements under Lonsdale to commence his march from the Umgazi camp to the Bay of Natal.

The Spies and Messages.

In the Volksraad there had been a good deal of discussion, and party feeling ran high. When it was too late, it was recognised that a great mistake had been made in entering into correspondence with Sir George Napier, and that the faction which favoured this course had, in reality, though unwittingly, played into the hands of the Cape Town plotters.

The Volksraad's Attitude.

J. N. Boshoff, who was then Landdrost of Pietermaritzburg, was requested by the Raad to draw up a despatch by way of protest against the Governor's proclamation of 2nd December. That able man had already rendered great services to the young Republic. His legal training, his knowledge of office work and of all formalities relating to the administration of justice, had enabled him to lay the foundation of the judicial department of the State, and to place the first courts of law established in the country on a good

J. N. Boshoff's Despatch.

footing. Now he had to voice the new nation's sense of wrong and injustice, to proclaim to the world the perishing Republic's accusation against England. His despatch was a masterpiece. It is a valuable historical document.

marginal note: The Perishing Republic's Accusation against England.

* "*To His Excellency,* Major-General Sir George Thomas Napier, K.C.B., *Governor and Commander-in-Chief, etc., etc., of the Colony of the Cape of Good Hope.*

"Pietermaritzburg, Natal,
21st *February*, 1842.

"Sir,—Assembled in our Council at this place, we, the undersigned, President and Members of the Volksraad, deem it right to inform Your Excellency of the receipt of your proclamation, dated 2nd December, 1841, in which it is announced that Your Excellency, in consequence of instructions received by you, has seen fit to resume military occupation of this country, and that we are considered British subjects, and cannot be acknowledged as a free and independent nation by Her Majesty the Queen of England, etc.

marginal note: Protest.

"Seeing that the friendly negotiations which we initiated with Your Excellency, and the representations made by us with the view of securing a lasting peace and alliance with the British Government, conditional only on our having an administration entirely our own —a privilege which has not been refused even to the Griquas resident on the frontiers of your Colony, although that nation, like ourselves, is entirely composed of emigrants from the Colony — that these

---

* Translated from Stuart's "Hollandsche Afrikanen," now out of print.

representations are now being made use of as a cause to overwhelm us with the most dire results, we, in order to become thoroughly acquainted with the opinion of our fellow-emigrants, have had the above-mentioned proclamation circulated among them, and have invited them freely to discuss this matter at public meetings, and to acquaint us with the result of their discussions.

"We can now inform Your Excellency that the general opinion of our fellow-emigrants is, and that they have requested us to declare, as we hereby do declare, that we regard your above-named proclamation as unjust in the extreme towards us, and as calculated, if brought into operation, to bring about what it states is its main object to avoid, viz., war and bloodshed.

"As this may possibly be the last communication which we shall have the opportunity of addressing to Your Excellency, we deem it necessary to treat of the subject more in detail.

"Especially, we wish to be well understood that it is not our object to insult, or make reproach, or in any way to give occasion for hostile acts, as it is our heartfelt wish and desire to preserve the peace with all people. Nothing shall induce us to take up arms and shed the blood of fellow-men,—nothing but the firm conviction that we cannot avoid doing so, when the protection of our property—possession of which has, in our opinion, been secured to our people by their fortitude and endurance—and of our national existence, demands such action on our part, or when we see that might and not right are the weapons of our adversary.

"We know that a God exists, who rules Heaven and Earth, that He is powerful and willing to protect the wronged, even although they are weak, against oppressors. In Him and in the justice of our cause we trust; and if it be His will that total destruction fall on us, on our wives and children, and all that we have or possess, we shall submit, and acknowledge to have deserved it of Him, but not of men.

"We know the power of Great Britain, and it is by no means our object to challenge that power; but, at the same time, we cannot in the least allow that violence instead of justice should triumph over us, without having tried all in our power to combat such violence. We do not accuse the British Government of being disposed as above indicated; but experience has taught us that false and unfounded representations (such as are, evidently, now once more in circulation with regard to ourselves), originating in a far-distant country, have but too frequently given rise to measures and enactments which have been both oppressive and unjust.

"We likewise deny most emphatically that we are actuated by an inveterate hatred of the English people. Every one is, naturally, more partial to his own than to other nations; but, as Christians, we have learned to cherish regard and affection for all men; and although we—South African peasants—have often been treated by the English with haughty disdain, yet, let many English people (among whom we also include the Scotch, with whom we were personally acquainted in the country of our birth, and some of whom were our ministers of religion, always held in high esteem by all of us), bear witness; let the officers and men, side by side with whom we have stood under arms, bear witness; let our former regents, judges, and local authorities, bear witness; and let even all respectable Englishmen, of those who at this present moment dwell and reside here amongst us in safety and security, bear witness whether it is a fact that such hatred is nurtured in our bosoms against the English people. But we shall not deny that the resolutions arrived at from time to time, with regard to ourselves, by the English Government in the Colony, as well as the proclaimed laws relating to us, have been the sole cause of our having left our native land and our kinsmen, and casting ourselves, as it were, on the waves of the wilderness, in order to be free from the rule of that Government. To refer to some examples of our grievances: Who was it that forced on us the growing evils and evil consequences of slavery? Who assured us of the right of ownership? Was it not the same Government which afterwards again deprived us of that right in such a manner that we ourselves had not the least voice in deciding as to the best or most suitable means to bring about the alteration? Who assured us of full compensation for our slaves? Was it not the same Government which palmed off on us a third of the true value of our property, and even then left us as a prey to greedy and grasping traders, who have been enriched at our expense? Who employed us, without reward, and at our own cost, for the protection of the frontiers of the Colony against the hostile, warlike, and plundering Kaffirs? Was it not the same Government which afterwards denied us all claim to compensation, falsely pretending that we ourselves, by robbing the Kaffirs, had brought down their just vengeance on our heads? Who took from us the best Governor we had ever had, simply because, as a man of conscience, he defended the wronged Cape Colonists, and, by punishing their marauding foe, sought their true safety and protection? Who then sent us political speculators—tied, hand and foot—whose dispositions as to our frontier line exposed us to be robbed and threatened by the Kaffirs unceasingly and with impunity, while the enormous expenses incurred by the country would ultimately be put to the cost of the ruined farmer? Was it not the same Government which left all the land free to wandering vagabonds, who followed an idle and savage course of life, and actually existed on the flocks and other property of the grievously oppressed peasant, so that the farmer—deprived of labourers, or, even if he had them, without all needful authority — lost heart, and, finding his repeated remonstrances and petitions unanswered or ignored, saw before him a dismally dark prospect?

"All these evils we ascribe to this one cause, namely, the want of a representative Government, refused to us by the executive authority of that same nation which regards this very privilege as one of its most sacred rights of citizenship, and for which every true Briton is prepared to give his life. And what did we do,

suffering from all these acts of oppression? Did
we, as the Canadians acted recently, take up arms,
demanding that justice be done to us? No; we gave
the coat also to him who had taken from us the cloak.
After having disposed of our landed property at a
ridiculously low value, we openly announced to the
Government that we would leave its dominions—our
country. We were allowed to leave; at least, we were
not prevented. We were even surprised to receive
information of a most fair and just declaration on the
part of the Lieutenant-Governor,—that it was an indisputable right that any one, dissatisfied with the rule of
his Government, was at liberty to leave its territory.
Immediately after our exodus we declared our independence; we established our own Government; we
waged war against those who had treacherously attacked
us; we concluded peace; we took possession of uninhabited regions — those which we had acquired
by friendly negotiations with savage tribes, as well
as those which we had bought with our blood.

"Meanwhile, what action did the Colonial Government take during the course of all these events? Did
it cause us to be informed that we could not rid
ourselves of our obligations as subjects, wherever we
might be? Or did it offer us any help when we were
in distress, and saw before us the prospect of at any
moment being destroyed by savage, bloodthirsty
heathens—when already over six hundred of our
people had been most treacherously massacred, without
having been guilty of any provocation? Or did it,
as long as they were threatened with total annihilation

and destruction, regard with indifference the great misery of its pretended subjects? But, what is more, were not their murderers assisted and helped as soon as the emigrants appeared to have some chance of gaining the victory? Was this not done by prohibiting our importation of weapons and ammunition? Yes, even by threatening us with a military garrison; by confiscating our own arms and munition of war; and this, at the same time, under pretence of philanthropically wishing to avoid further bloodshed, when there was no question of shedding Christian blood, but when vengeance was to be dealt out to those whose hands were still stained with it! Further, by restricting trade, so that many of the emigrants, during a visitation of infectious disease, died from want of the necessary remedies or of food which was necessary and indispensable at such a time! Has not the same Government invariably treated us as aliens, even in relation to our trade over sea? How, then, is it possible, that, with all such justification on our side, Your Excellency can expect that we should regard ourselves as transgressors or rebels against our lawful Government? We declare that we cannot see how the British Government can, under the above-mentioned circumstances, with any shadow of justice or fairness, claim us as subjects; unless it is that this only happens from other political motives, or that on account of jealousy, reasons are being sought for to bring under the yoke once more the despised emigrant, abandoned to misfortune. We doubt much whether, if we had moved towards the interior of Africa, or to

Delagoa, we should have been molested there also. But we still cherish the hope that, when the present Government of Her Majesty the Queen of England, and the British nation, have become fully and accurately informed of all the circumstances of the case, other means than by the sword and by bloodshed will be found to give satisfaction to both sides. We, therefore, pray your Excellency to further consider the matter, and not to resort to any measures by which we should be compelled to take — however much against our inclination, and however painful they may be to us — such steps as would become unavoidable for our life and security, and as would bring on Your Excellency a responsibility which, sooner or later, might become burdensome.

"As regards the pretext for this military occupation mentioned in your proclamation—namely, our resolution concerning the Kaffirs, which was passed here on 2nd August, 1841—we only wish to say that, as is generally the case, Your Excellency's informants either themselves did not know the true state of affairs, or intentionally concealed it from you. We are in a position to be able to convince any real philanthropist that our policy in respect to the Kaffirs—both old inhabitants and more recent arrivals—when we made our arrangements for removing and locating them (by the resolutions already referred to, as well as by another resolution which, since then, we have passed in relation to the same subject), is founded on true humanity, inasmuch as we have by these measures attempted to prevent and to avoid the probability of hostilities and bloodshed, which otherwise would have been the inevitable consequence, had we allowed Zulus and other natives to continue to leave their old homes in thousands and to settle amongst us—as is now the case; for, first made secure by us against their enemies, and, thereafter, having become strong and powerful, they could have had the finest opportunity in the world to exterminate us, only in order to become possessed of our cattle; or, their plans being discovered, they would have placed us under the necessity of at once attacking and repelling them by force of arms.

"We have therefore taken measures to guard against the possibility of such an event, in time, as far as we are able, so as not to let the evil grow and increase, or become quite irremediable, and then to bestir ourselves. A statement now of all we have to say on this point would become much too lengthy. We shall thus pass on to indicate that, even if Faku had any claim to that part of the country mentioned in Your Excellency's proclamation, he alone would be to blame had we made use of the land. In the first place, we have proofs that he himself, already in the year 1834, had declared that he had no claim whatever to that country, and that, as far as we have been able to find out, his people never inhabitated it, if we except a few small scouting and spy kraals. We have also had published the agreement entered into with Dingaan by the late Mr. Retief, as well as our proclamation fixing our frontiers as far south as the Umzimvubu. Besides, Faku himself came to a friendly agreement with us, and we obtained from him, and gave him in return, assurances of friendliness, and even of protection, so that nothing stood in the way to prevent him from protesting, had we disposed of any of his territory for ourselves; but, in addition, he himself voluntarily acknowledged to our delegate that the country, as far as the Umzimvubu, had lawfully belonged to Chaka and afterwards to Dingaan, and that he admitted our claim to it as founded on justice and right, both by reason of the contract or agreement above named, and because of our victory over the nation (the Zulus).

"He went further, and said that Chaka and Dingaan had conquered even the country beyond the Umzimvubu, and that he regarded himself and his people as being there by our permission. May we not then ask where, among the colonies and territories at present in the possession of Great Britain or of any other Power, is there one to which ownership can be claimed with more right? We are convinced that there is none; but if Faku can prove that neither Chaka nor Dingaan ever had any claim to the land in question, and that this desert and uninhabited tract of country has always been in his own possession, who can convince us of our having, notwithstanding this, insisted on the occupation of the land for ourselves, and that thus, on the ground of such action on our part, any shadow of reason for the threatened military occupation of our harbours and our territory can be advanced?

"We are free to admit, further, that we cannot by any possibility of means, as far as the matter relates to us, understand the law of subjects by birth and otherwise, as brought forward by Your Excellency in your proclamation. But, putting aside this question, we are bound to state our conviction that we should not be able to be secure, or even to exist, in this country, were we once more to place ourselves under the jurisdiction of Colonial rule, as formerly. The land, over which Your Excellency already disposes in anticipation, threatening to deprive us and our children of it, would then also be of no value to us. What prospects have we of obtaining better protection than that which is now enjoyed by the inhabitants of the frontiers of the Colony, and by reason of which many of our number have been under the necessity of leaving that country? What prospects have we of even enjoying that amount of protection?

"Your Excellency's actions give us more than reason to suspect that your concern and care exist only for uncivilised nations, and that, were we, our wives and children, and our servants, to be slaughtered by them like sheep, no great concern would be caused to any one; that even then the present-day philanthropists would discover false accusations enough to inform the world that we had richly deserved our lot, and that we were ourselves to blame for what had happened.

"Fate, then, seems to drive us to the choice of one of two alternatives: either to bow our necks to the yoke, willingly—like patient beasts of burden—to bear the load which is laid upon us, until, as before, finding its weight too heavy, we begin a new emigration, when we shall have to leave here all that we have in the world;— or, in defence of our just rights, of our possessions, yea, even of our existence, to grasp our rifles, do battle against our oppressors, and, perishing in the struggle, with our fall to make an end of our earthly difficulties. We leave to Your Excellency's own judgment, and to that of every right-minded Englishman, which of these two is the most desirable. Let it no longer be supposed that we seek to mislead, or that we ourselves are being misled. Experience has given, more or less, all of us dearly bought lessons, and, whatever may be our political differences concerning our civil administration, Your Excellency will find that there is very little divergence of opinion amongst us regarding this one point. When, at the cost of much blood and money, we have been subdued, the fire will then only be damped and pent up, to break out with all the greater fury in the day of vengeance. It is in Your Excellency's power to prevent these evils, and, if Your Excellency is really of a mind to avoid further bloodshed, then Your Excellency will easily find reasons enough to stay your projected military expedition, and to go to work by other means, which will have a more humane and a more happy issue.

"It has caused among us an intense feeling of regret to learn how, ever since the commencement of our emigration, we have been represented to the world as rough people, who, tired of civilised laws and church discipline, sought to live in licentiousness, every one after his own inclination. We have more than once put to shame our accusers. Although we are inexperienced peasants, who in their native land were never allowed to take any part in the public affairs of their own country, we have, nevertheless, succeeded in placing our form of government on such a footing that, from day to day, we are beginning more and more to gain public confidence. Religion itself and religious observances find due recognition among us. Cultivation of the soil and agricultural progress are daily on the increase. We have already built quite a respectable edifice for the purpose of public religious worship, and the education of our youth has been placed on a good footing.

"The martial Zulus surrounding us have been checked in their incessant warlike enterprises, so that they even, from fear of us, have recourse to arms only stealthily and infrequently. Two missionaries are already at work among them, under our protection; and we have the best prospects that the civilisation of that people will be capable of being promoted more speedily than that of the Kaffirs bordering on the Colony. All this has already been accomplished, now that we are only just beginning to emerge from our great difficulties.

"Your Excellency can, therefore, well understand how it would grieve us to see destroyed the foundation of all our hopes and expectations. Serviceable agents are already at work to rouse the Kaffir tribes against us, to their or to our misfortune; to impress on the natives that we are their oppressors, the English their protectors; and that, should they side with the English, our cattle will become their booty. Possibly Your Excellency has not given permission for this action. Still, what we state is taking place. Will it be possible for the civilised world ever to blame us when we, under such circumstances and under such inhuman persecutions, do and dare our utmost to preserve our lives? And if we have to yield to superior numbers and seek security further inland, where we are more concentrated and can do battle with our adversary to more advantage, can we then be reviled if we make good the losses sustained by us in the Colony and since our emigration from there—if we, in return for our lands, houses, and other property, which we have been compelled to leave a prey to destruction, seek compensation from our old debtors the Kaffirs, and even further? We pray that the Almighty may prevent this, and that it may please Him to vouchsafe us a happier lot.

"Finally, we must, both in our own name and at the special request of our fellow-emigrants, emphatically protest against the occupation and seizure of any portion of this country—as threatened in Your Excellency's proclamation of 2nd December above mentioned. We must declare that, in our opinion, we, from this instant, are not responsible for the evil consequences of such a step; and that we are free from blame before God, before our own conscience, and before the world.

"We have the honour, with all possible respect, to name ourselves—Sir, Your Excellency's obedient servants, JOACHIM PRINSLOO, *President;*
Besides all the Members of
the Raad,
J. J. BURGER, *Secretary.*"

Although General Pretorius and the Volksraad, confident of the justice of their cause, were determined not to submit without a struggle, the country was ill-prepared for war with a powerful European nation. The Emigrants had not yet had time to recover from the effects of the long continued hostilities against the Zulus. They had not completely rallied from the stunning disasters in the early part of the great contest against the armies of Dingaan. There was hardly a family among them which had not lost some relative, and a great many of those who had escaped massacre had been reduced to poverty. Provisions were not plentiful; for the country was only just recovering from the famine and distress which had followed the Zulu massacres, and during the war agriculture had, unavoidably, been neglected. *Unpreparedness for War.*

The State's treasury was empty. There was scarcity, not only of ammunition (the supply of which was now again completely cut off by England), but also of horses; for the horse-sickness had broken out, at the time of the last commando against Dingaan and subsequently. All this was well known in Cape Town as well as in Major Smith's camp on the Umgazi, and the column which was now massed on the southern frontier for the invasion of Natal made its preparations accordingly. When the Rev. Mr. Jenkins and the other missionaries of the Gospel of Peace instigated Faku—a Chief who, as they were well aware, had previously acknowledged himself to be a vassal of the Republic—to place himself under British protection, and at the same time to claim territory much further to the north than where he and his nation had ever had any dominion or authority, they, the honest Christian delegates, executed a master stroke in diplomacy, a *coup* which proved that Sir George Napier had made no mistake when he chose his messenger. The ministry in England had to be considered. They had previously refused their sanction to the annexation of Natal. They had now to be convinced that the military occupation of the country was absolutely necessary in the interests of the natives. Those interests were, in Downing Street, believed to be synonymous with those of the Chiefs, and the Africander Emigrants were supposed to be the tyrants and oppressors of the original inhabitants. As has already been pointed out on pp. 168—171, the advent of the Republic in the north and the downfall of the dominion of the Chiefs, in reality meant new life and salvation to the survivors of massacred thousands upon thousands—to the remnants of the numerous nations which were threatened with total extermination by Dingaan's and Umsiligaas' armies. The true friends and protectors of the natives were, not the British Government and the Aborigines Protection Society, who championed the cause of the Chiefs, but the Emigrants, who broke the power and subdued the armies of those Chiefs.

The true Friends and Protectors of the Aborigines.

Reference has been made to the arrival in Port Natal of an American trading ship. To the greedy Cape Town shop-keepers it was a terrible calamity that there should be any other harbour than their own in South Africa. And now, in the early part of 1842, there came to Table Bay the news of the departure from Holland (bound for Natal) of a small sailing ship called the *Brazilië*, which had been sent out from Amsterdam by Messrs. Ohrig and Klijn with a cargo of cloth fabrics and general merchandise, as well as some Bibles and hymn-books and some copies of a pamphlet, entitled, "The Emigrants at Port Natal," in which publication much sympathy was expressed for the cause of the Republic in Africa, and at the same time, the commercial interests of the house of Ohrig, Klijn & Co., and of other Dutch houses, were not forgotten. This was altogether too terrible a manifestation of foreign interference in the affairs of South Africa, and quite as great a shock to the irritable nerves of the Table Mountain Imperialists of those days as was the German Kaiser's cablegram the other morning to their descendants and the gallant Rhodesians. The British force, which had been massed on the Umgazi, was, therefore, ordered to invade Natal and seize the harbour. Captain Smith began *his* Jameson Raid on 1st April, 1842.

Meanwhile, on 24th March, the *Brazilië* had reached Durban. The Captain, Reus, and the supercargo, Smellenkamp, proceeded to Pietermaritzburg, where they were received with a perfect ovation of welcome. They were escorted into the town. An address was presented to them. They were feasted and fêted for a week. In compliment to them, the flag of Holland was displayed everywhere. The Emigrants did not look upon them as merely the representatives of a private trading firm, but also as the harbingers of that bond of union between the infant Republic and the outer world, the lasting bond of commerce and maritime trade, for which Pieter Retief had fought and died.

Now for the first time receiving full and authentic accounts of the sympathy and enthusiasm which existed in Holland for the cause of the Republic in South Africa, the Emigrants also welcomed Smellenkamp and Reus as citizens of that country which, in the days of the Batavian Commonwealth, had still been regarded as the Fatherland by many Africanders. The greater part of a generation had passed away since those days. The tie of allegiance, as well as most of the bonds of attachment which formerly bound Africa to Holland, had long since been severed. In the stress of adversity and of battle, in the long-continued and arduous struggle against barbarism and against British diplomacy, the different European elements of the new nationality in Natal had been consolidated into a homogeneous mass of pioneerdom and of frontier life—a community in which almost every vestige of the original Netherland stock had been completely obscured, and even obliterated, by African associations and the influences of the now distinctive Africander type. The new nationality was already clearly and sharply defined, and as distinct from the old as the South African landscape from that of the Low Countries. The rugged mountain ravine, the rocky boulders, the long dry grass, the waterless plain with the bounding *springbok* and *wildebeest*, the thorny acacias, the wild geraniums and heaths, the scarlet flowers on the Kaffir-thorn trees, with the sunlight and the lizards, and the dust, and the flies—these form a picture very different from the dunes and the windmills, the broad canals and green meadows, the *trekschuit* and the tulip beds, the beech trees and the mists, of Holland. As widely distinct and different as are these two pictures, were the national characteristics of the Africander and the Hollander, even in the days of the Natal Republic. And yet, among the older Emigrants of those days, there were many who kept a warm corner in their hearts for the country and the people of their former Governor, General Janssens. To them Holland still stood for liberty, for free institutions, for enlightened administration. The officials and the authorities representing the great name of England in South Africa, had, ever since the battle of Blauwberg Beach, taken pains to prove to all—young as well as old —that Great Britain was the foreign oppressor, the despotic and autocratic ruler, the enemy of popular government and of the Africander nationality. They had succeeded; and now, even with the British troops threatening invasion on their very frontier, the honest burghers of Pietermaritzburg took delight in showing how they hated these officials and the grasping Power at their back, by welcoming and doing honour to the Hollanders, Smellenkamp and Reus. This suited the plans of the plotters in Cape Town and London. It was "magnificent," but it was not diplomacy. It was like the little rabbit defying the fangs and coils of the huge boa constrictor.* [Magnificent, but not Diplomatic.]

Smellenkamp himself was an enthusiast for the

* Although the British troops were at the southern frontier, full details of the plot were not then known at Maritzburg, where an attack from the seaward side, rather than an invasion overland, was expected (*see* pp. 210—212).

cause of the Emigrants, and the Volksraad was foolish enough to imagine that it was possible to obtain help from Holland. The terms of a treaty of amity and commerce were drawn up, agreed to, and signed by the supercargo as "accepted in the name of H.M., the King of the Netherlands, by J. A. SMELLENKAMP." Then this wise Daniel, stepping boldly into the lion's den, travelled overland from Maritzburg to Graaff Reinet, whence he was proceeding to Cape Town, with the object of taking ship to Europe, in order to act as the delegate of the Republic to Holland, when, at Swellendam, he was arrested—*for travelling without a pass!*

Smellenkamp's Treaty of Commerce.

His Arrest.

CHAPTER XXV

A BLOW FOR FREEDOM

THE SMITER SMITTEN

Captain Smith's March—British Diplomacy—The Volksraad—Taken by Surprise—Preparing for Defence—Captain Smith Encamped near the Berea—Pretorius forms his Laager near Congella—Burghers rally in Defence of the Republic—Pieter Joubert, Sen.—Strength of Captain Smith's Force—The Burgher Force—Reconnoitring—Captain Smith receives Stores and Ammunition by Sea—English Cattle and Horses Captured—A Night Attack—Disposition of Burgher Patrols—The Night March—The Aged Sentinels—The Fish in Uniform—Queen's Birthday—Salute of the Elephant-guns—Night Encounter near Congella—Rout of the British Force.

AFTER leaving Faku's kraal on the Umgazi, Captain Smith crossed the Umzimvubu by the main ford, high up the stream. It had rained heavily in the mountains, and the volume of water in the river was considerable. The current, also, was strong, and thus great difficulties were encountered in crossing; but many of the waggon-drivers with the column were experienced South African frontiersmen, traders and hunters, who knew the country. From the Umzimvubu drift the expedition travelled to Faku's deserted kraal on the Umzimhlava, and then along the coast region, crossing the difficult fords of the Umzimkulu and other coast rivers, all of which were in flood—owing to the heavy rains which had fallen in the inland districts and in the Drakensbergen.

<small>Captain Smith's March.</small>   On 3rd May, the northernmost of these streams, the Umlaas, was crossed. Here, as well as at the Illovo, Umkomanzi, and all the other rivers further to the south, the fords were found to be undefended by the Emigrants. The details of the plot and the plan of the attack had been so skilfully concealed and kept from the knowledge of the Farmer Government at Maritzburg, that not even a suspicion of an intended march overland, instead of an onslaught from the sea side, was entertained by the Volksraad and the authorities. It was not even known that British troops had been massed on the frontier for months past, in readiness for the invasion. Sir George Napier took good care to keep this a secret, after his interview with Jenkins.

<small>British Diplomacy.</small>   When the British Government is preparing for a raid in South Africa, it knows how to manage such matters. The intended seizure and annexation of the Diamond Fields in 1871 was not previously advertised to the world. Sir Theophilus Shepstone, when starting on his *friendly mission* to Pretoria in 1876, did not announce from the housetops that he had in his pocket Lord Carnarvon's fiat for the incorporation of the valuable territories of the Republic with the British Empire. Sir Henry Loch did not publish his interview with Mr. Lionel Phillips in 1894, and took care that, when he thought of collecting a British force at Mafeking, intelligence of such a concentration of troops should not leak out. Even those heroes of the music-hall stage, the Administrator of Matabeleland and the Thinker in Continents, the Napoleonic Privy

Councillor—the Colossal Unpunished One—managed to conceal from the world, for a period of several months, their preparations for enlarging the British Empire by acting the Elizabethan Englishman, playing the land-pirate, and bringing about the much-desired and much-talked-of union of South Africa, by attempting to shoot down the despised and maligned "*Boer*" in time of peace.

If in this age of newspapers, and special correspondents, and railways, and telegraphs, such scheming secret preparations are possible, how much easier were they in 1842? There were no newspapers, no telegraphs, no railways, not even a regular postal service, in Natal. The missionaries and traders were in the plot. No other white men came anywhere near Faku's kraals. All the southern frontier district—indeed all the southern half of the Republic—was practically uninhabited.

Full intelligence as to what was passing in Pondoland did not reach Maritzburg. That many of the natives in Natal were getting restless, as natives generally are when their shrewdness leads them to foresee a conflict between the white races in South Africa, was known to the Volksraad, as also that some of the Kaffirs were being instigated to take sides against the Republic. This is plainly stated in Boshoff's Despatch of 21st February. But it was believed that the instigators were acting without the consent and without the knowledge of the British Government. There were rumours of the missionary intrigues with Faku, and it was known that the chief had left his new kraal and gone southward; but all the country

_{The Volksraad.}

beyond the Umzimvubu and between that river and the Kei was a *terra incognita* to the Emigrants, who, moreover, had to keep all their available forces near to Port Natal, in order to be prepared for an attack from the sea side. The previous British occupation had been effected from this quarter, and the march overland presented so many difficulties and obstacles, that an invasion from the south was not thought likely, and no precautions whatever were taken to guard against it. Besides, the honest burgher Volksraad had itself such a respect for the rights of nations, and had such confidence in the justice of its cause, that many of its members in all sincerity deemed the British Government incapable of such an act of barefaced buccaneering as the seizure and invasion of the Republic's territory without a previous declaration of war. They had the Cape Governor's proclamation —in which it was expressly stated that they would still be regarded as British subjects—before them, and yet many of them refused to believe that that proclamation was more than a threat.

Taken by Surprise.

When, therefore, Captain Smith's column appeared north of the Umlaas and advanced towards Durban, the Emigrants were taken completely by surprise. Had the southern frontier and the Umzimvubu drifts been guarded by burgher patrols when first the threat of a British occupation was heard of, the march would not have been so easily accomplished. The English force had advanced in a long, straggling line of waggons. Had they been attacked on the march, only the waggon-drivers and the Cape Rifles would have been of much use for defensive purposes; for they alone could shoot. The regular troops would probably have been of no more avail than they were at a later date at Bronkhorst Spruit. Even a check in the northward advance would have meant the destruction or surrender of the invaders; for their retreat could have been effectually cut off by the defending forces. On the other hand, had the burghers been defeated at any point in the south, they could easily have retired northward and resumed the struggle at another place. Each succeeding river, every range of hills, would have offered an almost impregnable line of defence for their mode of warfare. Then, in case of continued defeat, they could still have taken their stand near the sea at Durban, where the struggle was now imminent.

The enemy—having been allowed to cross all the southern, and even all the central, natural strategic positions of Natal without a blow having been struck in defence of the soil—was on the point of establishing communication with the Indian Ocean, and was already actively engaged in negotiations with the Uitlanders at the Bay, when Pretorius despatched express riders over the Drakensberg, by way of Van Reenen's Pass, to proceed to Winburg district and summon the burghers from there and from Mooi River (Potchefstroom) to the assistance of their countrymen in the conflict that was impending. At the same time, a commando was called out from Pietermaritzburg and Weenen districts. Preparing for Defence. Instructions for these measures of defence were issued by the Volksraad of Natal; but that assembly was more than a month too late in taking action.

Captain Smith Encamped near the Berea.

On the 3rd of May, when Captain Smith's column was on the march some distance to the north of the main ford of the Umlaas river, two burghers rode up from Pietermaritzburg with a letter of protest from the Volksraad against the violation of the territory of the Republic by the British troops. The English officer refused to receive this letter, and continued his march northward. On 4th May, he reached the base of the Berea Hill, near Durban, and formed his camp. On that, as well as on the following day, the Volksraad again sent their written protest to the British Commander, who ignored it. Then the Volksraad messenger announced that the Government at Pietermaritzburg considered the Republic to be under the protection of Holland. Andries Pretorius, however, and the citizen-soldiers, who were now coming to join his standard at Congella, where he was forming his laager, were

Pretorius forms his Laager at Congella.

not so foolish as to expect any help from without. They did not allow themselves to be deluded into the belief that any reliance could be placed for defensive purposes on the agreement which the Volksraad had entered into with Smellenkamp. To shield their country from oppression and from wrong, they trusted to their rifles alone—to the firm determination of the handful of Republicans in Natal to resist annexation to the British Empire. From all those farms which were not at a very great distance from the

Burghers rally in Defence of the Republic.

laager, recruits were already arriving. Most of them had horses, but some came on foot. There were boys from the age of twelve and upwards among the first arrivals, and there were old men who, by the law of the State, were exempt from military service, but who, nevertheless, desired to assist in the defence of the beloved Republic. Among these aged volunteers was the grey-haired Pieter Joubert. When a young man, he had fought for the Republic of Graaff Reinet against the British. Afterwards, he had taken part in the Kaffir wars in Cape Colony. At the time of the Great Emigration he had been one of the Voortrekker leaders. Then, when an old man, he had served in the campaigns against Dingaan's armies. Many of his relatives had fallen in battle. He himself was reduced to poverty through the losses which he had sustained during the trying times through which his adopted country had passed, but was held in great esteem by all who knew him. On presenting himself at the Congella laager, this veteran, bent and stooping though he was with the weight of more than seventy years of a frontiersman's life, but still resolutely grasping his heavy *roer*, requested that he might be allowed to serve with the foreposts of the commando. Pretorius felt constrained to refuse this request, although he at the same time attempted to mollify and moderate the effect of his refusal by asking the old man's advice on various points connected with the plan of campaign and with the disposition of the burgher force already in the field.

Pieter Joubert, Senior.

When, however, soon after that, the Commandant was riding out to one of the advanced patrols, he met the aged volunteer going forward in the same direction —on foot, with rifle resting on the bent and feeble shoulder, muttering and mumbling, evidently very much disconcerted.

"Well, uncle! this is not the way to our laager. Whither art bound now?"

"Ah, Commandant, leave me alone. I have come here to fight. Your laager officer, Moolman, and I can't agree. He wants to make a cattle-herd of me. I am not used to that kind of work. I wish to help in the defence of my country."

Such was the old man's answer. As persuasion was of no avail, Pretorius had to order him to return at once to the laager.

The encampment of the British force was on the north-western side of the Bay, on a small hill below the Berea, and about half a mile distant from what was then the township of Durban. Earthworks had already been thrown up in the form of a triangular-shaped fort, and the position was defended by two field-pieces and a howitzer gun. Including the armed volunteer riflemen, who had acted as waggon-drivers while the column was on the march, but who, being experienced frontiersmen, formed, perhaps, about the most efficient part of the force, the full fighting strength of Captain Smith's command numbered 323 officers and men.

Strength of Captain Smith's Force.

The Africander laager was at Congella, nearly opposite the central part of the horseshoe-shaped bend formed by the beach of the inner harbour. The commando which had been called out by Volksraad order numbered 200 men only; but, according to English accounts, based on statements contained in an intercepted letter (Theal), the actual number of burghers

Strength of Burgher Force.

in laager, at the date when hostilities commenced, was 264. Roughly constructed earthworks served for mounting the two old field-pieces which had already seen service in the Zulu War. A path led from the direction of the British camp towards the head of the Bay.

On the 9th of May, Captain Smith attempted to surprise and disperse the Emigrant force which was then collecting. He advanced along the path with a force of about a hundred men; but, when less than half the distance between his camp and the laager had been traversed, the column came upon some mounted videttes, and Pretorius' Adjutant, riding forward, handed the commanding officer a note informing him that the Africander leader was awaiting instructions from the Volksraad, and would make no forward movement unless he was attacked by the English. Captain Smith was further informed that, should he persist in advancing, he would immediately find himself opposed by fighting forces from the laager. At the same time, numbers of mounted burghers appeared along the slopes of some sandhills on both sides of the road. A parley ensued, and the British officer, finding his further progress blocked by his vigilant opponents, at once fell back on his camp. *Reconnoitring.*

Pretorius now had to wait for further instructions from the Volksraad, which did not meet until the 17th, when it was resolved to demand the evacuation of Natal by the British troops. Captain Smith, refusing to comply with this demand, was meanwhile receiving further arms and ammunition, as well as stores of *Captain Smith receives Stores and Ammunition by Sea.*

provisions, by sea. These were brought by the vessels *Pilot* and *Mazeppa*, and were landed on the Point, where an eighteen-pounder gun was now mounted.

On the evening of 23rd May, some cattle and horses, which had been grazing at a distance from the Congella laager, were being brought in by one of the burgher patrols. On the same part of the veld, there were at the time some cattle and horses belonging to the English camp. These had strayed and become mixed up with those from the laager. A patrol of English soldiers coming on the scene, and probably imagining that their own cattle were being raided by the burghers, fired a few shots. The Africander patrol immediately fell back on one of their outposts, where the order to mount and advance was at once passed round. A rush was then made on an outlying English cattle kraal, and a large number of the cattle swept off towards the laager. This movement was so sudden, and apparently so unexpected in the British camp—although, from their patrol having fired on the Natal videttes, the English officers might well have inferred what would follow—that it was carried out without a single shot more being fired on either side. No guard had been placed over the cattle, the loss of which was, under the circumstances, a serious blow to Captain Smith, who at once determined to make a night attack on the laager. But Pretorius was on his guard once more. Instead of waiting for the assault at Congella, he had pushed forward a commando of one hundred and fifty men to take up a position considerably to the north, at a spot where the path, from the direction of the British camp, led through some thickets of mangrove bush and over some sandhills. This night-patrol had thrown out scouts and skirmishers to the right and left, in order to prevent any secret forward movement from the English side. There were not enough men, however, to extend the line of scouts eastward (*i.e.*, to the right) as far as the sea; and so Pretorius, foreseeing the possibility of Captain Smith attempting a flanking movement by working his way down along the beach and attacking the laager from the eastern side, had stationed another detachment of twenty or thirty of his men as a night-patrol on that side, close to some bush and mangrove trees. He himself had command of this patrol. Further east still, on the beach, was a small guard of old burghers—five or six in all—among whom were Jacobus Davel, sen., and the aged Pieter Joubert, who was still incorrigible in his determination to help to fight the English. The laager itself was occupied by little more than a dozen men. Far out on the plain to the rear and to the left (west) of the encampment, individual burghers were placed as scouts to watch any possible movements of Kaffir spies, who had been observed in the neighbourhood.

Disposition of Burgher Patrols.

Such was the disposition of Pretorius' fighting force on the night of 23rd May (*see* Sketch-Map, p. 223). It was a full hour before midnight when Captain Smith started from his camp with one hundred and thirty-seven men (infantry, artillery, and Cape Mounted Rifles;—the first-named arm being represented by more than one hundred men of the 27th Regiment of the line, and the Mounted Rifles by only two men and horses. There were eight or ten sappers, eighteen men of the artillery, and two field-pieces). The route taken was, first, to the north-east, towards the rear of the Camp; then eastward through sandhills and bush; and then, after this detour, southward to near the Point, where stood the buildings and stores belonging to the firms of Maynard of Cape Town, and Owen Smith of Port Elizabeth. From here a boat with a heavy eighteen-pounder gun was despatched to a point situated near the head of the bay or inner harbour, almost due east of Congella, and, therefore, very nearly at the exact spot where Pieter Joubert and his small guard of veteran burghers were already waiting and watching, as if by intuition.

The Night March.

After midnight, the troops resumed their march from near the Point, along the beach to the bend of the Bay, where their piece of heavy ordnance (the eighteen-pounder) was to meet them.

The expedition had not proceeded very far, when it was discovered that a search-light was flashing on them from the sky; for the African moon, whose tell-tale rays had apparently been left out of their calculations altogether by the British officers, was illuminating the landscape far and wide. The heavy gun, also, was not forthcoming, for the simple reason that the boat could not cross the dry land, as the tide was out.

High in the firmament blazed the bright constellations of the Southern Hemisphere. These, with the moonlight, increased the dangers of the advance towards the Africander laager. The very heavens, the stars in their course, and the waves of the ocean, fought for the Voortrekkers that night, and seemed to sympathise with the cause of the brave little Republic, which was being hounded to its death by the greedy shop-keepers and hungry land-sharks of Cape Town— backed up by the might and unscrupulous power of Great Britain. To the English column on the march, the shadows of the clumps of bush and jungle-like thickets along the line of advance loomed large and weird, ominous and threatening.

* * * * * * * *

While the troops were moving forward towards the spot where they should have taken over the heavy gun from the men in the boat—had the tide permitted—Pieter Joubert, Jacobus Davel, and their aged companions, who with them formed the small guard on the beach, stood listening and watching with as much vigilance and alertness as if they were all youths of twenty-five, instead of feeble and grey-headed old men of three score and ten. The cause for which they had fought and suffered nearly all their lives, and to which they had first sworn fealty in the previous century, was in danger. They would once more stand sentinel under the African stars and in the African moonlight. Soon their weary limbs would rest, and their bones repose in Africa's dear soil—the land of their fathers. Soon they would sleep their long sleep. Now, they would watch and stand guard for the cause. Once more they would help in trying to save the beloved Republic.

"Listen," said one; "do you hear how the fish are splashing in the water up there? They seem to have come quite close to the shore to-night."

The Aged Sentinels.

The aged sentinels were crouching low to the ground. They were listening intently. Now one inclined his head somewhat more to one side, and stooped so as to bring his ear nearer the ground. Then another shaded his eyes from the glare of the moonlight, and peered intently along the curved line of the beach bordering the inner harbour.

Half a minute, or thereabouts, elapsed.

It was Pieter Joubert who spoke first. "Yes," he said; "they are fine fish those; they wear the red coats of Queen Victoria's line regiments. And they are marching against us with cannon."

The Fish in Uniform.

Then there was a pause.

"*Wat seg jy? Is dit soo?*" spoke another.

"Let us go to Andries and tell him. He will be ready for them. We shall show them what a handful of men can do when they are defending their country!"

Quietly Pieter Joubert and his companions slipped away from the shore, and proceeded in a westerly direction, until they came to the shadow of the clump of mangrove thicket where Pretorius and the night-patrol of twenty or thirty rifles with him were stationed. The old men at once reported what they had observed on the beach, and then they took their stand in the small thin line, which now prepared to do battle for the cause for which

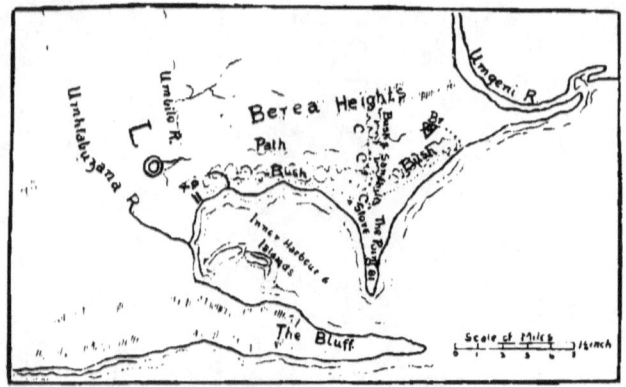

SKETCH MAP OF CONGELLA BATTLEFIELD.

the martyrs of Slachtersnek and Weenen had died.*

* * * * * * * *

When it was nearly one o'clock in the morning of 24th May, the British column had reached the point marked **X** on the accompanying sketch map. Before leaving their camp, the officers had been informed by their scouts that Pretorius had his night-patrols at C. C. C. They had not the least idea that there was another Africander patrol at *a*, right in front of them. They believed that they had completely out-flanked their opponents by the clever night march which they had just accomplished, and that the so-called "*Dutch*" laager, which they were now on the point of attacking from the rear or eastern side, was completely at their mercy.

<small>The Queen's Birthday.</small>

Brightly shines the Southern Cross overhead, and the African moonbeams glint on the gun-barrels, on the cannon, and on the cold steel which the Christian missionaries, in league with the merchants of Cape Town and of London, have sent forth to kill those true and brave sons of South Africa, whose only sin and sole crime was that they had refused to fall down and worship before the idol of Imperialism and dominion from across the seas.

Who are the presumptuous men who dare to resist the authority of England in South Africa? A handful of ignorant, of uneducated, farmers and peasants. The representatives of Britain's might

---

* This is the narrative (as told by those who fought at Congella) of the way in which Pretorius received intelligence of Captain Smith's approach to surprise the laager.

march forward with measured and steady tread. The Queen's bayonets will establish the Queen's rule in Natal, whether the inhabitants wish it or not.

But—not yet, for a few months. From the dark shadow-line of the edge of that bush on the right, there is a sudden bright flood of fire; there comes a roar as of thunder; then a second flash, and another thundering report. The heirlooms of last century— the elephant guns of Pieter Joubert and of one or two other old Voortrekkers—speak first; and their words are not gentle whispers. Then follows a volley —flashes, accompanied by more loud reports, succeeding each other so quickly, all along the extended line of the small detachment of the burgher force, as to make the sounds produced by the different shots appear like one continuous volume of noise. There are gaps in the ranks of the troops. The right flank and the front lines have suffered most. For a moment, there is confusion and wavering; but before the smoke, which hangs dense on the night air between the contending forces, has quite rolled away, some of the soldiers have been wheeled to the right and deployed into line, ready to return the fire of the Farmers.

As usual under such circumstances, the aim of the Regulars is far too high. Branches and leaves of trees are knocked down and scattered in profusion; but the small band of Africanders are unharmed, have already reloaded, and pour in another volley with such telling effect as to make more gaps in the British ranks. Now

Salute of the Elephant Guns.

Night Encounter near Congella.

the two field-guns have been wheeled round: but many of the oxen drawing the carriages are dropping; others are wounded, break loose from the yokes, and run about bellowing. The artillerists fire wildly. A plot of dry grass, which appears white in the moonlight, is torn up by the cannon balls. Pretorius and his riflemen are still unscathed; for the musketry fire of Captain Smith's skirmishing line is as harmless as the artillery practice.

The entire British column is now falling back.

With a force about four times as strong in numbers as that of the patrol under Pretorius, and with the further advantage of artillery on their side, the troops have been unable to advance even a step further towards the laager. The large number of casualties which have already occurred in the English ranks; the superior shooting of the Africanders; their dexterity in loading and reloading; and, perhaps above all, the effective utilisation of every available inequality of the ground as cover by the burgher riflemen—all this tells so much in favour of Pretorius, that the disparity in numbers is more than counterbalanced.

Brightly shines the Southern Cross. The star of the Africander is still in the ascendant.

Meanwhile, Gert Viljoen and Bart Pretorius, in command of the patrol of one hundred and fifty men stationed among the sandhills and bush at C.C.C.* (more than four miles north of the laager, and on the path between it and the British Camp), hearing the noise

* (See Sketch-Map, p. 223).

of the battle that was in progress, came down with
some of their men to reinforce Pretorius; while others
of the burghers, led by Gert Rudolph, moved forward,
and commenced firing on the British camp, in order to
feign an attack on the position and prevent strong
supports being despatched from there to Congella.
By the light of the stars, Viljoen and Bart Pretorius,
with their detachment, made their way through the
jungle and thickets, gradually approaching the spot
where, as evidenced by the heavy platoon firing of
musketry and by the occasional thunder of the British
artillery, the combat was still proceeding. The narrow
Kaffir footpaths, which traversed the bush, were so
intricate and winding in their course, that a considerable section of the reinforcements lost their way in
attempting to make a detour towards the beach and
get to the rear of Captain Smith's column. These did
not come up in time to cut off the retreat as they had
intended. The others, joining the patrol under
Andries Pretorius, at once came into action, and
poured in such a heavy fire on the British that
neither artillery nor infantry could maintain their
ground any longer and fell back precipitately towards
the shore.

It was half-past one in the morning. The greater
part of Captain Smith's column, including the artillery, was in full retreat northward along the shore
of the inner harbour, marching by a route somewhat more inland than that by which they had
advanced to the attack. A line of skirmishers, forming a rear-guard, was attempting to keep back the

burgher patrol, which was pressing forward in pursuit, reinforced by all the men who had been left in charge of the laager—about a dozen—and by the first arrivals of Gert Viljoen and Bart Pretorius' detachment. A steady musketry fire was being kept up on both sides; but, so far, not one of the Africanders had been hit. Suddenly more of the burgher reinforcements appeared on the left flank of the retreating British column, and opened fire. The retreat became a rout. The line of skirmishers was soon driven in on the main column. Then most of the oxen which were left to draw the gun-carriages were shot down. The combined Africander force, rushing forward in extended line, and now fighting over the open sandy plain, reserved their fire till within twenty-five yards of the English rear-guard. Captain Smith attempted to hold them back by a bayonet charge, but failed. The main body of the British column had already passed the store near the Point, and were making their way towards the camp, from which the howitzer was firing shell. A good many of the soldiers however, in the rear, who had fought bravely, and attempted again and again to drive back the burgher force by bayonet charges, were completely cut off from the column. A shower of bullets swept down on them from the sandy plain. With a rush, the guns were captured by the Africanders; the remnant of the British infantry, which still attempted to stand, was driven into the sea; some were drowned; others swam out to the small island in the harbour; and still others, after throwing away their

Rout of the British Force.

weapons, dashed through the waves and ran northward along the beach in the direction of the store of Maynard & Co., where they were rescued. The wreck of the main body of the defeated force reached the camp.

Thus ended the battle of Congella, the first contest of arms between European troops and the burgher forces of the Republic of Natal. The British troops had fought bravely, and had been in vastly superior numbers during all the first half hour of the fighting—in which time the issue of the engagement was practically decided. That the new nation's commando of citizen-soldiers was more than a match for regular troops was a revelation which the British officers—who had committed their usual mistake of under-estimating the prowess and courage of the enemy—were slow to admit. As to the Cape Town and Port Elizabeth public of narrow-minded office-seekers and ignorant shop-keepers, it was actuated as much then, as now, by malignant hatred of the Africander farmer; and so the convenient fiction, that the British troops were defeated because they were outnumbered, was invented. The legend is believed in to this day in some of the towns of the Cape Colony and in London.

The figures given in the foregoing narrative as to the numbers engaged on the side of the Africanders are from oral statements, made to the author, by surviving Voortrekker Farmers in Natal and in the Transvaal, in 1881.

CHAPTER XXVI

THE RAIDERS BESIEGED

The Morning after the Fight—Critical Position of British Force—Procrastinating Citizen Soldiers—Tender-hearted Samaritans—Captain Smith's Preparations for Defence—Dick King's Ride—Capture of Block-House on the Point—The much maligned "Boer" is a Generous Foe—Magnanimity Appreciated—In the Trenches—Captain Smith appeals to the Zulus for Help—Reinforcements for Pretorius—Richard King's Exploit—Lieutenant-Colonel Cloete to the Rescue—The Sortie—The Struggle for the Bastion.

THE pale light of the moon and of the southern stars gave place to the rose-and-purple flush of dawn over the waves of the Indian ocean. The tops of the mountains in the west became aglow with light. Occasionally a rifle-shot broke the stillness of the early morning. Now and then was heard the booming report of the howitzer in the British camp near the Berea, where the troops had retired. Here and there a horseman rode across the plain to and from the Africander laager, where the wounded were receiving such attention and succour as was available.

In their hour of victory the first care of the sturdy peasants of Natal was for the stricken foemen. Forty-seven killed and wounded were found on the battlefield. All belonged to the attacking force. The Farmers themselves had lost only one man—young Greyling—who was killed by a rifle-shot fired from the store near the Point, towards which he was riding immediately after the defeat of the troops (not knowing that the building had been barricaded and loopholed in the night by some of the Uitlander residents at the Bay, who were secretly acting in support of the English). The British wounded, after having been attended to at the laager by the German doctor, Schultz, and by the American medical missionary, the Rev. Dr. Adams, were all sent to Captain Smith's camp, so that they could at once be placed under the care of the army surgeons. The Africander officer who carried Pretorius' flag of truce at the same time informed the British commander that all his dead would be sent to the camp, in order that their comrades might bury them with military honours. That was done. The total British loss is given by Holden in his "History of Natal" as 34 killed, 63 wounded, and 6 missing. Captain Smith's own report is that, when the roll was called in the camp on the morning after the battle, there were left, to answer to their names, 88 out of the 138 who had started on the expedition.

The Morning after the Fight. Casualties

The farmer-soldiers, as already stated, had but one man killed. This was the young burgher, Pieter Greyling,* who was shot from the store near the Point. The building had been erected some time previously by Mr. Cato, the representative of Messrs. Owen Smith of Port Elizabeth.

The following statements, written down by the author at Newcastle, in Natal, and at Schoonspruit,

---
* Theal gives his Christian name as Abraham.

near Potchefstroom, in May, 1881, were made by Nicolaas Meyer, sen. (of Utrecht, Transvaal), and J. H. Visser, sen., of Schoonspruit, both of whom, when young, served under Pretorius in the war in Natal:—

(1) "Die eerste man aan ons kant gesneuweld was Greyling—een jonge man. Cato syn *store* was daar, en met ons aanval het ons nie verwag dat Cato aan die kant van ons vyand sou wees; want hy en andere handelaars het trou gesweer aan die Republick. Hy het sig self verontskuldig deur te seg dat hy wel trou gesweer het betreffende ons oorlog met Kaffers, dog nie wat aangaat oorlog met Engeland nie."

(*Translation*)—"The first man who fell on our side was Greyling—a young man. Cato's store was there (near the 'Point'), and, at the time of our advance, we did not expect to find him on the side of our enemy; for he and other traders had sworn fealty to the Republic. He stated, as an excuse for his conduct, that he had taken the oath of allegiance only as regards our war with the Kaffirs, and not in relation to war with England."

(2) "Greyling is geval toe ons kamp die nag deur Smith aangeval is. Cato syn *store* was verskans, en daar vuur die vyand toe een sarsie uit. Ons het nie geweet dat daar vyande was."

(*Translation*)—"Greyling fell when our camp was attacked at night by Smith. Cato's store had been barricaded, and it was from that building that the enemy fired a volley. We did not know that there were foemen there."

These statements, written down word for word as

spoken in the Africander vernacular, clearly indicate the view which the Emigrants entertained as to the attitude of some of the traders in Natal. The first burgher who fell in the hostilities with England lost his life through Uitlander treachery.

The only other casualties in the battle of Congella on the side of the Republicans were four wounded. One of these, Johannes Greyling, afterwards died of his wounds. The full list, as given by the Natal Volksraad in their report of 19th June, 1842, is as follows:—Killed: Pieter Greyling; Johannes Greyling. Wounded: J. Prinsloo; P. Nel; T. Schutte.

On the 24th and 25th of May there was no further fighting.

Practically, although the prolongation of the armistice, which had been agreed upon for part of the first mentioned date, was not secured by any formal stipulation, such a cessation of hostilities was brought about. Burgher scouts were surrounding the British camp, which was now isolated and cut off, from its supplies in the block-house on the Point and from the loopholed building close by where the Uitlander allies were entrenched; but the investing lines were not so close and complete as to prevent communications and messages passing from Captain Smith to these outlying points.

Critical Position of British Force. Immediately after the battle, *i.e.*, at dawn on the morning of 24th May, the position of the British force was critical in the extreme. The division which had attempted to surprise and crush Pretorius had itself been routed. There was a casualty list equal to nearly a third of the entire force. The artillery was gone. The stores and supplies were more than three miles off, in the block-house on the Point, where there was only a Sergeant's guard of twenty-three men. There was nothing to prevent this position being taken by assault on the instant, instead of two days later; nothing to hinder the burghers from at once arresting all the Uitlanders who were assisting, or suspected of assisting, the enemy; nothing to stop Pretorius from instantly investing the British camp closely—instantly, instead of six days after. To the trained European strategist, playing the game of war according to the universally recognised rules: that, when hostilities have actually commenced, the boldest and most daring offensive tactics provide best for defence, and that to strike hard as well as to strike swiftly spells victory, whilst delay means defeat—to the military critic, and to the soldier by profession—it must seem as if the Emigrants threw away all their chances of continued success, at least in the earlier phases of the struggle, by these apparently unaccountable delays. But they were citizen-soldiers, defending their hearths and homes. Their leader was a simple burgher of the veld, and not a world-conqueror.

Procrastinating Citizen Soldiers.

After that first night of strife, at break of day, when the battlefield from which the British force had been driven was in possession of the Africanders, they were moved to pity and compassion by the groans of the wounded, and by the sorrowful cries for water and for succour. Forgetting that victory was not yet secured for their side, and that it was absolutely necessary to follow up their first success by striking further blows at once, their main concern was—to their credit and honour be it spoken—to ease the sufferings of the enemy's wounded. As in after years, at Bronkhorst Spruit, Laing's Nek, Ingogo, Majuba, and Doornkop, the Republican Africanders showed themselves to be kind Samaritans and good-hearted Christians.

<small>Tender-hearted Samaritans.</small>

Meanwhile, Captain Smith, who had expected to be instantly attacked in his camp, finding that no immediate danger threatened him, made such preparations as he could to maintain his position, and, if possible, retrieve the disaster which had befallen his expedition.

While the armistice lasted, it was given out that the British officer was ready to consider terms of surrender. According to the statements of several of the Emigrants, Pretorius proposed that the English forces should have their cattle restored to them, and should be allowed to retire overland. The Volksraad, it is said, objected to this proposal, and insisted on absolute and unconditional surrender. It seems quite improbable, however, that Captain Smith meant to retire, much less to surrender; for on the night of the 24th May, he was getting provisions into his camp from some of the English residents of Durban, who had managed to pass through the Africander lines; at the same time he was in active communication with other Uitlanders, and arranging for the transmission of a message overland to the Governor of the Cape, asking him to send reinforcements. Mr. Richard King and Mr.

<small>Captain Smith's Preparations for Defence.</small>

IN SOUTH AFRICA

Cato, taking advantage of the darkness, swam two horses from the Point to the Bluff on the southern side of the Bay. It had been arranged that King should take the message. When starting, he was fired on by scouts from the Congella laager. But he rode boldly, and escaped, making his way to the southern frontier, and thence to Port Peddie. Intelligence was then sent from there to Cape Town concerning the critical position of the British force in Natal, and reinforcements were at once despatched by sea to relieve Captain Smith. *Dick King's Ride.*

At nine o'clock in the evening of 25th May, a commando of one hundred burghers, under Gert Viljoen and Bart Pretorius, mustered outside the laager at Congella. Their object was to carry by assault the British position at the block-house on the Point and capture the stores. All that day active preparations for defence had been observed to be in progress at Captain Smith's camp. This fact, and Richard King's departure in the previous night, made it evident to the Farmers that the British commander meant to continue the struggle; and so they had determined to strike another blow.

At daybreak on the 26th of May, their attacking line surprised the Sergeant's guard of twenty-three men on the Point. A detour of some eight hours had been made to avoid the Kaffir scouts on the British side. A summons to surrender having been rejected, the assaulting column at once opened fire. Two soldiers were killed and two wounded. The others scattered and fled towards the block-house store. *Capture of Block-house on the Point.*

The Sergeant and three men managed to escape to Captain Smith's camp. Seventeen, who had taken refuge in the store, surrendered. The eighteen-pounder gun and all the military stores fell into the hands of the burghers. The vessels *Pilot* and *Mazeppa*, which had been used for conveying stores and ammunition for the British expedition from Cape Town and Algoa Bay, and were then lying in harbour, were also taken possession of by order of the Volksraad. The captains of the vessels were ordered on shore, and all property belonging to British officers was seized. The burghers who executed these orders of the Volksraad were under the leadership of the Heemraad, Michiel van Breda, and his son Servaas.

Seizure of Mazeppa and Pilot.

And now another armistice was agreed to with Captain Smith. English accounts say that this truce was proposed by Pretorius. The Emigrants state that the British commander asked for it. It matters little which is the correct version. It is, however, quite certain that the Africanders gained nothing by this procrastination. A proposal from Pretorius, that the English force should embark in the *Pilot* and *Mazeppa* and leave Natal, was supposed to be under consideration by Smith, who took good care to lay in such a store of provisions as was available every night, when Mr. Cowie—one of the English residents who managed to make his way through the thin line of burgher pickets—supplied him. Cattle and sheep thus smuggled into the English camp were slaughtered, and the meat was salted. Grain and vegetables, also, were obtained in this way.

IN SOUTH AFRICA 237

When, on the morning of the 31st of May, it became evident that Captain Smith had no intention of yielding, and the armistice terminated, the investing lines were drawn closely round the British camp. Siege trenches were constructed. The eighteen-pounder and the two captured field-pieces were served with ammunition which had been taken at the Point. A hot artillery fire was opened on the English from these guns, and from the two cannon which had seen service in the Zulu war.

But once more Pretorius and his officers were too chivalrous and humane to press their advantage to the utmost; for, when the siege had lasted twenty-four hours, they sent word to Captain Smith that he was at liberty to send all non-combatants—the women and children in his camp —on board the *Mazeppa*, where they would be in safety. This proposal was at once accepted by the British officer. It was an arrangement which relieved him from his chief anxiety and care, and enabled him to hold out until relief came. No parole seems to have been exacted from those on board the *Mazeppa*; and the crew of this Port Elizabeth vessel, soon after, showed their appreciation of Africander magnanimity, by running the ship and all on board out to sea in search of a British man-of-war. <small>The Much-Maligned "Boer" is a Generous Foe. Magnanimity Appreciated.</small>

Interesting details of the progress and some of the leading incidents of the siege of Captain Smith's camp by the Emigrants under Pretorius, are given in the personal narratives of some of the Voortrekkers.

"Now, we had completely invested Captain Smith on all sides," says one of the officers, dictating to the author at Schoonspruit on 29th and 30th May, 1881. "Soon his supply of provisions began to run short. The soldiers often shot crows and rooks which were flying across the camp. Horses also were slaughtered to obtain meat." Describing the construction of some of the trenches, he says: "One morning I stood with Louw Erasmus on one of our batteries, and told him that I would undertake to dig a trench that night—closer to the enemy's position than any of those we had already constructed. I pointed out the spot to him. 'Can you do it?' he asked. 'Do you think you will succeed?' That night, when it was dark enough, I crept forward with about twelve men to within one hundred or one hundred and twenty yards of the English advanced posts. Here we commenced to dig very carefully (we had all brought spades with us as well as our guns). When we had succeeded in making a small furrow, we were joined by about twenty-five more burghers. Our work progressed rapidly. All at once, however, they opened fire on us from their fort. One of our spades must have glittered in the moonlight and betrayed us. But our trench was already quite serviceable, and we were able to return the enemy's fire from behind the breastwork of earth. Now we completed our work by digging deeper still."

Then he tells of the death of one of the burgher force — a young Farmer named Marais (another

Voortrekker in his statement gives the name as Liebenberg). "There was a small fort in one of our trenches. It was constructed of sandbags, and was exactly similar to the other forts which we had made at various points along our line. Marais was stationed here; but he never would keep behind cover, or seek any shelter whatever, when he was firing at the enemy. We used to shout to him: 'Take care!' but he never would listen to us. 'Ik is nie een meid nie!' ('I am not a woman!') he would shout in reply. 'When I am fighting, I always stand in the open. I do not wish to be sheltered.' And then the bullets from the English camp would whistle through the air, and fly close past him. One day he was blazing away as usual, standing erect on the earthworks of our little fort. A great many balls were coming in his direction, and some seemed to come very close to him. 'Do stoop down!' we shouted to him. 'He will certainly be killed,' said one of the older burghers. At that very instant, some of us plainly saw one of the Hottentot riflemen on the British side taking aim. The report of the shot was heard almost at the same moment, and our brave young comrade fell backward into the trench, with a large bullet wound through his head."

On another occasion a young burgher named Klopper was walking from the beach in the direction of the trenches, when a shell from the camp went screaming past one of the Natal earthworks—and cut him in two.

In the Trenches.

The defence of the British camp was conducted

with bravery, skill, and determination. Wells had
been dug to supply the garrison with water, of which
there was no want. Provisions, however, ran very
short; for the investing lines were now so close and
complete that no more cattle could be brought in at
night by English residents at the Bay. Besides, all
the Uitlanders who had assisted Captain Smith
were under arrest at Pietermariztburg. To eke
out the small quantity of provisions available,
the soldiers were getting smaller rations every
day, until, towards the end of the siege, camp-
biscuits, sun-dried horseflesh, and water, made up
the bill of fare. Deep trenches had been constructed
all round the fort, and the earthworks formed an
efficient protection against the rifle fire and the
artillery of the burghers, who had five guns in all,
but whose artillerists were raw, untrained young
farmers. The howitzer on the English side was well
handled. Undoubtedly the best part of Captain
Smith's fighting force were the Hottentot riflemen of
the Cape Corps and the European waggon-drivers
who had come with the expedition. All these men
could shoot well, and they formed the real back-bone
of the defending force. It is a question whether the
regular troops alone would have been able to hold out
and prevent the encampment being rushed and taken
by assault. But the troops also, and their officers,
were brave men. It is to be regretted that their
commander sullied his good name, and that of his
Government, by asking aid of the Zulus.

 "When Captain Smith," says Theal, "was in almost

desperate circumstances, he managed to communicate with the Zulu chief, whom he vainly entreated to come to his aid." This was returning evil for good, with a vengeance. The English commander knew what a Zulu invasion of Natal at that time would have signified, for the memory of the massacres of women and children in the neighbourhood of Weenen was still fresh in all men's minds. Pretorius and the Farmers had been charitable and merciful to the British wounded, kind to the prisoners of war, magnanimous towards Captain Smith himself—in allowing him to send the women and children from his camp to the *Mazeppa*, where they were safe. The appeal to savages, to attack the Africanders, testified to a British officer's appreciation of all this kindness and courtesy and magnanimity. It was an act in every way worthy the traditions of the self-styled philanthropists and of their administration.

<small>Captain Smith Appeals to the Zulus for Help.</small>

Early in June, Pretorius had been reinforced by some two hundred and fifty or three hundred burghers from Winburg and from the district between the Lower Caledon and the Orange River. They were under the leadership of Commandant Jan Mocke, and had come in response to the appeal from their countrymen in Natal. Hendrik Potgieter, however, had refused to send assistance from Potchefstroom. His contention was that the Volksraad of Natal had made a mistake in asking for the acknowledgment of the Republic's independence by England; that he and his burghers had formed a separate Government to the north of the Vaal river;

<small>Reinforcements for Pretorius.</small>

that they had had no share or voice in the negotiations; and therefore would take no part in the hostilities against England.

Richard King's Exploit.

When Richard King, the young Englishman who rode with Captain Smith's message, started from the harbour of Natal on the night of 24th May, he had before him a journey of four hundred miles on horseback, through an inhospitable and, for the greater part, an uninhabited country. Detained on the way by sickness, by swollen rivers, and by all sorts of hardships and dangers, he still managed to reach his destination—Fort Peddie (not very far from Grahamstown)—in nine days. On board the schooner *Conch*, which was then just ready for sea in Algoa Bay, one hundred men of the 27th regiment were at once embarked, with stores and ammunition, for Natal. At Cape Town, the 25th regiment was on the point of proceeding to India, when intelligence of the disaster to the British force arrived. Among the members of some of the old Cape families who, at that time, held commissions in the British army, was Lieutenant-Colonel Abraham Josias Cloete, whose father was the owner of an estate and famous vineyard at Constantia. That officer received instructions to take command of the troops which should, in the ordinary course of events, have gone to India; embark on board the frigate *Southampton* in Simon's Bay; and undertake the subjugation of the Africanders in Natal. He set sail on the 14th of June.

Lieutenant-Colonel Cloete to the Rescue.

Meanwhile, Andries Pretorius and his burghers were hotly pressing the siege of the British camp,

and were bringing their trenches nearer at every
point. One of the trenches ran in a zigzag
direction from a sandhill, where the Farmers had
constructed a battery and mounted one of their
cannon, to a point much nearer to the enemy. This
point was a small hill, round which the trench had
been carried. Breastworks of earth had been thrown
up here, and the defences of the little fort had been
further strengthened by sandbags piled up along its
front face. Sentries were constantly posted at
either end of the bastion, and a vigilant guard was
kept on this advanced portion of the siege works.

In the night of the 17th of June, however, when it
was very dark, Lieutenant Molesworth succeeded in leading a sortie party to within six or seven yards; then, pouring in a volley, his troops attempted to capture the trench by a bayonet charge. *Lieutenant Molesworth's Sortie.*

There were, at the time, only ten burghers holding the position. Their names were Strydom, Hattingh, Casper van Zyl, J. H. Visser, Christiaan v. d. Merwe, Klaas Dekker, J. Vermaak, Joachim Koekemoer, Jan Landman, Stefanus Bothma. One or two others had rushed back along the trench towards the main battery, in order to summon help. Reinforcements soon appeared on the scene, and then the English were driven back towards their camp. But meanwhile a desperate struggle had been in progress in the bastion. Two of the burghers had been killed by the volley fired at close quarters by the soldiers, five of whom fell in the bayonet charge that followed. These were all shot as they were in the act of *Struggle for the Bastion.*

jumping into the trench. Their rifles, with the bayonets attached, were seized by the defenders. Several of the troops who followed were thrust back by these bayonets. Others were struck down with the butt ends of the heavy elephant guns. It was a fierce contest; but it was soon over. When the burgher reinforcements from the large battery rushed along the trench into the little fort, it was found that, of the ten Africanders who had defended it, two—Strydom and Hattingh—had been killed; and four, viz., Klaas Dekker, Stefanus Bothma, Jan Landman, and J. Vermaak, wounded. On the British side there were six or eight, altogether, killed and wounded.

CHAPTER XXVII

THE LAST STAND IN DEFENCE OF THE HARBOUR

Relief for Captain Smith—Disposition of Emigrant Forces—Battle of Durban Bay—Retreat of Pretorius—Kaffir Marauders made Use of by the British Commander—Atrocities in the Service of the Crown.

BY the 24th of June, when the siege had lasted a month, the position of the British force under Captain Smith was desperate. There was no more food, except a very scanty ration of biscuit-crumbs and dried horse-meat—barely enough to keep the soldiers from absolutely dying of hunger. The water, also, was turning brackish, and there were some cases of enteric fever in the camp. Relief was sorely needed by the besieged. That night the schooner *Conch* arrived opposite the mouth of the Umgeni river, and sent up some sky-rockets. The frigate reached the outer anchorage in the following night. *Relief for Captain Smith.*

On the morning of Sunday, the 26th, the disposition of the Africander forces was as follows:— *Disposition of Emigrant Forces.*

At the mouth of the Umgeni river, Commandant Louw Erasmus was stationed with about a hundred burghers.

At a point on the Coast, about midway between the Umgeni mouth and the Bay, was a patrol of some twenty-five or thirty men under Commandant Gerrit Rudolph.

Another small patrol of twenty or twenty-five men was stationed at the head of the Bay or inner harbour.

On the Point, there was a detachment of between thirty and forty burghers, with the Commandant-General himself at their head. Here was also a battery commanding the entrance to the inner harbour. The gun mounted on this was a four-pounder. But there was practically no ammunition for this or any of the other guns. The supply had become exhausted, and all the cannon balls now available were masses of lead, moulded round hard pieces of iron or chain links. These missiles had been manufactured by some of the Farmer amateur-artillerists, and were not of much use.

The trenches and siege works surrounding the British camp were held by only about twenty-five men, with whom was J. H. Visser—from whose statement all the foregoing figures are taken.

According to Theal, there were on the Bluff, or headland which forms the prolongation of the southern shore of the Bay, three hundred and fifty Farmers. Most of these were men who had come with Commandant Mocke from the western side of Drakensberg.

With his forces distributed as described, Pretorius now attempted to prevent Lieutenant-Colonel Cloete landing and effecting a junction with Captain Smith. The latter had still a force (including his

Battle of
Durban Bay.

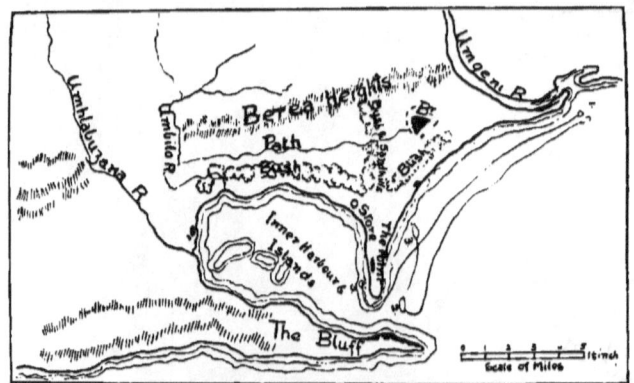

SKETCH MAP TO ILLUSTRATE DESCRIPTION OF THE BATTLE OF DURBAN BAY.

■ Afrivander Positions at noon on June 20th, 1842 (just before the battle began).
■ British Land and Sea Forces.
1. Position of *Southampton* Frigate and Schooner *Conch* at noon. 2. *Southampton* at about 2 p.m.
3. *Southampton* and *Conch* at about 4 p.m. (boats landing from both).
From narratives and pencil drawings by J. H. Visser, the late Servaas van Breda, M.L.C. (Natal) and others.

irregular troops) of over two hundred men who were not actually on the sick-list or wounded, although they were all much exhausted, and many of them more than half famished. The total relief forces on the *Southampton* and *Conch* were seven or eight hundred strong. Their base of operations, the ships, being movable and transportable, gave them the advantage of choosing their own point of attack, while the Emigrants, although inferior in numbers, had to spread out and divide their forces, so as to be prepared to defend a tract of coast-line nearly twenty miles in extent. We have already seen what the actual numbers were at different points along the coast line. It will be readily understood, therefore, that, were any one of these points to be attacked by the ships before reinforcements could come up, the disparity in numbers would be at once enormously increased to the further advantage of the British. This was precisely what happened in the engagement.

At early morning, the ships were both opposite the mouth of the Umgeni river. Here the burghers under Louw Erasmus had been scouting and patrolling for three days. Ever since the arrival of the *Conch* they had been on the alert, in order to be prepared to resist an attempted landing. At noon of the 26th, the burgher Commandant, who was no longer a young man, sought repose. The wind was then unfavourable to any attempt at landing. The patrol had taken the saddles off their horses, which had been allowed to graze. But it was no time for rest; for,

<small>Battle of Durban Bay.</small>

suddenly, the wind veered round, and a light breeze began to blow from the north-east. Both the frigate and the schooner at once made sail for the south, and shaped their course straight for the bar opposite the entrance to the Bay. Erasmus had instructions from Pretorius, in the event of a contingency such as had now arisen, to at once move southward and effect a junction with the detachment under Gerrit Rudolph —which was stationed midway between the Umgeni mouth and the Point.

This movement was attempted; but there was considerable, and what seemed unaccountable, delay in its execution. Afterwards, it was explained how the delay had occurred. The horses had strayed away from the camp, and could not be found at once. At about two o'clock in the afternoon the heavy guns of the frigate (a sixty-four), then lying in the outer anchorage, began to play on the Bluff as well as on the Point. Gradually she moved nearer to the bar; and, as broadside after broadside swept the slopes of the headland— that position becoming untenable—all the burghers who occupied it had to fall back and go the round of the entire course of the inner harbour, before they could attempt to reinforce those on the Point—where the attack was now made. At about three o'clock, the effect of Colonel Cloete's admirably executed tactics was that the Emigrants had four hundred and fifty of their men absolutely excluded from the field of operations.

The three hundred and fifty men who had held the position on the Bluff or headland were now making their way along the beach towards the Point. The patrol of a hundred, under Louw Erasmus, had failed to reach the point of attack. The *Conch* had, meanwhile, crossed the bar. It had some boats in tow. In these there was a naval detachment of eighty-five men under Captain Hill. On the schooner there were a hundred and thirty-five men, under command of Colonel Cloete himself. Andries Pretorius—with about thirty-three men now reinforced by the patrol of twenty-five under Gert Viljoen, which had previously been stationed on the beach at the head of the inner harbour—still held the Point. In skirmishing line along the beach, the burghers kept up a steady fire on the boats, which were advancing to the attack. But, meanwhile, the frigate had moved nearer to the position occupied by Gerrit Rudolph. Before the reinforcements under Louw Erasmus could come up from the north, several boatloads of soldiers, decked by the guns of the *Southampton*, managed to land—the small number of burghers of Commandant Rudolph's patrol (twenty-five or thirty in all) being unable to stand their ground. Those on the Point were now compelled to retire, for their position was threatened in the rear as well as in front.

Thus ended the battle of Durban. Falling back on the Africander battery situated on one side of the British camp, the Commandants found that the advancing troops were so well protected by intervening sandhills, that it was not possible to check their march by artillery fire from that point.

The patrol of one hundred burghers, under Louw

Erasmus, had now come up; but there seemed no possibility of immediately renewing the contest. Pretorius discovered that his supplies of ammunition were running short; that many of the burghers were discouraged and disheartened by their failure; and that a great many more, although too much devoted to the cause of their Republic to entertain the idea of submitting to the British, were anxious to return to their homes for a time, in order to make provision for the safety of their families. Those who had come from a long distance—more especially the men from the western side of the Drakensberg and from the Zulu frontier—were apprehensive as to what might happen, now that the natives knew of the struggle between the two white nationalities and had been invited to take sides with what had become the winning Power. It was decided, therefore, to retreat inland and await developments.

<small>Retreat of Pretorius.</small>

At about four o'clock, Colonel Cloete, without further opposition, marched into Captain Smith's camp, and thus raised the siege. Pretorius fell back with a small commando of burghers, and took up a position a few miles inland—near where the village of Pinetown is now. Here he formed a laager. Being then called upon by the British commander to submit to the authority of the Queen, he refused to do so—hoping still to be able to make a stand against the invading force, when reinforcements from the interior should have reached his laager.

But he was compelled to give up this idea by reason of the shamefully dishonourable means resorted to for the purpose of extending Her Majesty's dominions. A band of Kaffirs had been got together by Ogle, King, and other Englishmen, when hostilities first commenced between Captain Smith and the Emigrants. They had been used as scouts and videttes by the British officer. These Kaffirs were now sent by Cloete to procure horses and cattle from the farms. Their instructions were to bring as many as they could capture, and to "take particular care not to *kill* any women or children."* No other restrictions were placed on the *noble savages.* No European officers were sent to superintend the work of these marauders, who murdered Cornelis van Schalkwyk, Theunis Oosthuizen and his son, and Dirk van Rooyen. The wives and children of these men were not killed. They were stripped stark naked; in that condition, driven across the veld; and left to wander about without food. After three days of misery and suffering, they were found and rescued by Bart Pretorius, who was scouting in the neighbourhood with a small burgher patrol.

For Empire.

* Letter of Lieutenant-Colonel Cloete to Andries Pretorius, dated 3rd July, 1842. But the word "kill" is here italicised so as to indicate clearly the interpretation which the Kaffirs undoubtedly put on the order which they had received.

From what follows, it will be seen that solicitude for the safety and security of women and children weighed as a heavy load of responsibility on the shoulders of the military representative of the British Crown in those days, just as in the case of a great Empire-extending Privy-Councillor-Director and his lieutenant (the Imperial Administrator) recently. We have been told that the distinguished men were, all three, actuated by high and noble motives. At any rate, the official sense of duty and responsibility found expression, then, as now—in words.

Still the order for the Kaffir marauding expeditions remained in force, and Colonel Cloete, in reply to a letter from Andries Pretorius, refused to withdraw it. "You have caused this state of things by rebelling, and you must bear the consequences." Such was the answer, word for word, of the gallant representative of England's might and England's honour to the man whose treatment of the non-combatants (women and children and wounded) on the British side had been nothing less than chivalrous and noble. The simple-minded, honest farmers had set an example in the methods of civilised warfare to mighty England, whose military commanders in the vanquished country now proved that they knew so little of such generosity of spirit as should actuate officers and gentlemen, and allowed their zeal in the cause of Empire so far to minimise the claims of humanity, that they did not hesitate to resort to unfair and dastardly means to attain their object—the establishment of the authority of their Sovereign.

CHAPTER XXVIII

HOW NATAL WAS LOST

The Cape Town Plot Succeeds—Terms of Surrender—Amnesty—The proscribed "Irreclaimable Rebels"—The Mote in the Eye of the Africander Farmer—Zulu Incursion into Natal—Flight of Mawa—Smellenkamp—The *Brazilië*—No Hollander Clergyman, Schoolmaster, or Books Admitted—Commissioner Henry Cloete—Meetings and Resolutions—An Armed Demonstration—Cloete Master of the Situation—A Mere Coincidence—More Light—Commandant Mocke—Debate and Discussion—Submission.

ONCE more the Emigrants found that an evil return was being made to them for their own good actions and magnanimity.

The little Nation of hardy pioneers was already impoverished and exhausted by the long-continued and cruel struggle against the barbaric Zulu Power. And now, with their harbour and their sea coasts in possession of a much more formidable foe—a civilised Power which carried on hostilities without strictly adhering to the rules of civilised nations; with all their supplies of ammunition cut off; threatened and coerced, not only by England's ships and cannon, and troops, but by the menace of another Zulu invasion, which, it was said, the British Commanders could no longer avert if submission to British rule were delayed or rejected, but which, as was well known, one of those Commanders had in reality invited; with their burghers actually being murdered, and their women and children maltreated by the Kaffir scouts and marauders attached to the British army: the brave peasants could no longer stand in defence of their national existence.

Nor could the leaders find it in their hearts to ask the people for further sacrifices in the cause of liberty. The burgher riflemen formed the only defensive forces of the new fatherland. The unfair and unmanly strategy now resorted to by the British Commander made it impossible for these forces to remain in the field without exposing their homes and families to the danger of being outraged and pillaged by the Kaffir mercenaries and marauders.

Submission.

There was, therefore, no choice but submission. By such infamous means was Natal made a British Colony. The plot—of the Cape Town and London merchants, the intriguing Governor, and the scheming missionaries and Uitlanders—had been entirely successful.

The Plot Succeeds.

Pretorius had retreated on Maritzburg and disbanded his commando, when, on the first Monday of July, 1842, the Volksraad met and began to discuss the question of submission. When it was proposed to abandon the contest, several members spoke excitedly against the proposal. J. N. Boshoff and Carel Landman, as well as Andries Pretorius himself, were convinced that the struggle could not be continued. They, and a great many other influential burghers, advised coming to terms with Cloete, in order to gain time and afterwards obtain the intervention of Holland; but many others were bitterly opposed to all negotiations with England. There were several stormy scenes in the Volksraad. There was a lamentable amount of violent invective and recrimination, all of which made the leaders despair more than ever of being able to continue to defend the Republic.

After much wrangling and quarrelling in the Volksraad, about half the members retired from the assembly, and returned to their farms. Then, when there was a bare quorum of the Raad, it was agreed to submit to the British *on condition that the oath of allegiance should not be subscribed to ;* to give up all the cannon and ammunition taken from the troops; to release all prisoners of war; and to restore all public and private property which had been seized by the orders of the Government of the Emigrants.

<small>Terms of Surrender.</small>

These terms of capitulation were subscribed to, on the 15th of July, by J. N. Boshoff, President, and eleven members of the Raad.

The British Government, through its military representative, Colonel Cloete, agreed on its part to respect all private property; to allow the Emigrant Farmers to return to their homes with their rifles as well as their horses; to protect them against any attack on the part of the Zulus; that there should be no tampering whatever with the existing ownership of land, this condition, however, to be subject to subsequent resolutions and enactments by Her Majesty's Government; that, outside the limits of the military occupation on the Bay, the existing Government should remain as it was until Her Majesty's pleasure concerning the point could be made known :

and that the Kaffirs should, in the first instance, remain in occupation of those parts of the country which they occupied when the troops landed—this condition also to be subject to such subsequent arrangements as might be found necessary in the interests of general safety and security.

With the exception of Boshoff, all the most influential men and tried leaders of the Emigrants were absent when this agreement was concluded. Of the twenty-four members of the new Volksraad, only eleven had subscribed to it; and the adjunct Raad of Winburg and Potchefstroom was not represented at all at the deliberations. It was, therefore, a question whether the treaty of submission was valid. In order to disarm further possible resistance, the British authorities at once issued a proclamation of general amnesty and free pardon for all concerned in the recent hostilities, excepting Joachim Prinsloo, A. W. Pretorius, J. J. Burger, Michiel van Breda, and Servaas van Breda. Joachim Prinsloo was one of the survivors of those who had witnessed the execution scene of Slachtersnek, and a near relative of the National leader, Hendrik Prinsloo. He had been President of the Volksraad during the war, and was one of the chief representatives of those among the Emigrants who were still bitterly opposed to submission. A. W. Pretorius was dangerous to the conquerors on account of his known skill as a military leader, and also because he, as well as J. J. Burger, the Secretary of the Volksraad, was much esteemed and respected, and possessed great influence among the Farmers. Michiel van Breda and his son

Servaas, were members of one of the oldest Western Cape families. They had led the party of burghers who had seized the *Mazeppa* and *Pilot*, on 26th May.

In the case of Pretorius, by a subsequent proclamation—in consideration of his humane conduct towards the prisoners of war and his "general moderation," as well as in recognition of his having used his influence to bring about peace—his name was removed from the list of the proscribed. The four others were outlawed.

Not one of these men had a stain or a blemish on his character. They were all universally esteemed and respected in Natal, as brave and honest men. Their only crime was that they had defended their country, and that they had dared to come forward as leaders of the people. They were now styled "irreclaimable rebels," and a reward of £250 was offered for the "bringing" of each of them, "dead or alive," to the British military authorities.

For a considerable time, although Pretorius had submitted, and Boshoff and the eleven Volksraad members acting with him had entered into the above-mentioned agreement with Lieutenant-Colonel Cloete, it remained doubtful whether, after all, hostilities would not be resumed. The English occupation was confined to the Bay and its immediate neighbourhood. At Pietermaritzburg, the Volksraad was continuing its sessions, as if the country was still an independent Republic. Indeed, the majority of the Emigrants now maintained that it was. Andries Pretorius had resigned the post of Commandant-General, and

Gerrit Rudolph had been elected in his place. There were in reality two Governments in Natal; for the authorities at Cape Town had already gone far beyond their instructions, and they had to wait for complete approval before taking further steps. That approval was obtained in the British Colonial Secretary's despatch of October, 1842. In December followed instructions for a Royal Commissioner to proceed to Natal, to investigate affairs and bring about an arrangement for the permanent tranquillity of the country.

Captain Smith, who (for his gallant defence of the British camp) had been promoted to the rank of Major, and who, on the departure of Colonel Cloete for India, had been left in command of the military forces at Port Natal, now found himself confronted by a serious difficulty on the frontiers of Zululand. The Chief, Panda, while he remained a vassal of the Republic, had never dared to permit any of those massacres and wholesale murders, among his people, which had been the order of the day in Dingaan's time all over Zululand. On the day of his accession to the chieftaincy, in the presence of all the great indunas and councillors, he had been solemnly warned and exhorted by Pretorius not even in war time to allow any women or children to be put to death (*see* p. 153). The compact entered into on the upper waters of the White Umveloosi between the Emigrants and Panda was kept to the letter, because he feared the power of the white people. This fear was, probably, the sole **restraining influence which had prevented the savages** from reverting to their former barbarous and brutal atrocities. Now that the white men had been fighting against each other, the case was different. The Zulu Chief was quick to see that he need no longer fear anything—that while the power of the Emigrants was broken, that of their conquerors was by no means so firmly established as in any way to threaten the independence of Zululand. Nor were the British forces so placed as to be able to overawe the Chief, whose vanity had already been flattered by the request that had been made to him to come to their aid. In Panda's eyes, the British commanders were not all-powerful; nor had they set him an example of chivalrous adherence to the rules and usages of civilised warfare, as Pretorius had done. In fact, Captain Smith's invitation to the Zulus to invade Natal, as well as Colonel Cloete's treatment of non-combatants, were nothing less than infamous violations and inhuman disregard of the law of nations.

The kind and well-meaning philanthropists of England had sent missionaries—noble, self-denying men—to preach the Gospel of Peace and of Mercy, to Chaka and to Dingaan—without avail; for murder and massacre had gone on unchecked in Zululand. Then the Africander farmer-Commandant had spoken to the nation. On the 16th of December, 1838, he and his countrymen had punished the evil-doers; and afterwards, standing on that rock in the heart of Zululand, he had preached his sermon—just one sermon—to Panda and his assembled chieftains and captains. Murder had ceased, on the instant; and there were no more massacres. Still, the English philanthropists and merchants were not satisfied; for, all the way from London and Cape Town and Port Elizabeth, they saw and judged that the "*Boer*" had done very wrong when he had used his rifle to defend his own wife and child from being murdered. The wise and good men, and the calculating merchants, saw the mote in the eye of the Africander Farmer; and then they, and the good missionaries, and the scheming Governor, sent the brave soldiers of Britain to extinguish the rule of the men who were so "unenlightened and reactionary and unprogressive" as to prefer their own Republican Government to that of the Empire-extenders and the worshippers of the Golden Calf. And now, when the regiments and the force of Britain had put down and suppressed the Africander, the words of the sermon from the rock no longer echoed in the ears of the Zulu Chief. Panda, no longer kept in restraint, had large numbers of his subjects put to death. The witch-finders were active, and all those who opposed, or were thought to oppose the Chief in any of his schemes, were doomed to destruction. The wives and children of those who were murdered were not allowed to escape; and all their adherents shared their fate. One of the first and chief victims was a brother of Panda. All those in his kraal were slaughtered. Women were ripped open; children had their brains dashed out against the stones; all the nameless horrors and atrocities which had disgraced the country in Dingaan's time were

[margin: The Mote in the Eye of the Africander Farmer.]

re-enacted. Once more murder and massacre were rampant in Zululand.

There was a beam in the eye of the philanthropist of England, who was indirectly responsible for all the outrages; but he saw only the mote in the eye of the Africander frontiersman.

A chieftainess of the royal house, named Mawa, as well as some rulers and indunas of less importance and influence in Zululand, managed to escape with large numbers of their followers. These all made their way towards the Natal frontier. They were followed by others—in thousands, for the former sybarite of the Umveloosi now proved himself to be possessed by the same demon spirit of maniacal frenzy, by the same passion for slaying and destroying, which had been characteristic of Dingaan; and bloodshed, murder, and outrage, raged unchecked and unrestrained in every part of the Zulu country. In less than a week, some thirty thousand fugitives had crossed the Tugela; in ten days, the number had increased to fifty thousand men, women, and children. Many of the Zulus brought their flocks and herds of sheep and cattle with them into Natal. They seized whatever pasturage and lands they wanted. They terrorised the farmers on the isolated and scattered homesteads, and drove many of the settlers into the towns for safety. The country soon became more disorganised and more disturbed than when it was at war with England. *The Flight of Mawa.* *Zulu Incursion into Natal.*

In the treaty of submission, concluded at Pietermaritzburg, the British Government had pledged itself to protect the Farmers against inroads or incursions by the Zulus; but the military authorities now found themselves powerless to render any assistance to the white inhabitants, who saw ruin staring them in the face.

<small>Smellenkamp.</small> Early in May, 1843, the Dutch ship *Brazilië*, with *Administrateur* Smellenkamp on board, had again appeared off Port Natal. On the occasion of its previous visit, part only of its cargo had been sold to the Emigrants. Captain Reus had then returned to Batavia, and afterwards to Holland. Smellenkamp, after having been arrested at Swellendam, as related in a previous chapter, had been taken to Cape Town, and then allowed to leave for Europe by mail packet. When he arrived in Holland he had again interested himself in the cause of the Africanders, but had received no encouragement whatever from the Government. A strict neutrality proclamation had already been published at the Hague, and copies of this document had been sent to Natal and to other parts of South Africa. The Farmers, however, absolutely refused to believe that the document was genuine. Although the Government of the Netherlands was bound, by the laws of neutrality, to prevent any of its subjects from fitting out expeditions intended to carry on or in any way assist in hostilities against the British forces in Natal, it could not be expected to restrain its people from showing their sympathy with the Emigrants; and when a society, which had been started in Amsterdam, sent out a clergyman, a schoolmaster, some books, and various

articles of merchandise, no objection was raised. The vessel chosen by the authorities in Holland for the voyage was the *Brazilië*, and Smellenkamp was once more on board as supercargo and chief director. *The Brazilië*

Arrived in the harbour of Natal,* however, he was informed by the British officers that he would not be permitted to land any of his cargo without a permit from Cape Town, which, of course, he was known not to have with him. No one on board was allowed to communicate with the Emigrants at Pietermaritzburg. The young clergyman and his wife, as well as the schoolmaster, were refused permission to land. Even the books were prohibited, and had to be taken on to Delagoa Bay in the *Brazilië*. This autocratic and unreasonable militarism was not calculated to impress the Africanders favourably with the advantages of British rule, and was regarded as a breach of, at least, the spirit of the agreement of the treaty of submission, while the inaction of the English Commander, in face of the Zulu incursion, formed a distinct violation of the letter of that agreement, which stipulated for protection against such inroads on the part of the Kaffirs. *No Hollander, Clergyman, Schoolmaster, or Books, Admitted.*

At Delagoa Bay, Smellenkamp and the clergyman— the Rev. Mr. Ham—and his wife landed and remained on shore, while the *Brazilië* proceeded to Batavia. The schoolmaster, Mr. Martineau, had died at sea between the ports of Durban and Lourenço Marques. At Delagoa Mrs. Ham died in childbed.

* 8th May, 1843. "Smellenkamp's Diary," published in Stuart's "Hollandsche Afrikanen."

Commissioner Henry Cloete.

Meanwhile, the English Commissioner from Cape Town had arrived in Natal. Advocate Henry Cloete, brother of Lieutenant-Colonel Cloete, and a member of the Cape Legislative Council, had up to then been known merely as one of the leading barristers of Cape Town. He was destined to make a name for himself by guiding and directing the peaceful incorporation with the British Empire of that province which his brother had seized, but not effectually subdued. That he was able to bring about this great work of aggrandisement and Empire-extension for England, without having further recourse to the keen arbitrament of the sword, proved his skill as a diplomatist. Born under the shadow of Table Mountain, and brought up in that atmosphere of worshipful adulation of Government House which was fashionable at a time when the autocratic representatives of the British Crown in South Africa ruled with almost unlimited powers, he had afterwards been fortunate in enjoying a very liberal European education. He had studied at the University of Leiden, and also in England, and was an accomplished classical scholar, as well as a distinguished lawyer.

On the 5th of June, 1843, Commissioner Cloete arrived at Durban. On the 8th, there was a mass meeting of burghers at Pietermaritzburg, at which it was resolved, almost unanimously, that no negotiations whatever should be entered into with the English Commissioner before Smellenkamp had been communicated with at Delagoa. On the 9th, Cloete addressed a meeting of some five hundred people at

Maritzburg, speaking in favour of a settled Government under British rule, which was to bring prosperity to the country. Then one of the Farmers present— Anthonie Fick by name—in a loud and clear voice, read out the resolution which had been adopted at the mass meeting on the previous day. A scene of confusion and uproar followed, and the meeting broke up without passing any resolution.

<small>Meetings and Resolutions.</small>

C. Bodenstein, the Secretary to the Volksraad, then wrote to the Commissioner, to inform him that that Assembly had adjourned until August, when members from the adjunct-raad of Winburg and Potchefstroom would take part in the deliberations. And now large numbers of farmers and ranchmen from the other side of the Drakensberg mountains began to emerge from the passes leading to Natal. They were all well armed and mounted, and travelled in separate parties, each under its own leader. Commandants Jan Mocke, Greyling, Jan Kock, and J. P. Delport, were the best-known of these leaders.

<small>An Armed Demonstration.</small>

It is said that Cloete ascertained that there were, in all, some ten thousand armed horsemen when they reached Pietermaritzburg. It is, however, quite impossible that there could have been so many. The communities of Potchefstroom and Winburg, with all the other smaller settlements north of the Orange river, could not then put a fighting force of more than one-tenth of that number in the field; and, besides, nearly all the Potgieter faction—by far the larger body west of the mountains—were holding aloof from the complications in Natal.

The objects of this armed demonstration seem to have been (1) to overawe the invading host of Mawa's emigrant Zulus; (2) to raise the drooping spirits of the party in favour of further armed resistance to the English; (3) to make an impression on the British Commissioner, by proving to him that the cause of the Natal Republicans had the support of their countrymen beyond Drakensberg; (4) in case of failing to save Natal from being annexed by England, to make sure of the Hinterland to the west of the mountains for the Republicans.

Cloete Master of the Situation.
As far as Natal itself was concerned, Cloete appeared master of the situation.

By their submission on the 15th of July, 1842, J. N. Boshoff, and the Volksraad members who acted with him, had cut the ground from under the feet of the party which was in favour of upholding the Republic. The English authorities took good care to insist on the agreement which had been entered into on that date being carried out to the letter—as far as concerned the obligations which the Natalians had undertaken. As to England's obligations, one of the first and foremost of these was deliberately ignored when the Zulu incursion was allowed to go on unchecked. It was,

A Mere Coincidence.
presumably, nothing more than an interesting coincidence that this sudden influx of fifty thousand savages into the country came at the very time when it was in the interests of England to make the position of those opposed to the dominion of the British Crown as insecure as possible. There are several startling coincidences in the history of

South Africa. Certain it is that the burghers of Natal, when they indignantly protested against this violation of the terms of the agreement, were not only left helpless and unassisted, but were expressly warned by Major Smith that they would not be allowed to take steps to protect themselves by driving out the Zulus. Here, at any rate, we have to deal with more than a mere coincidence. If we remember that, before Captain Smith's raid into Natal, the Emigrants, in their letter to the Cape Town Governor, dated 21st February, 1842, had complained of emissaries visiting various native chiefs and inciting them to range themselves and their warriors on the side of the British, and to obtain for reward the flocks and herds of the farmers (*see* p. 201); if we further bear in mind such facts of history as the British officer's shameful appeal to Panda to invade Natal, and Lieutenant-Colonel Cloete's barbarous *foraging parties* with the accompanying murders of peaceful farmers and outrages on women ; then we can see more light thrown on the disgraceful means by which the British Representatives established the authority and the rule of their Sovereign.

More Light.

With Mawa's hordes, in their thousands, terrorising the land, and occupying whatever tracts of country they chose to seize ; with these savages not only unhindered and unchecked in their aggressive attitude, but actually encouraged by the English Commander, when he refused to allow the Farmers themselves to call out a commando to punish the intruders ;—all **further agricultural progress and industry at once** became impossible. In order to safeguard the lives of their families, the burghers had to remove to the towns, or to form laagers for security, in many cases submitting to the loss of their property. The Port and its revenue were in the hands of the British. The former was now closed to all commerce from abroad.

In face of the great danger of further native atrocities in case of a resumption of hostilities, the Volksraad, which met on the 7th of August, declared that they had no choice but to accept the Commissioner's conditions.

But this resolution was not arrived at without considerable discussion and violent argument between the different parties and factions. Pretorius, Landman, Prinsloo, Burger, and many others, had taken no part in the deliberations in July, 1842; but it was quite well known that most of them now despaired of success, in case the struggle had to be resumed immediately. Not so the leaders from the other side of the mountains. The most determined of these was Commandant Mocke. With some hundreds of his adherents, he came forward, and demanded that a new Volksraad of thirty-six members should be chosen to represent all the Emigrants. Those already elected for Natal would not agree to this, and they carried the day. It was then ascertained that Cloete would not regard the agreement of submission already entered into, and now to be further defined and ratified, as applying to any part of the country west of Drakensberg. Thereupon all those from the other side

Commandant Mocke.

of the mountains withdrew from the deliberations, and *Debate and Discussion.*
it was decided by the Volksraad of Natal to bow to
the inevitable and accept the conditions of surrender *Submission.*
laid down by the British Commissioner. But this
was done only after long continued debate and discussion, and after every possible attempt to obtain
better conditions. The Volksraad first proposed that
England should take a strip of coast territory only,
and that the rest of Natal should be allowed to
remain an independent Republic. Cloete replied that
he had no authority to accept anything short of
complete surrender. Then the civil equality of
Black and White inhabitants, on which principle the
British Commissioner stated that he had instructions
to insist as a *sine qua non* of the new order of things
to be inaugurated by English rule, was objected to
by the Farmer assembly. But the objection was
without avail.*

* *See* Appendix: "England's Native Policy, Past and Present, in South Africa."

CHAPTER XXIX

ONCE MORE ACROSS THE MOUNTAINS TO LIBERTY OR DEATH

A BRIGHT RAINBOW IN THE BLACK CLOUDS

Conditions laid down by Cloete—Futility of Further Resistance—Petition and Deputation of the Women of Maritzburg—The Face of the Cards—Ownership of Landed Property—The Crown Lands obtained—Demands of the Volksraad—Autonomy not Granted—Subjects in Place of Citizens—Recommendations of the Volksraad ignored—Annexation of Natal to Cape Colony—Treaty with Panda—The Proscribed Leaders—Pardon for Pretorius—Death of Prinsloo and Michiel van Breda—Arrest of Wife and Daughters of the Latter—Servaas van Breda Pardoned—Volksraad Abolished—Natal overrun by Zulu Refugees—The Locations—Ruin of the Farmers—Once more through the Mountain Passes—Lost.

THE other conditions laid down by Commissioner Cloete for the acceptance of the Volksraad (besides that of complete civil equality for Black and White) were the following :

That there should be equal rights for all religions and all creeds; that slavery or any modification of it should be prohibited; that no association of men, nor any individuals, should be allowed to molest or attack the natives beyond the borders.

Other Conditions of Surrender.
To all these conditions the Volksraad readily assented. The two last-named were principles already acknowledged and provided for by the Grondwet or elementary Constitutional Law of the Republic. To

say, as Anti-Africander writers say, that the British Government, when it annexed Natal, put a stop to slavery, is untrue. Had it been a fact that slavery existed in Natal, then, surely, the British Government, after the annexation, would have proceeded to take steps to liberate the slaves. That there is no record of such measures on the part of the new rulers proves that there were no slaves to set free.

If the system of apprenticeship as it existed in the Republic—although to a much more limited extent than in the Cape Colony—is to be called a modified form of slavery, and brought into court against the "Boer," then the British Government itself stands condemned; for its officials had introduced the system, long before the Natal Republic came into existence.

As to the wars which the Republic had had to carry on against the natives, these cannot, with fairness and justice, be called wars of aggression; for they were hostilities which had been forced on the burghers. The Zulu war was a struggle for national existence. The campaign against Ncapayi was an expedition to protect the frontiers of the State from robber incursions and raids.

On the evening of 8th August, the Volksraad agreed to accept all the conditions proposed by the British Commissioner, including that of civil equality for Black and White. There had been a good deal of discussion before an understanding could be arrived at on this point; but discussion was quite useless; for the Commissioner stated that he had no authority to make any alteration whatever in the conditions which he had laid before the Volksraad for acceptance. Even the party most determined not to submit to British rule now saw the hopelessness of any further attempts at armed resistance. They had already made up their minds to seek a new home beyond the mountains of the Drakensberg range. As on a former occasion, the women again showed their attachment to the Republic, and to the cause of independent nationality. They sent a deputation to the British Commissioner. He received them in the Landdrost Court at Pietermaritzburg, where he listened patiently to a pathetic recital of the people's grievances and of the reasons why they could never submit to be ruled by England.

Futility of further Resistance.

It was the wife of the aged missionary chaplain, Erasmus Smit, who spoke. The hardships and sufferings which the Emigrants had already undergone were eloquently described. Their poverty and distress were only referred to in order to emphasise their determination to remain true to the cause of the Republic. They could not give up the ideals and the aspirations of the heroes—men, women, and children—who had fallen in the great struggle for freedom.

The Women of Pietermaritzburg.

"You have invaded our country. You have seized our harbour. You have allowed the Kaffirs to overwhelm us. You have suppressed our flag and ruined our land. We are footsore and weary with wandering and suffering; but we shall march once more across those mountains to liberty or death."

Her voice was feeble; but her words may yet some day make a grand refrain for the hymn of liberty of the Federal United South African Republic. She clearly saw what was coming — she predicted the future.

While the twenty-four simple farmers, who were then the remaining members of the Volksraad—the twelve representatives of the *Overberg* or Trans-Drakensberg country had retired from the assembly—deluding themselves with the vain hope that the existing institutions, the official language, the rights to property, etc., would remain under British rule as they had been under the Republic and as they had been guaranteed by the British officers on the occasion of the first agreement of capitulation, finally signed away the independence of their little State, the people, "without seeing the face of the cards," as Motley says of some of their ancestors, "suspected the real truth." "The Face of the Cards."

Troops and artillery had already been moved to Maritzburg; and then, when all was ready, it was made known that the British Government would only acknowledge titles to landed property where it could be claimed and proved that the ground had been in actual occupation by the claimant for a full year previous to the arrival of Commissioner Cloete in Natal. As during part of that time the burghers had been in the field against the British, and during the remainder encamped in laagers to guard against attacks from Panda's Zulus, who were then overrunning the country by permission of the British, such proof was entirely impossible in the case of more than three-fourths of all the farms in Natal. Thus, the British mode of determining ownership amounted to confiscation of nearly all the property that was left to the unfortunate inhabitants. That this high-handed procedure would have such an effect was quite well known to the British Commissioner and the officials who acted with him; for their Government had itself been instrumental in bringing about the conditions which made it impossible to produce the very proofs which were now asked for. It is hardly necessary to add that this confiscation was a distinct violation of the agreement of 15th July, 1842, by which England had solemnly bound herself not to interfere with the rights to property.

Ownership of Landed Property.

Thus did the British Government obtain the Crown lands of the Colony of Natal.

The Crown Lands Obtained.

But, before the seizure could become an accomplished fact, the Volksraad had to be got rid of. The British Commissioner had requested that assembly to make known the wishes of the inhabitants of Natal as to the future form of government. This was done in the Volksraad's letter to him, dated 4th September, 1843.

That the country should retain representative Government and corresponding institutions—a Legislative Council chosen by the burghers (with the right of veto to the Governor), Landdrosts or Magistrates elected by the people, and Heemraden or Councillors chosen and appointed by the Governor out of a certain number nominated and elected by the burghers—a Court of Appeal and Circuit Courts; that there should be equality for all religious denominations and creeds and no State church; that education should be fostered and provided for by the legislature; that trade and commerce with all nations should be allowed, but that the sale of firearms to the Kaffirs and other natives should be prohibited; that the English and Dutch languages should have equal rights in the courts of law, English being acknowledged as the official tongue in districts where the majority of the inhabitants were British, and Dutch receiving the same recognition where the opposite condition of affairs existed, *i.e.*, in districts where those of Dutch-Africander descent were in the majority.

Demands of the Volksraad.

Such were the principal recommendations made to the British Commissioner by the Volksraad. There was nothing in these requests which in any way threatened British supremacy or interfered with British rule in the new Colony. All officials other than the Landdrosts and Heemraden were to be appointed by the Governor, and not elected by the people. Even the Heemraden were to be elected by the Crown from among a certain number of candidates nominated by the electorate. Under the circumstances in which the country was then placed, nothing could be more fair or more moderate than these demands made by the Volksraad in the name of the inhabitants of Natal. Large numbers of the Emigrants had already left the country, recrossing the mountains in order to be once more in a position to maintain their Republic, the cause of which they regarded as lost in all that region which lay east of the Drakensbergen. Others, however, were ready to remain in Natal and become

British subjects, on condition that they were fairly treated.

Autonomy not Granted.

In order to conciliate these, the British authorities might have granted the scheme of limited self-government which the Volksraad recommended. Such a policy of conciliation would have gone far to prove that the new rulers of the country were making an honest attempt to keep faith with the people, in interfering as little as possible with the existing laws and institutions, and in acknowledging and granting such a measure of autonomy as would, to some extent, satisfy the popular aspirations, and yet, at the same time, be quite compatible with allegiance to the British Crown. It was not to be expected that men who had dared and endured as much as had these brave Africanders, since they left the frontiers of Cape Colony behind them in order to found their own State and raise aloft their own flag, would be contented to give up not only their nationality, but likewise every vestige of the free political institutions and of the popular representative government which they cherished, and to place themselves once more under British rule as it then existed at the Cape—an unlimited, or, at most, only a slightly limited, despotism.

Subjects in place of Citizens.

But, the distinguished Peninsular and Waterloo veteran who was then Governor at Cape Town was more concerned with making British subjects of the Emigrants than with conciliating and persuading them to become citizens of the Empire.

Great Britain, it was said, was the Paramount Power. Republicans were not wanted; but their farms were—for Crown lands. The report and recommendations of the Volksraad were, therefore, simply ignored. It was then announced that Natal should have no representative government whatever; that its laws should be made by the Governor and Council of Cape Colony; and that its territory should be annexed to that of the Cape. This was in May, 1844.

Recommendations of the Volksraad ignored.

Annexation to Cape Colony.

Meanwhile, the British Commissioner had proceeded to Panda's country, to conclude a treaty with that Chief, and to inform him that he would be required to cede to Great Britain the harbour of St. Lucia Bay and the triangular-shaped area of Zululand lying between the Upper Tugela, the Buffalo River, and the Drakensberg. This territory was to be added to the new Colony of Natal. The Zulu King, making a virtue of necessity, agreed to this territorial rearrangement; but it seems open to doubt whether, even at the present day, England's title-deeds to the country and the harbour thus ceded are valid. Panda had been made Ruler of Zululand by an agreement entered into between the leaders of the Emigrants and all the Chiefs of the Zulu nation, and had acknowledged himself a vassal of the Africander State. His country was a separate subject State of the Republic of Natal. The Volksraad, in surrendering Natal, had not ceded Zululand, any more than it had given up the country to the west of the Drakensberg; and, even had it so disposed of the territory to the north of the Tugela, the consent of the Volksraad of Winburg and Potchefstroom would still have been necessary before England could lawfully take

Treaty with Panda.

possession of any Zulu territory. But the English authorities in South Africa deemed it necessary to extend the Empire by fresh annexations, and thus to prevent the Republicans from attempting in future to obtain a harbour of their own. The Home Government approved.

The Proscribed Leaders.
Pardon for Pretorius.

Major Smith and the military officers were now in possession of Pietermaritzburg. The arbitrary sentence of outlawry on Andries Pretorius had been rescinded; but Prinsloo, Burger, and the Van Bredas, had not been so fortunate as to obtain pardon. In spite of the sums of money which the British Government had offered to any who would undertake to apprehend or "*bring*" them, they had remained scatheless and uninjured at or near Maritzburg from the 11th of August, 1842, when the outlawry proclamation was issued, until the end of the following year, when parties of soldiers were employed to search for them. In 1844, Joachim Prinsloo, having succeeded in reaching Delagoa Bay and communicating with Smellenkamp, was returning to Natal, when he died of malarial fever. Burger had by that time crossed the Drakensberg mountains, and was in safety. Servaas and Michiel van Breda, after having been for some time concealed by their friends at Pietermaritzburg, had also got away overland to Delagoa Bay. There a rumour reached them that they had been pardoned. Returning to Natal, however, they, when on the frontier, received a message from their friends informing them that the British Government had refused to grant them an amnesty. Once more they

Death of Prinsloo and Breda.

retraced their steps through Zululand and through the fever swamps of Lourenço Marques. Struck down in their camp in the forest by the deadly fever, Michiel van Breda closed his eyes in death, after having received the tidings that the English Government, not satisfied with hunting him to death, had had his wife and daughters arrested at Pietermaritzburg and taken as prisoners to Cape Town. Thus, even these helpless women, on whom the heavy hand of adversity and misfortune was already pressing with much severity, were made to feel the displeasure and the bitter resentment of the same Paramount Power whose officials at a later date—in 1880-1—showed their consistent adherence to the old policy of not sparing the defenceless relatives of "*irreclaimable rebels*" by imprisoning, in the vermin-crowded cells of the common gaol at Pretoria, three ladies whose only crime was that the husbands of two and the father of the third were prominent men on the Republican side. *Arrest of Wife and Daughters of Michiel van Breda.*

The young Servaas van Breda, having placed in the earth the mortal remains of his brave father, once more travelled overland to Natal—as Trichard had done before him. One or two faithful Kaffirs accompanied him to Pietermaritzburg, where public opinion and sympathy were now so strongly in his favour that the British Government deemed it wise to leave him unmolested. *Servaas van Breda Pardoned.*

The majority of the Volksraad which was elected in August, 1844, taking the view that the English officials had broken the agreement entered into in

July, 1842, refused to subscribe to the oath of allegiance to the Queen. The British military commander, Major Smith, at once dismissed the newly-elected legislature, and again called together the members of the old Volksraad; but they, also, refused to agree to the high-handed proceedings of the Administrator, who thereupon found it most convenient to do without the Volksraad altogether.

The Volksraad Abolished.

Zulus in large numbers were now swarming all over Natal, and more were coming from Panda's country. All these immigrants were great thieves, and so many complaints came from the Farmers in the outlying country districts, that the British officers, though still refusing to allow burgher commandoes to be formed for the purpose of repelling the Kaffir invasion, agreed that something should be done to render life and property again secure among the white population. Recourse was therefore had to the plan of forming Zulu Locations in different parts of Natal. Of course, this was a departure from the principle of civil equality for Black and White. The black man could no longer go and roam about where he liked. The policy of restricting and curtailing the Kaffir's range of free movement, when attempted by the Republic of Natal, had been so severely censured and condemned by the Cape Governor and the British Secretary of State in the name of the philanthropists of England, that its adoption by the officials as soon as Natal had become a British colony was, to say the least, very inconsistent. But that was a small matter.

Natal overrun by Zulu Refugees.

The Locations.

The way in which the Location system was worked and utilised to still further injure and ruin the Farmer was nothing less than scandalous. By the arbitrary edict as to the method of determining the ownership of farms a great part of the lands which the Africanders regarded as their lawful property already stood confiscated to the Crown, which had seized on the sovereignty of the country; and now the remaining farms, those with indisputable title-deeds according to the new English law, were made worthless to the owners by having many relatively small native Locations placed adjacent to them. Wedged in among the different Africander estates all over that part of the country where the Farmers had established themselves, these numerous Kaffir kraals and squatting grounds for marauders and robbers at once brought about such a reduction in the value of land, that the remedy was almost worse than the disease.

Ruin of the Farmers.

Even those among the Farmers, who, had they been fairly treated, would have been content to remain in Natal under British rule, now made up their minds to join the ranks of those who were looking for a new home and a new Republic on the other side of the Drakensberg range.

With nests of cattle-thieves constantly located on the frontiers of most of the grazing grounds, successful cattle-grazing and stock-farming became impossible. Away, then, from England's Government and from the Kaffirs. "Across the mountains: to liberty or death!"

The cause of the Republic in Natal was lost; but

those who had fallen in the struggle had not died in vain. The flag of the fathers would float over other lands; the spirit of nationality would not perish.

Once more through the mountain passes of the Drakensberg trudged the pilgrims—old and feeble men, young and stalwart burghers and yeomen, brave women, and little children. Westward lay their route.

At sunrise the women had wept when they looked back from the mountain slopes on that fair land where they had left their homes, and where so many of the loved ones lay buried. At eventide, by the camp fire, among the silent mountain peaks, they sang their hymns of hope, and trust, and faith in God. When the dark clouds and the mists rolled over the crags down the ravine, and the drenching showers descended in torrents, the old men pointed towards the rainbow in the western sky, and the children admired the bright colours;—red, white, blue, and green, they seemed.

The wanderers were often hungry, weary, and faint. The weakly and feeble ones among them, the little children, and some of the aged Voortrekkers, suffered much from the privations which they had to endure. The heat was at times excessive during the day, and the nights were bitterly cold among the mountains. Worn out with hardship, and toil, and battle, and sickness, and distress; their own beloved land, for which they had suffered and bled, in the grasp of that Power which they now regarded as the oppressor and the spoiler; homeless outcasts, in misery and poverty; with barren rocks and inhospitable crags around, and the wilds of the wilderness in front of them: the pilgrims did not yet lose heart.

The White Man's Republic was not dead.

The Cause was not lost.

There was a rainbow in the clouds.

Onward went the wanderers. Beyond the mountains, their countrymen awaited their coming.

Though Natal was lost, the flag of the Africander would still wave over the country north of the Orange river; and beyond the Vaal, onwards to the great Limpopo, the banner of the Voortrekkers would hold its own against fraud and force. The sons of those who had suffered and died for the cause of liberty would know how to defend the great heritage entrusted to their care by the martyrs of Weenen and Umkungunhlovu.

> "For Freedom's battle once begun,
> Bequeathed by bleeding Sire to Son,
> Though baffled oft, is ever won."

APPENDIX

APPENDIX

APPENDIX

ENGLAND'S NATIVE POLICY, PAST AND PRESENT, IN SOUTH AFRICA

EQUALITY FOR BLACK AND WHITE ON AFRICAN SOIL

Civil Equality for Black and White—British Rule—The Case of the Bushman—The Hottentot—Historical Review—Philanthropic Legislation—Effects—Barbarous Punishments—Extermination of the Hottentots—The Case of the Kaffir Nations—British Native Policy of To-day—Christianity and Civilisation in Mashonaland—The Mashona's Prayer—England's Armenia in Zambesia.

To such an extent was the policy of England in South Africa, in the early forties, guided and directed by the group of ill-informed philanthropists afterwards known as the Aborigines Protection Society, that what were presumed to be the interests of the Natives were everywhere placed first and foremost. It often happened that these imaginary interests clashed with those of the white community, but the wiseacres of Exeter Hall and Downing Street never wasted any sympathy on White people. To them Africa was, and had to remain, a Black man's country. The whites were there on sufferance, and had no such claim on official consideration as to be allowed to resort to measures for their own defence and protection by territorial rearrangement or alteration of boundary lines, to safeguard the frontier settlements from being swamped and destroyed by the hordes of savagery. The Glenelg Despatch, and numerous other

State papers, are there to prove that this is no exaggerated statement.

In the British Isles, it has taken centuries of constitutional struggle and of reform to bring about such changes as Catholic Emancipation and parliamentary representation for the Jewish race. Even at the present day, there is no such thing as complete civil equality in England; for the eldest son of the nobleman is born to the privileges of a legislator, whether he has the qualifications for the position or not. But in England the political situation is simplicity itself to what it is in a country where there are different races in occupation of the soil. Is the Africander unjust in his criticism, or does he want to know too much, when he asks what length of time it took the English conquerors to grant complete civil equality to Ireland, where even now, in these glorious Jubilee days of Imperialism, the condition of thousands of the unfortunate inhabitants is infinitely worse than that of many Kaffir tribes who are supposed to be groaning under "Boer" tyranny?

In South Africa, with its complex problems of different races and distinct nationalities, English statesmen and English writers have ever presumed to apply a different criterion to that which, judging from the history of Europe, one might suppose to be a just and a fair one; and so in Natal, as in the Cape Colony, the idea of civil equality of Black and White was insisted on by the British authorities.

Civil Equality for Black and White.

Now, the Oriental element in the nature of the Kaffir renders him quite unable to understand this

APPENDIX

principle of equality without, at the same time, doing violence to our commonly accepted ideas of right and wrong. Among barbarous warrior nations such acts of robbery and theft as, *e.g.*, cattle-lifting, are looked upon as accomplishments, and not as crimes. Fear of punishment by some power able to inflict it becomes the only restraining influence at work to prevent these enterprises. To the Kaffir all power and authority is centred in the Chief; and every White man is a Chief in the eyes of the savage. But where he himself is placed on an equality with White men, there is to his mind an end to all authority and all power, and then he no longer fears punishment. The result is that the white settler and colonist is harassed and annoyed, and that life is made intolerable to him by lawless vagrants and robbers, who prevent all progress and banish all prosperity from the community. This was the history of Natal from the time when it became a British possession until the English Colonists set them- *British Rule.* selves to undo—and to some extent succeeded in undoing—the evils which stupid and ill-advised legislation by the Home Government had created for them. The case of the ruined and depopulated eastern districts of the Cape Colony has been fully referred to in previous pages as another glaring example of the harm that had been done to South Africa by British rule. To the White man that rule meant the ignoring of his rights, the denial of his claims to justice and fair treatment. Did it really protect the true interests of the Natives? Were the philanthropists of England able to show, as the result of their policy, that they had done some actual good to the natives whom they affected to serve, to benefit, and to protect? It is quite certain that those whose party then formed the Government of England had, before 1844, done some of the aborigines of South Africa much injury, and caused them much suffering.

Now, to prove this assertion by putting before the reader some absolutely undisputed facts in the history of two out of the three great groups of native races in the country. Let us consider what happened to the Bushmen and to the Hottentots during the first half century of the British "*Paramountcy.*"

The power of the missionary philanthropist-politician of those days was similar to that of the financier Empire-extender of to-day. In territories even beyond the dominions of the British Crown—in lands where England had *no claim whatever* to exercise any authority or any rights of government, the missionary could arrange with the chiefs for the carrying out of whatever political programmes he had in view.

North of the Orange river, before the Emigrant Farmers came there, the plains had been inhabited by the Bushman nation. The name Philippolis still commemorates the sweeping results of one of the schemes of that great Apostle of the Philanthropists, the Rev. Dr. J. Philip. The region surrounding the town (which was then a mission station) was, in 1826 (*see* p. 181, vol. i.), given by him to the Griqua chief Adam Kok. The Griquas were half-breed Hottentots, and Dr. Philip had a theory that the Bushmen were Hottentots who had become stunted in growth, deteriorated in physique, impoverished as regards worldly goods, and savage in habits, through ill-treatment by white people!! So the Griquas were placed at Philippolis to shield and protect the Bushmen. The result was the almost complete extermination and extinction of the latter. On Sundays Adam Kok and his robber clan sang hymns and psalms at the mission station; and inflated their souls with self-righteousness and their stomachs with the vile brandy supplied by itinerant representatives of the Cape Town and Port Elizabeth merchants, who likewise supplied them with guns and ammunition. On week days, the guns were loaded. The unfortunate Bushmen found on the plains were shot down without mercy. Others were dragged out of their hiding-places, and—bound, hand and foot— had their throats cut like sheep, or were roasted alive over slow fires.*

The murderers knew that their captain had had presented to him from London and Cape Town (under the government of Lord Charles Somerset) a large coin-medal, with an engraving and an inscription on it—the former representing a Farmer-

The Case of the Bushman.

---

* "It was hoped that the Griquas would protect the Bushmen of this missionary station, but soon after the settlement there was not a single Bushman to be found. They were chased and shot down like wild animals by the tribe of Kok, and their lands and water fountains were taken possession of by the Griquas. . . . In 1830, it was proved before Mr Melvill (representative of the Colonial Government) that these same Griquas exterminated two large Bushman kraals, and that these massacres were characterised by an unparalleled degree of inhuman cruelty." (Sir Andries Stockenstrom: *Report on the State of the Griquas*, September, 1839. Dutch text in Hofstede's "Geschiedenis van den Oranje Vrijstaat.")

George-like individual shaking hands with a naked Hottentot (or, to speak more accurately, a savage with bare legs, and with a skin kaross thrown over his shoulders), and the inscription running: "We are all brothers." (*See* plate in Dr. Matthews' "Ingwadi Yami.") As they had been thus officially declared to be the equals and brothers of the white men, Adam Kok and his people presumably intended to signalise their attainment to equality, and to express their sense of security from punishment by a higher authority. The ferocious deeds referred to were the result. The London Missionary Society and its agents knew of the massacres, for the facts were proved by official declarations and reports. They did nothing whatever to put a stop to the outrages—to this deliberate extinction of the remnants of a nation. The abused, reviled, and calumniated Africander-farmer—the despised "Boer"—when he appeared on the scene, stayed the blood-stained hand of the murderer, and saved the remnant of the Bushman race from further persecution and destruction. And what thanks did he get from humane and justice-loving England for his work of mercy?

Her missionary and philanthropic societies carried on the campaign against him with more virulence than ever. Writers, who either knew nothing whatever about the subject, or who were guilty of deliberate and intentional untruth, informed the European public that the "Boers," and not the Griqua protégés of the London Missionary Society, had massacred the Bushmen.

APPENDIX

To crown all, the Government of England itself, at a later date (in 1845)—after having actually entered into a treaty with the chief of the robber gang of Griquas, agreeing to pay him a subsidy of £100 a year and to supply him with arms and ammunition—openly took the side of the savages and murderers against the Emigrant-Farmers, and marched troops into the country to uphold the authority of the son and namesake of that precious scoundrel and ruffian—the exterminator of the Bushmen—Adam Kok.

So much for what the British philanthropists did for the Bushmen.

Let us next consider the case of the Hottentot. Did the doctrine of civil equality for Black and White—as insisted on by the British Government, and as finally placed on the statute book in that much-vaunted so-called South African Magna Charta, the 50th Ordinance of 1828—do him much good? Has he been improved, benefited, and protected? *The Hottentot.*

In 1823, the total population of the Cape Colony was somewhat over 110,000. Of those, some 30,000, or thereabouts, were Hottentots. These received more than the regulation doses of missionary teaching. They were taught to spell (and in some cases the teachers succeeded in getting them to read), to write, sing hymns, etc. They looked upon all these accomplishments as marks of a superior civilisation, certainly; but they would seldom set themselves to any task that required continued effort or perseverance, unless they were constantly supervised and watched. True children of the Sun, they had an inexhaustible *Historical Review.*

Philanthropic Legislation.

fund of droll humour ever at command, hated looking at the serious side of things, and yet were often seen with an extremely sad expression on their countenances. The fact is, most of them were in their proper senses only for occasional brief intervals. They were nearly always under the influence of strong drink, the sale of which the Government did not sufficiently restrict. Conscious of their own degradation and debasement, they laughed at the very idea of any of their nation being able to exist without being under authority and under restraint,—not to mention being considered the equals of white men. They were all supposed to be Christians. A law had been passed, therefore, by which all chieftainship among them was abolished, and they were all placed under direct European rule. At the same time, a vagrancy law was put in force, to prevent them from wandering about and getting into too much mischief. This was in 1809, during the administration of the Earl of Caledon (*see* p. 109, vol. i.) In 1812, Sir John Cradock introduced a law providing for the apprenticing of Hottentot children. These enactments had a salutary effect in arresting and preventing the further debasement and destruction of the race. But the English philanthropists raised such an outcry against the "veiled slavery" and the "cruelty" which they pretended to see in such measures, that the laws were all repealed, in 1828, by the publication of what became known as the 50th Ordinance, which stipulated that Hottentots and other free natives should no longer require passes and be subject to the provisions of the Vagrancy Act; that

Hottentot children could not be apprenticed for service; and that all the Hottentot tribes, who were now subject to European laws, should be placed politically on an equality with the white people.

As regards its effects on a nation situated as the Hottentots then were, no more cruel — no more unjust—law than this could have been devised. The most accursed despotism could have invented no more ingenious measure for destroying the helpless and the weak than this very 50th Ordinance—the crowning achievement of the philanthropists. The Hottentots were savages who had become acquainted with European vices before being placed under European laws. The vices, especially that of drunkenness, had completely overmastered their weak natures — had already, in effect, become part of their natures. Plainly, the law as ordinarily applied was not enough for their case. To allow them to go about unrestrained, unwatched, and unchecked by any additional safeguard other than the reserve force of the ordinary machinery of the law when set in motion—which reserve force could only act by way of punishment, and not as prophylactic—was not merely unfair: it was barbarous. It was like permitting the maniac or the confirmed white drunkard to go about without restraint, and then punishing him when he transgressed the law. *[margin: Effects. Barbarous Punishments.]*

The Earl of Caledon's and Sir John Cradock's laws were wise, humane, and beneficial enactments for protecting the Hottentots against themselves. Those laws did more good to the unfortunate people than all the mission stations and psalm-singing institutions put together; and undoubtedly they should have been strengthened instead of abolished. But the silly philanthropists and Boer-haters thought otherwise; and, as they alone had the ear of the Government of England, the unfortunate Hottentots were doomed to destruction.

There were, as stated, some 30,000 Hottentots left in the Cape Colony in 1823. It was in 1828 that the so-called 50th Ordinance became law. Were these people benefited in any way by the Government of England as manifested in philanthropic legislation? From the official point of view, they were now the equals of the white people. They could go where they liked, without let or hindrance. They were not obliged to work. They could at all times choose their own masters, and suit their own tastes. They did. To them Christianity and civilisation meant drinking Cape brandy until they became besotted, sleeping off the fumes, and then recuperating themselves at the nearest mission station by hymn-singing and sheep-stealing. Punishment would follow—sometimes, when the delinquents were caught, which was often not an easy matter. Occasionally it was noticed that the culprits rather liked the punishment—imprisonment—and would commit some crime, with apparently no other object in view than that they might be locked up in gaol. This statement may seem hardly credible, but is, nevertheless, absolutely correct. The reason commonly given in explanation of this strange taste is that they found themselves fairly well housed and fed in the prisons. But the prisons of the Cape Colony have the reputation of being by no means oriental palaces of delight and luxury, even at the present day.

Is it not just as likely that the vagrant Hottentots were attacked by these occasional fits of what has somewhat facetiously been termed *nostalgia*, because there dwelt in their own minds the inward conviction that restraint was good for them, and that they ought to be protected against their own weakness?

But, the *philanthropic* British Government was not consistent in its action and in the carrying out of the details of its so-called *humane* policy. Had it been so, it would not have resorted as frequently as it did to the punishment of flogging in its prisons in the Cape Colony. Had the crime-preventive measures, which were recommended and brought into enactment by the two able and experienced administrators mentioned, been kept in force, amplified, and strengthened, instead of abolished, then the floggings would not have been necessary quite as often. But when there were no longer any legislative restrictions on vagrancy and laziness; when Government and law were no longer doing their duty in supervising, guarding, and safeguarding the best interests of the weak-minded, more than half-demented, dying nation; when the free sale of vile, poisonous spirit by canteens and traders was allowed to go on unchecked, for the mere sake of the revenue which this nefarious traffic brought in: then punishments and penalties became more frequent, because there was more crime. In spite of evidence to the contrary all over the world, the British Government in South Africa had assumed and taken it for granted that what was in reality an inferior race could be sufficiently protected and shielded from complete deterioration—and from extinction—by merely the ordinary application of the law. It obstinately refused to believe that in the struggle for existence between nations and races, as between individuals, the weakest goes to the wall; it had further been guilty of neglecting its duty as a Government, in refusing to protect the weak race; it had failed or refused to see that civil equality for such a race meant destruction. Only the vices of civilisation were attractive to the savages. As crime increased among them, and imprisonment was found not to be a sufficient deterrent, the penalty of flogging came to be resorted to more and more frequently. The philanthropists failed to perceive that they were acting barbarously as well as unjustly. They were punishing the irresponsible; for, under the circumstances, and largely owing to the action of the same British rulers who were posing before the world as a most humane and a most just Government, the Hottentot could not be otherwise than a criminal. There was nothing left in the law of the land to make him apply himself to industry and work; to keep him from laziness, vagrancy, and evil; to save him from utter ruin, body and soul. While the Government had either wilfully or carelessly ignored the palpable fact that it would still take, perhaps, some centuries before this nation could—by education suited to their wants, and by constant supervision and restraint from evil—be brought to such a level of intelligence as to benefit at all from civil liberties, the missionaries, taken as a body, were absolutely doing harm instead of good among the Hottentots. Let us say—the missionaries, taken as a body; for there were honourable and notable exceptions. First and foremost among these, the *Moravian Brothers* must be mentioned. They taught the natives thrift and industry. They did not encourage the equality idea. On the contrary, they made it part of their system of teaching to send the Hottentots out for service among the farmers; and they insisted on obedience and orderly conduct in and around their mission station at Genadendal, among the Baviaanskloof mountains to the south of Worcester. They had authority to "expel unruly persons from the place, and maintained strict discipline among the Hottentots; but it was the kind of discipline that parents enforce upon children, tempered by love and interest in their welfare" (THEAL).

[margin: Extermination of the Hottentots.]

Had the rulers of the land been half as intelligent and sensible as these humble German missionaries, then civilisation and Christianity would have been a blessing, and not a curse—as, if we have any regard for historical truth, we must admit that they were—to the Hottentots.

The agents of the London Society, and most of the other missionaries in South Africa, continued, as they had done previous to 1828, to emphasise the civil equality of Black and White men, and spent more of their time in preaching politics and reviling the

Africander farmer, than in teaching what was really useful to the native. The Gospel, according to the Rev. Dr. John Philip, signified a gospel of strife, in place of a message of peace and good-will. The Hottentots were encouraged to live in laziness and idleness, many of the missionaries maintaining that, in order that their teaching might have effect, it was necessary for them not only to place themselves on an equality with their pupils and congregations, but actually to live in the same way as the savages. Some of them, therefore, married Hottentot women. Others lived in Hottentot huts, and adopted Hottentot clothing—such as it was, and what there was of it.

No wonder that the natives began to entertain the idea that many of the missionaries were fools; and, in truth, the natives were not so far wrong. It is even probable that some of the political "gospel-bosses" were knaves as well as fools. Says Cloete, who—as British Commissioner entrusted with the task of forcing on the Africanders in Natal the acceptance of this very principle of civil equality for Black and White now under consideration—was well qualified to speak impartially :—

"Appearing as I do for the sacred cause of truth, my duty compels me to say that in the period with which I am now dealing there were among those who arrogated to themselves the responsible position of teachers in the mission schools within the Colony several persons so illiterate, and so possessed by narrow-minded prejudice, that they were quite unsuited for the task of educating and training the

Hottentot youth of both sexes; while there were even some among them who, by their dishonourable intercourse with women of that race, had forfeited all that respect to which a good moral character can always lay claim." (" *Three Lectures on the Emigration of the Dutch Farmers,*" as translated in Stuart's " *Hollandsche Afrikanen.*")

In some of these so-called schools, the missionaries had themselves established what they were pleased to designate Courts of Justice. Here the Hottentots accused of any transgression were tried, and punishments of various degrees of severity were inflicted. Thus, within the Colony, the missionaries arrogated to themselves the functions of government. Beyond its boundaries they—with the sanction and under the patronage of Government—were disposing of large areas of territory (which were not theirs either to retain or to give away), and deciding the fate and the destiny of native races;—as if South Africa, with its Bushmen, and Hottentots, and Kaffirs, and white inhabitants, had been created by God Almighty for the express purpose of allowing the London Missionary Society and Downing Street to carry on political experiments at race extermination, which they, in their misguided zeal, deemed necessary to secure peace and tranquillity in the land.

What has become of the thirty thousand Hottentots who were in existence before the 50th Ordinance came into force as law? From what has been already said on the subject of the alteration in the law as to vagrancy, and on that of the prevalence of drunkenness and crime among them, the answer can be readily obtained. They have been improved—off the face of the earth. To-day there are only a few individuals of unmixed Hottentot blood to be met with here and there throughout all Cape Colony. The nation is in effect extinct. British Government—the 50th Ordinance, aided by the missionaries and by Cape brandy—has done this work of destruction.

At the period with which this narrative deals, British policy towards the native races in South Africa was shaped and outlined by the missionaries and the philanthropic societies in England, and British rule meant the application of missionary and philanthropic schemes and theories to the problems with which administrators and nominated legislators had to deal. The result has been seen in the case of the Bushman and Hottentot nations. As to the various divisions of the Abantu or Kaffir race, only one section of the Amakosa nation was under British rule in 1843. The rest of Kaffirland Proper or Amakosaland, was independent and unconquered by either British bayonets or missionaries. Pondoland, Basutoland, Zululand, Bechuanaland, Matabeleland, Mashonaland, and other Kaffir countries were to receive the benefits of British rule at a much later date, when, towards the century's close, the strong pro-consuls and the empire-extending financiers were to join hands; when the map of Africa was to be painted red and dotted over with battlefields; when the useless mask of sham philanthropy was to be cast aside. Then, after a sham investigation by an Imperial Commissioner, who subsequently confessed to

The Case of the Kaffir Nations.

not always being in the habit of speaking the whole truth, the seal of British official approval was to be set —on a system of spoliation and slaughter of the natives more ruthless and cruel than that practised by Cortez in Mexico and by Pizarro in Peru—on a mode of warfare characterised by atrocities as barbarous as those which disgrace the annals of the gold-seeking Conquistadores of the Sixteenth century.

Time has indeed wrought strange transmutations in the course of British native policy in South Africa since 1843. The same Power which then prided itself on championing the cause of civil equality for the Kaffir has, in the numerous wars undertaken for the extension and enlargement of its dominions, butchered and shot down so many thousands of all the Kaffir nations—Kosas, Fingoes, Galekas, Zulus, Basutos, Matabele, Mashonas, and Bechuanas—that the survivors may well look upon its Government as an exterminator, not as a protector. The beautiful theory of civil equality on African soil offers but small consolation and comfort to the brave Zulu or Matabele warrior whose comrades and whose chiefs now lie under that soil, whose lands and whose cattle have been taken, and who finds himself reduced to serfdom and forced against his will (by the representatives of that very Power which still boasts of having abolished slavery even in Zanzibar) to dig and burrow in the earth—in a fruitless search for that extremely fabulous gold of Ophir and Sheba, which the Dukes and Princes in London fondly imagine some day to obtain as a reward for their enterprise and patriotism.

When the English merchants and army-contractors of Cape Town and Port Elizabeth magnify their own political importance by arrogating to themselves the *rôle* of representatives of South African public opinion, they love to sing the praises of the "flag that braved a thousand years, the battle and the breeze," and make pathetic allusions to the noble figure of Britannia leaning on her shield, and, armed with the classic trident, making "freemen of slaves."

At these Imperialist glorification meetings one still sometimes hears a great deal of all the benefits conferred on the natives by that humane and enlightened Government, whose name is synonymous with justice, and mercy, and freedom;—of the affectionate regard which the Kaffirs show for the British flag.

Let the Mashona make answer in his own words in reply to this pious fiction of the modern Conquistador.

Driven to bay amid the rocks and mountains of his native country, where the official declarations and proclamations say there is peace, he is alone with the dead—with the mangled remains of his women and children, and of his comrades in arms, whose cave-shelters have been blown up, and whose bodies have been shattered by the dynamite charges of the civilising Paramount Power. In yonder cavern, further up the mountain side, his chief, with a small band of warriors, made a last stand against the forces of the white men, surrendered on condition that his life should be spared, and was handcuffed to be led out to die—to be shot by the order of a British officer.*

* *See* the accounts of the death of the Mashona chief, Makoni, in 1896.

APPENDIX

Where is that land? Is it Cuba? Is it Armenia?

To the throne of Heaven have ascended the groans of the wounded and the dying black men who have fallen in defending their country. The relatives of the murdered white people—of the men and women who were shot by means of the weapons which had been put in the hands of the savages by Government itself—are still calling aloud for that full investigation and that impartial enquiry which has been promised. They are calling in vain for justice. The high and mighty in the distant land across the sea are accomplices in the national crime. "Territory is everything."

Yes; there is equality now. Equality on the soil of Africa.

The bones are all bleached white on the African veld—the bones of the black and white victims of the cupidity and greed of a cattle-annexing* association of financiers and speculators, ruled and directed by a Privy Councillor of the British Crown.

Does the widowed mother; do the sorrow-stricken parents whose sons—deceived and sent to slaughter by the Mammon Colossus—now lie in those nameless graves of Doornkop; do the white bleached bones on the hillsides of Matabele- and Mashona-land; do the victims of the Moloch of Modern Imperialism; do they all now appeal in vain to Heaven for retribution?

Hark! The bells are tolling their warning in the great echoing belfry of the temple of History. Is it only a warning? Or are they sounding the death-knell of an Empire?

* *See* Sir Richard Martin's Official Report.

INDEX TO VOL. II

INDEX

A BLOW for freedom, 209
Aborigines benefited by Emigrants, 169 ; true friends and protectors of, 204
Africander aspirations, 17
,, Balboa, the, 15
,, Farmers, ruin of, 281
,, women, notable, 59, 130, 272
,, Samaritans, 234
Annexation of Natal refused, 5, 72, 121 ; enforced, 277
Apprenticeship laws condemned by British Government, 184 ; adopted by British, 185
Armed demonstration by Emigrants, 265 ; objects of, 266
Association of South African Emigrants, 71; proclamation at Bay of Natal, 136 ; sovereignty of Zululand, 155

BACAS, the, 179
Badenhorst, Commandant, 131
Bantjes, J. G., diary of, 89
Barends, Gert, 56
Basson, W., massacred, 46-7
Battles of Bloed River, 97, 101 ; Bushman's River, 53 ; Congella, 224 ; Durban Bay, 247 ; Italeni, 62 ; White Umveloosi, 110
Batts, H., 68
Bay of Natal, 5 ; Volksraad proclamation at, 135
Bechuanaland, Southern, annexed, 28
Beer, de, 35 ; massacred, 46
Beer, de A., assists Van Rensburg, 53
Bergs, Van den, massacred, 53
Bester, Barend, killed, 114
Bezuidenhout's laager attacked, 51 ; massacre at, 52 ; Daniel escapes, 53
Biggar, Alexander, 60, 88 ; death of, 114

Biggar, Robert, 67 ; killed, 68
Blanckenberg, C., 68
Blauwkrans River massacres, 52
Bloed River, battle of, 97, 101
Bodenstein, C., 265
Boshoff, J. N., 71 ; accusation against England, 188 ; subscribes terms of capitulation of Natal, 255
Bottomley, W., 68
Bothas, the, 35 ; massacre of, 46, 52
Bothma, Stefanus, 243
Bothmas, the, 35 ; massacre of, 46, 52
Brazilië, the, 204, 263
Breda, S. van, 142, 236 ; proscribed, 266 ; pardoned, 279
Breda, Michiel, 236 ; proscribed, 256 ; death of, 279
British Emigrants at the Bay of Natal, 5
British Immigration Scheme, 134 ; Volksraad proclamation against, 135
British Government refuse to annex Natal, 5 ; annex Natal, 277
Burger, J. J., Secretary to Natal Volksraad, 182 ; correspondence with Governor Napier, 183, 202 ; proscribed, 256 ; escape over the Drakensberg, 278
Bushman's River laagers attacked, 53

CAMPAIGN of the Mariqua, the, 27
Campbell, T., 68
,, J., 68
Cane, John, 19 ; accused of treachery, 40 ; attacks Dingaan, 65 ; killed, 86
Cape Colony, condition of, in 1840, 166
Cape Town merchants, jealousy of, 173 ; in alliance with British, 175 ; some grievances of, 176 ; Sancho Panzas, 177 ; malignant hatred of Emigrants, 228

INDEX

Carden, T., 68
Charters, Major, 40; seizes Port Natal, 124; evidence of, 130
Chlooma Amaboota massacre, 46; avenged, 104; deed of cession to Association of S. A. Emigrants discovered at, 106
Cilliers, Pieter, with Retief, 35; massacred, 46
Cilliers, Sarel, in Potgieter's campaign, 26; at defence of Maritz's laager, rescues Gert Barends' laager, 56; restrained by Pretorius, 95; at Bloed River battle, 99; White Umveloosi, 104
Cloete, H., British Commissioner, 264; obtains submission of Natal Volksraad, 269; annexation, 277; treaty with Panda, 277
Cloete, Lieut.-Col., 242; attack on Durban, 248; relieves Capt. Smith, 250; employs Kaffir marauders, 251
Combezana the spy, 134, 145; tried and shot, 149
Comet, the, English settlers retreat to, 68
Conch, the, 247
Congella, Pretorius at, 214; night attack on, 224; rout of British, 227; casualties, 230; capture of British stores, 235; capture of British ships, 236
Cowie, W., 131, 236
Crown lands of Natal, how obtained, 274

DANCE OF DEATH at Umkungunhlovu, 44
Davel, Jacobus, sen., 319, 321
De Beer's Pass, the, 32
Dekker, Klaas, 243
De Klerks, the, 35; massacred, 46
Delegorgue, A., 142
Delport, J. P., Commandant, 265
Dingaan, chief, 4; cession of territory to Retief, 22, 43; his telegraph service, 38; a message from the Cape, 40; his character, 41; treachery, 43; massacre of Retief's party, 46; attacks laagers on Bushman's, Mooi, and Blauwkrans Rivers, 49; repulsed by Maritz, 59; defeated by Pretorius, 102; stronghold destroyed, 114; agrees to terms of peace, 133; again prepares for war, 138; flight and death, 139, etc.
Drakensbergen, the, crossed by Retief, 7, 28; by Emigrant Farmers, 32, 282
D'Urban, Sir B., 5
Durban Bay, battle of, 247; Emigrant forces at, 245, 246
Durban township established, 129; British encampment near, 216

EMIGRANT Farmers at Winburg, 1; move eastward, 7; on the Klip, Bushman's, Mooi, Buffalo, and Tugela Rivers, 36; on the Upper Umgeni and Umkomanzi Rivers, 36; attacked by Dingaan, 49; *diagram* of laagers, 50; the Win Commando, 86; the vow to God, 91; victory, 118; stores, etc., seized by British, 125; poverty, 129; Major Charters' evidence, 130; again across the mountains, 273, 282
Empire-extenders, 177, 182, 210, 260, 264
English and Cape Town adventurers in Natal, 4; at Durban, 18
Erasmus Commandant, S., 86, 88
,, Louw, 247

FAKU, chief, 179; and missionaries, 181; and Governor Sir G. Napier, 184
Federal United South African Republic, 273
Fourie, Commandant, 142

GARDINER, Capt., 5; mission-station at Berea, 6
Garner, Wm., 181
Gelato mountain, 94
Glenelg Despatch, a, 5; Cape Punishment Bill, 6; despatch, 72, 128
Goossen, M., killed, 114
Greyling, A. C., with Retief's trek, 7, 35; witness to Dingaan's cession of territory, 43; massacred, 46
Greyling, Commandant, 265
,, Johannes, 232
,, Pieter, 230
Grondwet of Winburg, 23

HALSTEAD, Thos., and Retief, 19; at Umkungunhlovu, 44; massacred, 45

INDEX

Ham, Rev. Mr., 263
,, Mrs., death of, 263
Hatting, Christiaan's letter, 89
Hattingh, 243; killed, 244
Helen, the, 124
Huguenot Ironside, the, 55
INCHANGA, mountain, 15
Indian Ocean, view of, 15
Italeni, position of, 50; battle of, 62, 63; Emigrants killed at, 64, 65

JACOBS, P., 1
,, P. D., 87
,, J. H., 87
Jameson Raid, the, 124; Napier-Jenkins-Faku-Smith, 176; Capt. Smith's, 205
Jenkins, missionary, 179; Sir G. Napier's messenger, 180; mission, 181, 203
Jervis, Capt., 128; fails to exert judicial authority, 129; negotiates with Dingaan, 130; Earl of Normanby's despatch, 135; recalled, 136
Joob, chief, 143
Joubert, —, at Doornkop laager, 55
,, Gideon, 69; mission to Natal, 70
,, Pieter, sen., 215; on guard at Durban Bay, 219, 221; fish in uniform, 222
Julavusa, chief, signs deed of cession of territory, 43

KAFFIR telegraph service, 88, 39
Kalipi, chief, 21
Kalahari desert, the, 160
Kemp, G., 142
King, —, and the Kaffirs, 251
King, Richard, 41; famous ride of, 242
Klopper, —, killed, 239
Kock, Jan, Commandant, 265
Koekemoer, J., 243
Krause, Dr., 142
Kruger, Paul, and the Cape Colonists, 176

LAAGERS on Klip, Bushman's, Mooi, Buffalo, Tugela, Upper Umgeni, and Umkomanzi Rivers, 36
Labuschagne, —, with Retief, 35; massacred, 46

Lalazi River, 19
Landdrost of Natal, 71
Landman, Jan, 243
,, Carel P., 68, 69; occupies Port Natal, 71; acting commandant, 78; ambuscaded, 107
Lange, J. (Hans) de, 88
,, saves the Commando, 109; guards the frontier, 141
Leonard, Chas., 176
Liebenberg, R., with Retief, 7, 35; witness to Dingaan's deed of cession, 43; massacred, 45
Lindley, Rev. D., 164
Lingen, Rev. G. W. A. van der, 89
Locations, Native, proposed by Emigrants, 185; condemned by British, 187; adopted by British, 280
Loggenbergs' laager, massacre at, 53
Lombaard, H. J., signs proclamation, 156
Lovedale, R., 68

MAKWANA, chief, Emigrants purchase territory from, 3
Malans, the, with Retief's trek, 35; massacred, 46; at Doornkop laager, 55
Malan, D., killed at Italeni, 65
,, Jac., *ibid*
,, Jan, *ibid*
Manondo, chief, signs deed of cession, 43
Maoro, chief, *ibid*
Marais, the, with Retief's trek, 35; massacred, 46
Marais, —, killed, 239
Marico, the, description of, 26
,, Poort, 25
,, River, 25
Maritz, G. M., at Winburg, 1; character of, 33; laager attacked, 55; repulse of Zulus, 59; illness, 74; death, 81
Martineau, Mr., 263
Mary, the, 124
Massacre at Umkungunhlovu, 46; names of victims, 47, 48
Massacre on the Mooi, Bushman's, and Blauwkrans Rivers, 50
Matabele defeated by Potgieter and Uys, 28

INDEX

Matabeleland annexed by Voortrekkers, 28
Matawaan, chief, 143
Matchawe, chief, 24
Mawa, chieftainess, 261; hordes terrorise Natal, 267
Merwe, C. v. d., 213
 ,, J. C. v. d., 52
Meyers, the, with Retief's trek, 35; massacred, 46
Meyer, Jan, 142
 ,, Nicolaas, sen., 231
Missionary, the, a power, 177; in Pondo country, 179; — and Faku, 181; — and Africander Farmers, 260
Mocke, Commandant, 265; demands a new Volksraad, 268
Molesworth, Lieut., 243
Mongala, chief, 24
Moordkraal, 51
Moroko, chief, in alliance with Retief, 2
Morwood, Mr., 142
Mosega campaign renewed, 24
Moshesh, chief, in alliance with Retief, 2

NAPIER, Major-General, 72, 73; attempt to seize Natal, 120, 128; plot and plan, 174; correspondence with Volksraad, 183, 186; Proclamation, 2nd December 1841, 187
Napier Charters Raid, the, 120
Napier-Jenkins-Faku-Smith Jameson Raid, 176, 184
Natal, British Government refuse to annex, 4; Retief's first view of, 9; abandoned by Potgieter, 66; Republic of, 162; Volksraad, 163; sovereignty of Zululand, 155; federation with Winburg, 165; extent of federated Republic, 166; proposed treaty with England, 183; Volksraad despatch, 186; accusation against England, 189; British troops ordered to seize Durban, 205; attempted treaty with Holland, 208; Pretorius surprised, 213; Potgieter refuses to assist, 241; the last stand, 245; annexation, 253
Natal Crown lands, how obtained, 274
Natalian flora and fauna, 12
Naude, J., 53

Ncapayi, chief, 179; depredations of, 180; expedition against, 181
Nels, the, killed at Italeni, 65
Nel, P., 232
Niekerk, J. v., 131
Nongalaza, chief, 111; defeats Dingaan, 147

OGLE, Henry, 41, 176; spy, 188; marauding expeditions, 259
Ohrig and Klijn, Messrs., 205
Olifants, Hoek, 68
Oliphant, Attorney-General, 73
Oosthuizen, Jan, killed, 114
 ,, with Retief's trek, 7, 35, 43, 46
 ,, Marthinus, 53, 54, 66
 ,, Theunis, murdered, 251
 ,, ,, son of, *ibid*
"Onze Groote God zeggen wij toen Dank," 126
"Ou Grietjie," 86
Owen, Rev., missionary, 22; drafts deed of cession for Dingaan, 42

PALMER, SAMUEL, 181
Panda, chief, 139; conspires against Dingaan, 140; alliance with Voortrekkers, 141; proclaimed King of Zululand under Republic of Natal, 151; cedes territory to England, 277
Parker, Mr., 92
 ,, John, 40
Philip, Rev. Dr., 179
Phillips, Lionel, 180, 210
Pietermaritzburg, encampment at, 68, 127; township established, 129; Volksraad and Panda, 142
Pieter Mauritsburg, see above
Plot and Plan, 120, 174, 176, 254
Pondoland, 178
Pondos, the, 178
Port Natal, see Natal
Potgieter, Andries Hendrik, at Winburg, 1; quarrel with Maritz, 3; campaign against Umsiligaas renewed, 24; march against Dingaan, 60; battle of Italeni, 63; retires north of Vaal, 65; abandons Natal, 66; agreement with Pretorius, 165; refuses aid to Natal, 241
Potgieter, Jacobus, 74, 89; signs proclamation, 156

INDEX

Potchefstroom district, 28 ; foundation of, 76 ; Republic, 159 ; old district boundaries, 160
Pretorius, Andries, W. J., founder of South African Republic,78; ancestors, 79; military career, 80 ; appointed Commandant-General, 85 ; address to army, 89 ; battle of Blood River, 98 ; wounded, 103 ; attacks Umkungunhlovu, 104 ; victory, 118 ; Mooi Valley laager, 131 ; correspondence with British, 135 ; invades Zululand, 139 ; forces in the field, 143 ; proclaims Zululand subject state under Natal Republic, 155 ; agreement with Potgieter, 165 ; attacked by British, 214 ; Congella laager, 214 ; forces, 216 ; rout of British, 227 ; Potgieter's supineness, 241 ; Battle of Durban Bay, 247 ; retreat, 250 ; surrender, 255 ; proscribed, 256 ; proscription cancelled, 257 ; resignation, 257
Pretorius, Bart, 88 ; at Blood River, 98 ; at Congella, 225
Prinsloo, Joachim, 74 ; President of Volksraad of Natal Republic, 202 ; proscribed, 256 ; death, 278
Prinsloos, massacre of, 52

REENEN's Pass, Van, 29
Rensburg's laager on the Bushman's River, 50 ; a fight for life, 53
Republic of Natal, *see* Natal
Republic of Winburg, 159, 161 ; Volksraad, 162 ; armed demonstration, 265
Republic of Natal and Winburg, federated, *see* Natal
Republic across the Drakensberg, 273
Retief, Pieter M., at Winburg, 1 ; mission to Natal, 3, 7 ; welcomed at Durban, 18 ; at Umkungunhlovu, 19 ; at Matawaan's Kop, 32 ; again at Umkungunhlovu, 34 ; restores Dingaan's cattle, 42 ; receives cession of territory, 43 ; massacred, 46 ; the cold sentinels on Chlooma Amaboota, 47
Reus, Captain of the *Brazilië*, 205
Rhenoster Poort, 28
Rhodesian Empire-extenders, 177
Roos, F., 142

Roscher, J. P., 182
Rooyen, D. v., murdered, 251
Roux, N. le, killed, 114
Rubramania, South African, a check to, 136
Rudolph, Gert, 226 ; elected Commandant-General, 258
Rudolph, Jan, 103
Knigte Spruit, the, 62
Russell, R., 68

SALELA, chief, 21, 34 ; attacks the Emigrants, 49 ; at Blood River, 102 ; defeated by Nongalaza, 147
Sapusa, chief, defeats Dingaan, 141
Schalkwyk, C. v., murdered, 251
Scheepers, M., 156
Schutte, T., 232
Sermon on the Rock, the, 153
Shepstone, Theophilus, 124 ; Sir Theophilus, 210
Sikonyella, chief, 2, 22, 34
Slachtersnek names at Umkungunhlovu, 35
Smellenkamp at Pietermaritzburg, 205 ; his treaty of commerce, 207 ; arrested, 208 ; again appears, 262
Smith Raid, the, 174 ; Capt. Smith's force, 184 ; Capt. Lonsdale's force 187 ; the march from Faku's kraal, 209 ; advance towards Durban, 212 ; encampment near Berea, 214 ; the night attack, 218 ; routed at Congella, 227 ; Dick King's ride, 235 ; Capt. Smith's appeal to Zulus, 241 ; relieved by Cloete, 250 ; promotion, 258
Smit, Erasmus, 164; Mrs. Smit's appeal on behalf of Republic, 272
Sotobo, chief, 141
Southampton, the, 247
South African Associations, 1842 and 1896, 173, 175
Spies, Andr., 156
Staden, G. v., killed, 114
Steenekamp, Anna, 74, 138
Stubbs, J., 68
Strydom, —, killed, 244

TAMBUSA, chief, 21, 34 ; attacks the Emigrants, 49 ; at Blood River, 102 ; as Dingaan's ambassador, 134, 145 ; shot as a spy, 149

Tawane, chief, Retief's alliance with, 2
Tobe, chief, 90
Toohey, Daniel, 40
Trichard, Carel, 17

UITENHAGE district, 68
Uitlander, the, 175; at Congella, 232, 240
Uitvoerende Raad, of Winburg, 23
Umgeni River, 19
Umkungunhlovu, position of, 50; massacre at, 46; kraal destroyed, 104, 118
Umsiligaas, second expedition against, 23
Umslatoosi River, 19
Umveloosi River, White, 20
Umvoti River, 19
Umzimvubu to St. Lucia Bay, coast-line, 157
Uys, name of, prominent in history, 2
 ,, Dirk C., 63; tragic death of, 64
 ,, Jacobus, at Winburg, 1; honoured by British settlers, 2
 ,, Pieter L., 2, 23, 24, 60; death, 64

VAN VUUREN, 35
Vechtkop Blood River laager, 94
Veld which the Voortrekkers fought for and won, 159
Vermaak, J., 243

Victoria, fort, 128; Republican flag hoisted on, 136
Viljoen, Gert, 225
Visser, J. H. Oud Commandant, 98; oral narratives of, 98, 109, 117, 231; in action, 243
Volksraad of Natal, 163; *see* Natal
 ,, ,, Winburg, 162; *see* Winburg
 ,, ,, Federated Republic, 165
 ,, ,, abolished, 280

WEENEN, village of, 50, 59
White Umveloosi, battle of the, 110
Winburg, first township of, 23; Republic of, 159, 161; Volksraad of, 162; federation with Natal, *see* Natal
Win Commando, the, 86; chief officers of, 88
Women of South Africa, brave, 59, 130, 272
Women of Pietermaritzburg, 272
 ,, outraged by Kaffirs in British service, 251

ZOUTPANSBERG boundary, 28
Zulu delegates in Natal, 131
 ,, incursions into Natal, 260, 280
Zululand, conquest of, 137; under sovereignty of Natal Republic, 155
Zyl, Casper v., 243

ERRATUM

Vol. i., p. 64, line 17.—*For* "views in favour to," *read* "view in favour of."

www.ingramcontent.com/pod-product-compliance
Lightning Source LLC
Chambersburg PA
CBHW021150230426
43667CB00006B/331